FAN FICTION AND COPYRIGHT

For Jenny
Live long and prosper

Fan Fiction and Copyright
Outsider Works and Intellectual Property Protection

AARON SCHWABACH
Thomas Jefferson School of Law, USA

ASHGATE

Published by
Ashgate Publishing Limited
Wey Court East
Union Road
Farnham
Surrey, GU9 7PT
England

Ashgate Publishing Company
Suite 420
101 Cherry Street
Burlington
VT 05401-4405
USA

www.ashgate.com

British Library Cataloguing in Publication Data
Schwabach, Aaron.
Fan fiction and copyright : outsider works and intellectual property protection.
1. Fan fiction. 2. Copyright–Fictitious characters. 3. Law and literature.
I. Title
346'.0482-dc22

Library of Congress Cataloging-in-Publication Data
Schwabach, Aaron.
Fan fiction and copyright : outsider works and intellectual property protection / by Aaron Schwabach.
p. cm.
Includes bibliographical references and index.
ISBN 978-0-7546-7903-5 (hardback : alk. paper) – ISBN 978-0-7546-9786-2 (ebook)
1. Copyright–Fictitious characters. 2. Fan fiction–Law and legislation. 3. Copyright–Fictitious characters–United States. I. Title.
K1447.95.S39 2011
346.04'82–dc22

2010050760

ISBN 9780754679035 (hbk)
ISBN 9780754697862 (ebk)

Printed and bound in Great Britain by the
MPG Books Group, UK

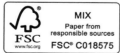

Contents

Introduction:
Who Owns Fandom?

Fan fiction, long a nearly invisible form of outsider art, has grown exponentially in volume and legal importance in the past decade. Because of its nature, authorship, and underground status, fan fiction stands at an intersection of issues of property, sexuality, and gender. This is a book about property; it looks at the various types of fan-created content, most of which are to some extent derivative works, and asks whether some or all of them can be protected as transformative uses. Among the more celebrated disputes over fan writings are a dispute between SF author Larry Niven and fan author Elf Sternberg over the latter's use in fanfic of a fictional species of alien beings created by the former; a dispute between SF author Marion Zimmer Bradley and fan author Jean Lamb over a work by the former that purportedly resembled a work by the latter; and the recent dispute between author J.K. Rowling and fan webmaster Steven Vander Ark over the Harry Potter Lexicon, which Rowling once praised and more recently succeeded, briefly, in suppressing, until the parties reached an accommodation.

Unlicensed fan fiction presents a dilemma for content owners: while fan fiction may infringe on the content owners' copyright and trademark rights, the fans who create and share it are the biggest, and for some genre works very nearly the only, market for the owners' works. Active enforcement of intellectual property rights may alienate consumers—fans—and harm future revenues. On the other horn of the dilemma, some rights-owners fear non-enforcement of those rights may result in their loss.

Fan fiction provides fans with an opportunity to enjoy, discuss, and most of all inhabit the canon texts in ways that would be impossible without it. Despite its essential role, though, fan fiction's legal status remains unclear. Many fans, including academic fans, believe that fan fiction is another type of information that just wants to be free: all or nearly all non-commercial fan fiction should be protected as fair use. In contrast to previous generations, today we live in a world of symbols and texts that are all, or nearly all, owned; fan fiction is a way of combating the inevitable alienation this produces.[1]

Balanced against this are the interests of copyright owners. U.S. copyright law protects some economic interests, but very few non-economic interests.

---

1 See generally, for example, Leanne Stendell, Comment, *Fanfic and Fan Fact: How Current Copyright Law Ignores the Reality of Copyright Owner and Consumer Interests in Fan Fiction*, 58 SMU L. Rev. 1551, 1581 (2005) ("The destruction of this 'modern folk culture' should be contemplated with hesitancy"); Rebecca Tushnet, *Legal Fictions: Copyright, Fan Fiction, and a New Common Law*, 17 Loy. L.A. Ent. L. Rev. 651 (1997).

Owners may object to fan fiction that alters the nature of the original work—the literary equivalent of scribbling mustaches on Grant Wood's *American Gothic* (which would earn the scribbler a quick trip to a Chicago jail cell), or perhaps of scribbling mustaches on a postcard of *American Gothic* (which is perfectly legal, if not original), but in the case of works of fiction on the page or on the screen, they are not likely to get very far: in the U.S. such rights in original works of art are protected by the Visual Artists' Rights Act, but there is no counterpart for works of fiction. Owners assert a more clearly economic interest when they object because fan fiction may anticipate elements of an author's own future works, precluding the author from publishing them. Although this, unlike the first, is an economic interest, it is not necessarily a protected one. But an owner may also object because a fan work borrows extensively from the author's own work; this may infringe the owner's copyright, although various limitations and exceptions exist.

The book that follows explores those limitations and exceptions, and attempts to address, as much as possible, the extent to which a safe space for fanfic has been defined and acknowledged, as well as the larger extent to which that space has been defined but not yet acknowledged by copyright owners. While there are some areas in which the law is unsettled, there are more in which it is settled but widely misunderstood by owners and fans alike. When, for example, the daughter of SF author Philip K. Dick threatens to sue Google for incorporating words from her father's work into its Nexus One cell phone and a writer for Wired.com responds "First, clearly … copyright lengths should be reduced (PKD died in 1982, 27 years ago),"[2] lack of education is as much to blame as lack of clarity. "First, clearly," if the plaintiff has a valid claim (which seems unlikely) it is in trademark, not copyright—and even that seems pretty shaky. Second, it is true that Dick's work is currently in copyright under the current U.S. copyright term of life plus 70 years, but so would it have been under the older term of life plus 50 years—and so would it have been under the Copyright Act of 1909, with its 28-year renewable term: *Do Androids Dream of Electric Sheep*, the work allegedly infringed upon, was published in 1968. To find a copyright term short enough to leave *Do Androids Dream of Electric Sheep* currently out of copyright, we would have to roll back copyright law by over a century. This seems an ambitious project, especially as in this case it is unnecessary; the Dick estate owns no copyright in individual words.[3]

Copyright law has become a subject on which any web posting instantly generates a score of instant experts. With any luck, in the future those debating fan works and copyright law will be able to stay a bit more focused by referring to this book, which would not have been possible without the support and patience of

2 Charlie Sorrel, *Nexus: Did Google Dream of Electric Lawsuits?*, Wired.com, December 16, 2009, www.wired.com/gadgetlab/2009/12/nexus-did-google-dream-of-electric-lawsuits.

3 Nor is there much of a trademark argument here; it seems highly unlikely that Dick's use of the words in a story gave him trademark rights in the commercial use of those words in the cell phone industry.

my employer, Thomas Jefferson School of Law, and the help and input of a great many people, including Mary Cheney, Kevin J. Greene, Lev Grossman, Seiko Katsushima, Akiko Kikuchi, Brian J. Link, James Leggett, Kathleen Lu, Andrea Maestas, Flavio Nominati, Sumit Raghuvanshi, Heidi Tandy, Rebecca Tushnet, Molly Winter, Julie Cromer Young, Qienyuan Zhou, and Daniel, Deborah, Jennifer, Jessica, Jon, Karen, Robert, and Veronica Schwabach, as well as many others I apologize for overlooking, in many cases because we know each other only through online fandom and I am not sure quite what name to use. Thanks to all of you who helped and saved me from many errors; I'm sure I still managed to slip a few by you, though, and must claim all the credit for them.[4]

And a final thought for any fans reading this: we all have our fandoms, our likes and dislikes. It may become evident as you read this, for example, that I quite like Harry Potter but am not (to put it mildly) particularly fond of James Bond. Nonetheless, all of us in fandom share a common interest, and we should respect all fandoms equally—yes, even Twilight. So if James Bond is your thing, I respect your right to post your Bond/Q fanfic at www.fanfiction.net/movie/James_Bond, and urge all fans and fandoms out there to do the same. (That is, respect each other's fandoms, not post Bondslash, although that's okay too.) We're all in this together.

4 Except, as noted in note 108 to Chapter 4, where I must cede credit for the errors to Google Language Tools.

Chapter 1
The World of Fan Fiction

Fandom and fan fiction

Some works of fiction create detailed imaginary worlds and acquire followings of fans who come to know these works as deeply as the "real" (or at least hyperreal) world—that is, the world known not through personal experience, but through text and other media. Much, possibly even most, of the pleasure these fans derive from the works comes not from reading the underlying texts or watching the underlying movies or television shows, but from discussing the works with others. Together these fans make up a community—a fandom. Part of any fandom's discussion may take the form of fiction, artwork, or videos based on characters, settings, or other story elements from the original work.

Much of the content of these fan works addresses the questions of "What if?" and "What next?" What happens after the credits roll, or after the last chapter? Is the Land of Oz really the seamless utopia L. Frank Baum presents, or does it have a darker side? How can Aragorn's government assimilate the displaced and disaffected populations who, voluntarily or otherwise, supported Saruman or Sauron during the War of the Ring? What is Holden Caulfield like as an old man?

Human beings being human, much, perhaps most, of this fan-created fiction addresses questions of love and sex. Will Ginny Weasley's marriage to Harry Potter last? Just how beautiful is the "beautiful friendship" between moody American exile Rick Blaine and effervescent French police chief Louis Renault? Do they ever acknowledge the romantic and erotic nature of their relationship? Do Holmes and Watson? Do Kirk and Spock?

Fandom and fan works pose special problems for the owners of copyrights and trademarks in the underlying works. Some fan works may infringe on these intellectual property rights, although rarely in a financially harmful way; yet enforcing intellectual property rights against fans can alienate the market for the protected works, with financially disastrous results. As a result, the most common state of affairs is an uneasy accommodation between fans and rights owners. Few authors want to risk poisoning their relationship with fans, and thus their livelihoods, unless the fans, through their works, are also threatening the author's economic well-being.

Occasionally the relationship between an author and fandom may turn toxic for other reasons. Some fans may develop a sense of entitlement, and chafe at delays in the release of the next installment in a series. After author George R.R. Martin had gone several years without releasing another volume in the Song of Ice and Fire series, some fans had grown sufficiently abusive that fellow author

Neil Gaiman wrote, in a blog post titled "Entitlement Issues," a counterattack, the central theme of which, in Gaiman's words, was that "*George R.R. Martin is not your bitch*."[1] The tone is scolding, even confrontational; Gaiman can afford to chide Martin's fans as Martin himself could not. The central point is that there is no contract between authors and fans requiring the former to continue to entertain the latter, a point that is likely to be far more appealing to authors than to fans. It also breaks down at the margins; one wonders what might have happened had J.K. Rowling decided, after the sixth Harry Potter book, not to finish the series. While the fans would have had no legal remedy, it might, at the least, have been regarded as socially improper.

Changes in a series' direction may also alienate former fans. Laurell K. Hamilton's "Anita Blake: Vampire Hunter" novels began as a series of stories about vampires in a world that more or less resembles ours, save for a touch of the supernatural. The setting is familiar enough to fans of *Twilight*, *True Blood*, or *Buffy the Vampire Slayer* (although the first novel in the Anita Blake series predated *Twilight* and *True Blood* and the novels on which both are based, as well as the *Buffy* TV series, though not the movie). Anita Blake acquired a loyal fan following. About 10 novels in, though, the series took a sharp turn into erotic fiction, at the expense, in the opinion of many readers, of characterization, setting, and plot. These readers reacted with fury, venting their feelings on fan sites and in the Amazon reviews.

Sometimes the causes of the shift to toxicity are mixed. The vitriol heaped upon another vampire story, Anne Rice's *Blood Canticle*, might seem, at first glance, to be purely a reaction to the shift in the direction and underlying religious values of the Lestat series ("The Vampire Chronicles"), and perhaps to the deterioration in quality when an author has a guaranteed market for stories set in a milieu of which she's become rather tired. But the reaction can also be viewed through the lens of the relationship between Rice and fan authors. Rice has been more hostile to fanfic than many authors, and through her representatives has taken steps to have works based on her characters removed from fan sites. This, more than Rice's public espousal of religious values that many of her fans share, has served to alienate her fandom, causing them to view her as an opponent rather than an ally and thus to view her later works with hostility. (Admittedly Rice did not help matters when she, or someone using her name, published a long and defensive response to her critics in the review section of the Amazon listing for *Blood Canticle*.[2])

Other authors who have been hostile to fanfic have also generated some backlash. A "literary" (as opposed to "genre") author like Annie Proulx does

1 Neil Gaiman, Entitlement Issues …, May 12, 2009, http://journal.neilgaiman.com/2009/05/entitlement-issues.html (last visited May 3, 2010).

2 Posting of Anne O'Brien Rice, From the Author to the Some of the Negative Voices Here, to Amazon.com (September 2, 2004). The review has since been removed from Amazon, but can be read at, among other sites, www.spiritus-temporis.com/anne-rice/amazon-incident.html (last visited May 3, 2010).

not depend on fandom for her commercial success, and can get away with more outspoken criticism of fanfic. Proulx, the author of the short story "Brokeback Mountain"[3] on which the 2005 film of the same name (with a screenplay by Larry McMurtry) was based, reacted unfavorably when fans sent her what she called "ghastly manuscripts and pornish rewrites of the story."[4] Apparently she was unfamiliar with the world of fanfic, in which, alas, ghastliness and pornishness are too rarely absent. Of the fans who write "Brokeback Mountain" fanfic, she said "They do not understand the original story, they know nothing of copyright infringement—i.e., that the characters Jack Twist and Ennis Del Mar are my intellectual property[.]"[5]

As we shall see repeatedly, her suggestion that the fanfic authors are violating her copyright is only partly right: the characters may be (and in this case probably are) her intellectual property, but her copyright in the characters does not mean that no one else can use them; they are protected but not untouchable. The exact limits of this protection are unclear, and neither Proulx nor the fanfic writers are to be blamed for not knowing exactly where they lie.

Genre writers depend less on mainstream media reviewers, book clubs, and Oprah, and more on word-of-mouth (or, more accurately, online) recommendations. The "Song of Ice and Fire" series is sold mainly not by television or magazine advertisements, but by readers who enjoy it and recommend it to their friends, the readers of their blog, the readers of the Amazon reviews, and anyone else who will listen. As more people read the books and share their impressions with other readers, a fandom coalesces; this fandom is the most powerful marketing tool a work of fiction can have.

But fandom can be fickle. The history of popular literature, music, and television is littered with works and artists suddenly abandoned by fans. Less dramatically,

---

3 Annie Proulx, *Brokeback Mountain*, The New Yorker, October 13, 1997, at 74; Brokeback Mountain (Focus Features, Paramount Pictures & Good Machine 2005). The screenplay for the movie was written not by Annie Proulx but by Larry McMurtry and Diana Ossana.

4 Catherine Shoard, *Annie Proulx Bemoans Torrent of "Pornish" Brokeback Fan Fiction: The Pulitzer Prize-Winner Calls the Film Adaptation of Brokeback Mountain "A Source of Constant Irritation" as She's Bombarded with Pornographic Fan Literature*, The Guardian, September 17, 2008, www.guardian.co.uk/film/2008/sep/17/heathledger.porn; Robert J. Hughes, *Return to the Range: Annie Proulx Goes Back to Wyoming for Her New Short-Story Collection*, Wall St. J., September 6, 2008, http://online.wsj.com/article/SB122065020058105139.html. Proulx was also criticized for her response. See, for example, David Lister, *Stop Whingeing about Your Fans, Annie*, The Independent, September 20, 2008, www.independent.co.uk/opinion/columnists/david-lister/david-lister-stop-whingeing-about-your-fans-annie-936189.html; posting of SB Sarah, Ownership, Creativity, and What Fans Do, on Smart Bitches Trashy Books (September 25, 2008, 02:31 AM), www.smartbitchestrashybooks.com/index.php/weblog/comments/ownership-creativity-and-what-fans-do.

5 Hughes, *supra* note 4.

what was cool becomes less cool, and sales drop. While it is impossible to trace the extent to which fanfic and authors' responses to it are a factor, attacks or outright bans on fanfic seem to cost authors some credibility with fans. (It's worth noting that these bans are not necessarily legally enforceable, but major online fanfic archives, anxious to avoid litigation and confrontation with authors, tend to honor them.)

Fan fiction and other fan works

So what, specifically, is fan fiction? For purposes of this discussion it will be necessary to attach definitions to several terms that may not exactly accord with the definitions in use in some fandoms, especially as fandom and fan vocabulary are ever-evolving. As used here, though, a "fan" is someone who enjoys works set in a particular fictional world or about a particular character or set of characters. The fans of a particular world or set of characters are, in the aggregate, a "fandom." A "fan work" is any work by a fan, or indeed by anyone other than the content owner(s), set in such a fictional world or using such pre-existing fictional characters. Fan works may be fiction or nonfiction, and may be created in any medium. When such works are fictional, they are "fan fiction." Fan fiction includes all derivative fiction and related works created by fans, whether authorized or unauthorized by the author of or current rights-holder in the original work. Some fan fiction is commercially published; some is invited by the original author. The vast majority of fan fiction, however, is published only online (or, in pre-Web days, in fanzines), without the express permission of the author or other rights-holders, for an audience of fellow fans. Fan fiction of this sort is "fanfic." "Fanfic" is thus, in this discussion, a subset of "fan fiction," which is in turn a subset of "fan works."

Fanfic, at least for the purposes of this book, refers to works derived from other works currently protected as intellectual property, but not explicitly authorized and not commercially published. As we shall see, the absence of such authorization does not necessarily mean that the fanfic violates an intellectual property right. Fan fiction that is authorized (such as the many commercially-published Star Trek novels and short stories)[6] or that is based on works no longer in copyright and characters not currently protected as trademarks (the works of Jane Austen or William Shakespeare, for example) presents no legal problems; these works are often mined for source material for works that are published commercially.[7]

---

6 See, for example, STAR TREK: THE NEW VOYAGES (Sondra Marshak & Myrna Culbreath, eds. 1976).

7 For fandom-related examples, see, for example, NICK O'DONOHOE, TOO, TOO SOLID FLESH (Wizards of the Coast, 1989) and *Star Trek: The Conscience of the King* (NBC television broadcast, December 8, 1966), both of which draw not only their titles, but also much of their content from HAMLET; and JANE AUSTEN & SETH GRAHAME-SMITH, PRIDE AND

Before the advent of the World Wide Web in the 1990s, fanfic reached relatively small audiences. It might be handwritten or typed and distributed to a few friends who might make copies and distribute them further. At the next higher level of formality and recognition, fanfic might be published in fan magazines (abbreviated to fanzine, and yet further to zine[8]). Some of these fanfics, or their authors, might attract the attention of commercial publishers. An important crossover moment for fanfic/fan fiction was the 1976 publication of *Star Trek: The New Voyages*, a collection of eight Star Trek short stories written by fans with introductions to each story written by actors from the cast of the television show.[9]

Star Trek: The New Voyages made fanfic respectable, or perhaps merely acknowledged that it had already become so. It also transformed the once mostly-male domain of fandom, to the subsequent enrichment of genre fiction as a whole:

> [T]o a whole generation of girls, *Star Trek* on television opened up the world of science fiction. And they had a new world to write about.
>
> * * *
>
> And, in a wave of amateur fiction completely unlike any phenomenon in science fiction history, these stories somehow got themselves published in amateur magazines. There were *hundreds* of them; or let me amend that; there were *thousands*, though I have read only a few hundred.
>
> * * *
>
> And some of these women … have gone on to write other things.[10]

The prevailing mood was one of bonhomie: Gene Roddenberry, creator of the Star Trek television series, wrote:

> Eventually we realized that there is no more profound way in which people could express what Star Trek has meant to them than by creating their own personal Star Trek things … It was their Star Trek stories that especially gratified me. I have seen them in meticulously produced fanzines, complete with excellent artwork. Some of it has even been done by professional writers, or by those

PREJUDICE AND ZOMBIES (Philadelphia: Quirk Books, 2009); JANE AUSTEN & BEN H. WINTERS, SENSE & SENSIBILITY & SEA MONSTERS (Philadelphia: Quirk Books, 2009).

8 Fan magazines have their own complex hierarchy, ranging from perzines (personal fanzines) to semiprozines (semi-professional fanzines), some of which may cross over into commercial territory and become prozines.

9 STAR TREK: THE NEW VOYAGES, *supra* note 6.

10 MARION ZIMMER BRADLEY, *Introduction* to THE KEEPER'S PRICE 10, 10–12 (Marion Zimmer Bradley, ed., 1980).

> clearly on their way to becoming professional writers. Best of all, all of it was clearly done with love.[11]

There is no sign that Roddenberry felt threatened by the fans' use of his intellectual property; rather, he welcomed and embraced it. And he was right: Star Trek fandom persisted, becoming the standard against which all other fandoms are measured, and eventually leading to the commercial publication of additional short stories and novels and an entire world of Star Trek movies, television shows, and merchandise. Roddenberry understood not only what Star Trek meant to the fans, but what the fans meant to Star Trek. One fan reports:

> In fact, there is a probably apocryphal story that George Lucas [creator of the Star Wars movies] once went to Gene Roddenberry to ask him what to do about all the copyright violations being perpetrated by fans. Roddenberry is supposed to have told Lucas "Leave them alone, they'll make you rich!"[12]

Regardless of whether Roddenberry actually made this suggestion, at first, Lucas followed it, albeit cautiously:

> At the height of the original Star Wars phenomenon, Lucasfilm was wary of giving its stamp of approval to the tremendous amount of fan fiction being published. Their solution … was to set up a no-fee licensing bureau that reviewed material and offered criticism about what might be considered copyright infringement. The ugliness of legal threats was avoided, and fans could still have their say.[13]

Many other authors and content owners were similarly relaxed about fanfic. But two developments were to upset this easy accommodation: slash and the Internet.

Slash

Much fan fiction explores romantic and erotic interactions between the characters. Fan fiction of this type is often referred to collectively as "slash," although other fans use the term to refer to the subset of romantic/erotic fan fiction that places male characters from the original work in same-sex romantic and/or erotic situations. The name comes from the punctuation mark used to divide the names of the characters, as in the archetypal slash pairing Kirk/Spock or the perennially popular Harry/Draco. Slash is subdivided into subcategories, a partial list of which

---

11 Gene Roddenberry, *Introduction* to Star Trek: The New Voyages (Sondra Marshak & Myrna Culbreath, eds., 1976).

12 Fan Works Inc., Star Wars! Policy: No Commercial Gain, Doesn't Sully Image, www.fanworks.org/writersresource/?action=define&authorid=112&tool=fanpolicy (last visited May 3, 2010).

13 Ibid.

might include yaoi (slash involving manga and anime characters), chanslash (explicit slash involving minor characters, such as Harry/Draco or Snape/Harry (also known as Drarry and Snarry, respectively) from the Harry Potter universe), and RPS (for "Real Person Slash," such as the Dom/Lijah pairing involving two of the actors from the Lord of the Rings movies). Related concepts include het (romantic and/or erotic stories involving characters of different genders, such as Harry/Hermione), femmeslash and femslash (slash with female rather than male characters, e.g. Buffy/Faith from the television series *Buffy the Vampire Slayer*), transgender slash, friendship fiction (indicated by an ampersand, such as Harry & Draco, to denote a story in which the two characters are friends, in contrast to their canonical relationship) and shipping (devotion to a particular non-canonical romantic relationship, or ship). Ships are often given names, such as HMS *Harmony* (for Harry Potter and Hermione Granger from the Harry Potter universe) or *Zutara* (for Zuko and Katara, characters from the animated television show *Avatar: The Last Airbender*). As noted, fiction in all of these categories—and others not listed here—with the exception of friendship fiction, is often collectively, though incorrectly, referred to as "slash."

Most writers of slash are female; slash thus stands at an intersection of issues of property, sexuality, and gender, and as a result, has attracted academic interest.[14] Much research has been done by academics, including Henry Jenkins, Rebecca Tushnet, and many of the scholars cited in this work, who are themselves fans and view the topic from within.[15] Research by non-fans sometimes violates accepted norms of fannish behavior and can trigger a backlash. Recently neuroscientists

---

14 See, for example, Mirna Cicioni, *Male Pair Bonds and Female Desire in Fan Slash Writing*, in THEORIZING FANDOM: FANS, SUBCULTURE AND IDENTITY 9 (Cheryl Harris & Alison Alexander, eds., 1998); Shoshanna Green et al., *Normal Female Interest in Men Bonking: Selections from the* Terra Nostra Underground *and* Strange Bedfellows, in THEORIZING FANDOM: FANS SUBCULTURE AND IDENTITY 153 (Cheryl Harris & Alison Alexander, eds., 1998); CONSTANCE PENLEY, NASA/TREK: POPULAR SCIENCE AND SEX IN AMERICA (1997); Sonia Katyal, *Performance, Property, and the Slashing of Gender in Fan Fiction*, 14 AM. U. J. GENDER SOC. POL'Y & L. 461 (2006); Rosemary Coombe, *Authorizing the Celebrity: Publicity Rights, Postmodern Politics, and Unauthorized Genders*, 10 CARDOZO ARTS & ENT. L.J. 365 (1992); Meredith McCardle, *Fan Fiction, Fandom, and Fanfare: What's All the Fuss?*, 9 B.U. J. SCI. & TECH. L. 433 (2003); Mollie E. Nolan, *Search for Original Expression: Fan Fiction and the Fair Use Deference*, 30 S. ILL. U. L.J. 533, 549–50, 562 (2006); Christina Z. Ranon, *Honor Among Thieves: Copyright Infringement in Internet Fandom*, 8 VAND. J. ENT. & TECH. L. 421, 447–48 (2006); Rebecca Tushnet, *My Fair Ladies: Sex, Gender, and Fair Use in Copyright*, 15 AM. U. J. GENDER SOC. POL'Y & L. 273 (2007).

15 The contributions of Professors Jenkins and Tushnet are too numerous to list here, but see generally Confessions of an Aca-Fan, www.henryjenkins.org, including descriptions of Prof. Jenkins' recent books on the "About Me" tab and Rebecca Tushnet's 43(B)log, http://tushnet.blogspot.com, as well as Professor Tushnet's *Legal Fictions: Copyright, Fan Fiction and a New Common Law*, 17 LOY. L.A. ENT. L. REV. 651 (1997), as well as other articles cited throughout this work.

Ogi Ogas and Sai Gaddam triggered outrage with a questionnaire revealing buried assumptions about fandom and fannish behavior. As one fan put it:

> We don't know how aware you are of your subject, but there have been multiple studies on fanfiction done over the last thirty years, and few if any of them have represented the community in an accurate or complex manner. Studies of fans, particularly female fans, tend to follow in the long history of pathologizing women's behaviour and women's desire, the history of male scientists objectifying queer/female desires in order to subjectivize themselves, the history of othering and shaming the weirdos as a form of boundary-policing. There is a similar history in relation to studies on kink, or on other communities relating to queer sexuality: policing, othering, pathologizing. And even in studies that don't think of themselves as policing, othering, and pathologizing, there is still a note—a note that is audible in your brief message, in your "fascination" with kink bingo—of a nineteenth century scientist with a particularly interesting bug under the microscope. We're not interested in being your bug.[16]

The present work has a somewhat narrower scope, being concerned mostly with copyright law. From a copyright perspective, slash and related categories of fanfic pose no problems not also posed by other forms of fanfic. Nonetheless, works of this sort seem to upset some content owners more than does non-slash fanfic.[17] While this makes little sense in copyright terms, it does make sense in trademark terms. Trademark law protects some marks—those deemed "famous" rather than merely "distinctive"—from tarnishment, even when there is no likelihood of confusion. Only commercial uses of the mark are covered, however; the average amateur website (or letterzine, like *Not Tonight, Spock*) is unlikely to be commercial.[18] At least one author has proposed that at least one federal district court has already applied a concept of "copyright tarnishment"

16 Eruthros, *Please Don't Take the Fanfiction Survey*, August 31, 2009, http://eruthros.dreamwidth.org/273840.html (quoting e-mail from Eruthros to Ogi Ogas). See also Carmarthen, *Deceptive Studies and Scientists Talking Back*, September 3, 2009, http://carmarthen.livejournal.com/322504.html; Shaggirl, *I Was Wrong*, September 2, 2009, http://shaggirl.livejournal.com/190980.html.

17 It must, as Penley observes, provide some amusement as well. Penley, *supra* note 14, at 100–101 (commenting on the implicit amused acknowledgment of slash in Spock's line "[p]lease, Captain, not in front of the Klingons" as Kirk tries to embrace him near the end of the movie *Star Trek V: The Final Frontier*). A hint of similarly amused acknowledgement can be found in J.K. Rowling, Harry Potter and the Half-Blood Prince 522–23 (2005), when Harry (literally) slashes Draco with the spell Sectumsempra.

18 See 15 U.S.C. § 1125(c)(2)(A) (2006); see also *Playboy Enters., Inc.* v. *Netscape Commc'ns Corp.*, 354 F.3d 1020, 1031–32 (9th Cir. 2004). See also, for example, William M. Landes & Richard A. Posner, The Economic Structure of Intellectual Property Law 160 n.28, 162, 270–73 (2003). Or, in the words of one slash writer's disclaimer, "I most certainly don't own these characters and haven't been paid for writing stuff like this."

analogous to trademark dilution by tarnishment.[19] However, such a rule lacks the statutory basis that trademark tarnishment has and would seem to pose fair use and First Amendment problems that are not necessarily (although occasionally) present with trademark tarnishment. To the extent that such a rule seeks to protect moral rights, it may also be inconsistent with policy underlying U.S. (although not international) copyright law.

How the Internet changed everything

Nothing in the Internet's early days gave a hint of the dramatic impact it would one day have on fandom, fiction, and the idea of discrete communities of "authors" and "audience." In 1969, when the U.S. Department of Defense's ARPANET first connected four computers at universities in California and Utah, networking computers was seen as a research tool rather than a mass medium. Though ARPANET grew dramatically, especially following the switch to TCP/IP networking protocols in 1983, it was not until the creation of the World Wide Web that the Internet became a part of daily life for hundreds of millions of people.

The first web page and the first web browser were created in 1990–1991 by Tim Berners-Lee computers at CERN, the European Organization for Nuclear Research in Switzerland. By 1992 the web was accessible to Internet users throughout the world. The release of easy-to-use web browsers, including Netscape and Internet Explorer, brought the web to the desktop of everyone with a computer. The public was quick to grasp the feature that made the web different from earlier mass media: everyone was not only a part of the audience, but also a part of the show. Anyone who wanted to communicate anything—anything at all—to the rest of the world could do so by posting it online. The World Wide Web grew by an order of magnitude each year during the mid-1990s; today it includes hundreds of billions of pages on hundreds of millions of sites. Many of these sites include user-generated content: original artwork, reviews of everything from recent movies to power mowers, ALL-CAPS rants about imaginary conspiracies, party photos, videos of cats falling into cardboard boxes … and fanfic.

In the generally permissive pre-Internet days slash and other fanfic mostly skated by. Entire zines, like *Beyond Antares* and *Alternative: Epilog to Orion*, were dedicated to Star Trek slash. But these zines circulated among a small number of people, all of whom were already dedicated fans.[20] With the advent of the Internet, and especially of the World Wide Web, the potential audience for

---

Fennelseed, *A Strange Ghost Indeed* (Frodo/Sam), March 15, 2004, www.fanfiction.net/s/1774878/1/A_Strange_Ghost_Indeed.

19 See Nolan, *supra* note 14, at 569 & n.269 (citing *DC Comics, Inc.* v. *Unlimited Monkey Bus., Inc.*, 598 F. Supp. 110 (N.D. Ga. 1984)).

20 For more background on Kirk/Spock, see Beyond Dreams Press, Jenna Sinclair, A Short History of Early K/S or How the First Slash Fandom Came to Be, www.beyonddreamspress.com/history.htm (last visited May 3, 2010).

slash and other fanfic began to grow exponentially, as did the number of fanfic authors. Fanfics and fan art pages number in the millions, each accessible to the entire population of the world—at least, the entire population with Internet access. Entire communities exist to address particular subcategories: what if Harry Potter turned evil, got arrested, and was sent to Azkaban?[21] What if, after Harry Potter defeated Voldemort, the Ministry of Magic imposed a "Marriage Law" requiring all pure-blooded witches and wizards to marry Muggle-borns?[22] Many sites collect fanfic and categorize it in archives; at least as much is uncategorized, recorded in individual fans' blogs or circulated by e-mail. "Squick" warnings may be attached to denote more than usually disturbing content, such as incest, torture, or pedophilia.

And the Internet complicates things by increasing the ease of creating and publishing fan works while accelerating the rate at which those works reach an audience. Writing and publishing a bound volume requires sufficient effort that the writer may have time to contemplate possible copyright issues. In addition, there is usually an intermediary—the publisher—who will raise copyright concerns even if the writer does not. No such contemplation is required for Internet publication; as soon as a Tarzan fan finishes writing his or her Tarzan/D'Arnot fanfic, it can be posted on a blog or fanfic archive, or even sent in an e-mail: instant publishing, and possibly instant copyright infringement. Internet service providers lack the resources to police content the way a book publisher might; the sheer volume of content would require the resources of an entire planet of copyright lawyers. And, thanks to the safe harbor provisions of 17 U.S.C. § 512 (the Online Copyright Infringement Liability Limitation Act, Title II of the Digital Millennium Copyright Act [DMCA]), they have no need to do so.

Internet service providers (ISPs) transmit and store enormous quantities of information at the direction of their customers. Most of the time the ISPs neither know nor have any reason to know anything about the information beyond technical data such as file sizes and types. The content is of interest only to the creators and end recipients. One user may e-mail another author's copyrighted content (or a fanfic that the copyright owner of the underlying work thinks is copyright infringing) to a second user, who then posts it on a website at the first user's request, where it is read by a third user. Multiple copies of the work, or of parts of the work, are created: by the e-mail sender's and e-mail recipient's ISPs and intermediate ISPs in the course of transmitting the e-mail, by the host of the website where the story is posted, by the ISP of the second and third user in the course of uploading the document to and downloading it from the website, and by

21 See, for example, Fanfiction.net, Dark Harry Crossovers, www.fanfiction.net/community/Potter_in_Azkaban_Dark_Harry_Cross_Overs/3512 (last visited May 3, 2010).

22 Fan History, *See Marriage Law Challenge*, www.fanhistory.com/wiki/Marriage_Law_Challenge; *The WIKtT [When I Kissed the Teacher] Archives*, www.themasque.net/wiktt/efiction/toplists.php?list=favstories; *The Marriage Law RPG [Role Playing Game]*, http://asylums.insanejournal.com/marriagelaw/profile (all last visited May 3, 2010).

various sites archiving Internet content. Any or all of these ISPs may make backup copies as well.

At one time each copy might have been regarded as a new infringement, subjecting the ISPs to liability for each occurrence. Given the enormous amount of content stored and transmitted by ISPs and the very short times involved, requiring ISPs to police everything stored or transmitted for possible copyright-infringing content would shut down the Internet. To deal with this problem, in 1998 the U.S. Congress enacted the Title II of the DMCA. Title II created a new section 512 of the copyright code, setting up and defining safe harbors for service providers for transitory communications, system caching, storage of information on systems or networks at the direction of users, and information location tools. Service providers whose activities fall within the scope of the safe harbor provisions and who comply with those provisions can not be held liable for damages for copyright infringement arising from those activities, and the availability of injunctive relief against those service providers is limited. The latter two safe harbors (storage at the direction of users and information location tools) provide notice and takedown procedures: a copyright owner who finds infringing content online can provide proper notice as set out in the statute, at which point the ISP must remove the content. There is also a counter-notification procedure; a user who disputes the purported copyright owner's claim can, by complying with the procedure, have his or her content put back up again.

The individual users, however, have no such protection and online fanfic content, preserved for eternity on Internet archive sites, is a potential liability bomb for the fans. Content owners have for the most part behaved relatively responsibly where fanfic is concerned, in contrast to, for example, the notorious campaign of lawsuits against individual music file-sharers by the Recording Industry Association of America (RIAA). The RIAA's legal position was stronger; the music file-sharers were, or mostly were, infringing the copyrights of RIAA's members, while much or even most fanfic is probably not copyright-infringing. And the negative publicity resulting from the RIAA's lawsuits may serve as a cautionary tale to future copyright owners inclined to pursue a similar course. (To lend a Dickensian poor-widows-and-orphans flavor to the music-sharing suits, among the first defendants was 12-year-old Brianna LaHara, who lived with her mother in public housing in New York City. Brianna said "I thought it was OK to download music because my mom paid a service fee for it."[23]) But this present accommodation is no guarantee that in the future a bankrupt, self-destructive, or malicious content-owner may not decide on a campaign of RIAA-type excesses, with teenagers who have posted fanfics involving sparkly vampire Edward Cullen from Twilight finding their college funds and future income streams jeopardized as a result.

23 Gary Younge, *US Music Industry Sues 261 for Online Song Copying*, Guardian, September 10, 2003, at 13, available at www.guardian.co.uk/technology/2003/sep/10/arts.usnews.

For the most part, content owners seem to be taking to heart the lessons of the recording industry's ill-starred attack on online file-sharing. Just as the Internet did not create music piracy, it did not create fanfic. As with music piracy, however, it transformed what had been small into something much bigger. Harry Potter fanfics alone number not in the hundreds or thousands but in the hundreds of thousands, if not millions. The music industry's ham-handed handling of online piracy has made business history, although not in a good way. Content owners have been treading more carefully with fanfic, perhaps having learned from the music industry's attacks on its own consumer base.

The claim is often made that online music file-sharing actually helps licensed music sales by introducing listeners to music that they might not otherwise hear.[24] While the merits of this claim are debatable and much-debated, it is easier to see, as Roddenberry did, the connection between fanfic and profits. Part of the fun of fandom—most of the fun, perhaps—is not in reading the books or watching the movies, but in talking about them with other fans. In the days before the Internet, this was not always possible. Now, though, however obscure a fandom might be, others share it. Those who, for example, think the adventures of the children's comic-strip detective Slylock Fox might be better expressed as pulp-era detective stories will find what they're looking for at *Reynard Noir*;[25] those who have wondered what might happen if the castaways of *Gilligan's Island* had been visited by Gomer Pyle or the Munster family can find others' answers or post their own.[26]

Larger, more current fandoms make possible a marketing synergy unknown to pre-Internet content owners. Harry Potter fandom is perhaps the best known example: fans who might otherwise have read the books and talked them over with a few friends found an entire universe of fanfic, fan art, and commentary online. What might have been entertainment for a few hours became entertainment for days and weeks—in some cases, years. Fans who might have spent a few dollars on books—or taken the books out of the library—became fans who spent thousands of dollars on books, movie tickets, DVDs, and merchandise. J.K. Rowling made canny use of the Internet with a series of teaser games on her own website and carefully timed releases of information to major fan sites, promoting upcoming books and movies.[27] The incredible success of the Harry Potter phenomenon—the

24 Compare Rufus Pollock, Miscellaneous FactZ, *Filesharing Costs: Dubious Figures Making the Rounds Again*, May 29, 2009 (discrediting figures posted by BBC story that music industry is losing revenue because of file sharing), *with* CNNMoney.com, Music's Lost Decade: Sales Cut in Half, February 2, 2010, http://money.cnn.com/2010/02/02/news/companies/napster_music_industry/index.htm (describing online file sharing services as "the disease of free").

25 Reynard Noir: The Seedy Underworld of Slylock Fox, http://reynardnoir.wordpress.com (last visited May 3, 2010).

26 Fanfiction.net, Gilligan's Island, www.fanfiction.net/tv/Gilligans_Island (last visited May 3, 2010).

27 See J.K. Rowling, Official Site, www.jkrowling.com (last visited May 3, 2010).

books alone have sold more than 400 million volumes—would not have happened without a devoted online fan following, and fanfic is part of that. Even critical fanfic serves a valuable market-building or market-preserving function, allowing fans to blow off steam about character or plot developments they dislike without abandoning the work altogether. For example, many readers of the Harry Potter series were dissatisfied with "Nineteen Years Later," the epilogue to the seventh volume, in which Harry is seen at King's Cross Station, complacently married to Ginny Weasley, with three children named, rather disturbingly, after characters who have died.[28] One fan wrote "Five Years Even Later," a short fanfic in which a middle-aged, not at all complacent Harry is again seen at King's Cross, talking to an equally middle-aged, equally non-complacent Hermione.[29] This time, though, Hermione is complaining about her marriage to Ron. Harry, it turns out, has had an affair with Luna Lovegood and is divorced from Ginny. The author's exaggerated mimicry accurately parodies J.K. Rowling's writing style:

> Harry turned to see his old friend Hermione. "Ron's here," he warned her warningly.
>
> I know that," she said knowingly.
>
> * * *
>
> "Still enslaving house elves?" Hermione asked finally.
>
> "The Wizengamot awarded 12 Grimmauld Place to Ginny in the settlement," he said simply. "Kreacher went with it."
>
> He, Harry, missed his Kreacher comforts.[30]

The fanfic serves as a useful antidote to the anodyne, even saccharine, epilogue in the book, as do others taking a darker view: In "And the Truth Will Set you Free," another fan rejects the book's ending, in which the central characters survive relatively unscathed. With Ginny Weasley dead and Ron Weasley suffering from a self-inflicted memory wipe, Harry and Hermione, both emotionally scarred, are married. Ron is living in Canada, where he encounters a disabled Neville Longbottom. After meeting Neville, Ron returns to England, his vanished memory inflicting further emotional suffering on those who remember but are not remembered by him.[31] Such revisionist fanfic may actually enhance the fan

---

28 J.K. Rowling, *Epilogue* to Harry Potter and the Deathly Hallows 753, 753–59 (2007).

29 Alaskaravenclaw, Epi-epilogue: 5 Years Even Later, July 27, 2007, available at http://alaskaravenclaw.livejournal.com/963.html (last visited October 19, 2010).

30 Ibid.

31 Rubymiene, And the Truth Will Set You Free, http://rubymiene.insanejournal.com/838.html#cutid2 (last visited September 21, 2009).

author's and readers' attachment to the original text, by allowing them an "out" from some unwelcome aspect of the original.

Other fan works are sillier, such as the Potter Puppet Pals puppet skit "The Mysterious Ticking Noise."[32] In the skit, Hogwarts Professor Severus Snape hears a ticking noise and begins to chant his name in time to the ticks. Various other characters appear and also begin to chant their names. The noise turns out to be a bomb, which explodes, blowing the puppets to shreds. Lord Voldemort then appears and, being somewhat more musically gifted than those who serve the side of Good, gleefully chants *his* name in an approximation of the 1958 Ronald & Ruby song "Lollipop" (covered by the Chordettes and the Mudlarks in the same year): "Voldemort, Voldemort, ooh, Voldy, Voldy, Voldemort!"[33] While the skit provides no deep insight into the characters or the story, no one who has seen a dozen schoolchildren spontaneously begin snapping their fingers in unison and chanting, "Snape, Snape, Severus Snape" can doubt its market-building power. Ultimately fandom is about shared experience, and the more experience the fans can share, the deeper their attachment.

Internet fandoms have become vast worlds of outsider literature and art and may have influenced commercially published writers. Fan fiction as criticism has become more common, as has meta-fanfic—fanfic commenting not only on the original work but on other fanfic commenting on that work.[34] Some works in these categories, including Neil Gaiman's "The Problem of Susan"[35] and David Langford's "The Spear of the Sun,"[36] are crossovers, achieving commercial publication as fiction. Gaiman, a long-established author with fans of his own who write fanfic based on his works, wrote "The Problem of Susan" to address and criticize what many fans find to be the most disturbing aspect of C.S. Lewis' Chronicles of Narnia: the exclusion of Susan Pevensie from salvation in the last book in the series, *The Last Battle*. Gaiman's fan fiction as criticism has in turn been incorporated into online meta-fanfic, such as this fan version of the scene

---

32 Potter Puppet Pals (Niel Cicierega et al.), *The Mysterious Ticking Noise*, www.potterpuppetpals.com (last visited May 3, 2010). The Potter Puppet Pals skits are among the many fan works that have enabled their creator to make the transition from fandom to professional career.

33 Ibid.; Ronald & Ruby, Lollipop (RCA 1958), available at www.youtube.com/watch?v=RHi_ECIFOHo (last visited November 8, 2008).

34 For a further discussion, see, for example, David A. Brewer, The Afterlife of Character, 1726–825 (Philadelphia: University of Pennsylvania Press, 2005); Kristina Busse, *Historical Memory, Affective Imagination: Fan Representation in Media Fan Fiction*, www.kristinabusse.com/cv/research/pca09.html (April 2009); Fan Fiction and Fan Communities in the Age of the Internet (Kristina Busse and Karen Hellekson, eds., Jefferson, NC: McFarland, 2006).

35 Neil Gaiman, *The Problem of Susan*, in Flights: Extreme Visions of Fantasy 393 (2004).

36 David Langford, *The Spear of the Sun*, in Year's Best SF 2 237 (1997).

immediately following Aslan's resurrection in the film version of *The Lion, The Witch, and the Wardrobe*:

> []AUDIENCE: I wish I knew what they were talking about.
> NEIL GAIMAN: Well, okay, but you're not going to like it.
>
> * * *
>
> ASLAN: For your loyalty, Lucy, I shall reward you. You shall always be my favorite.
> SUSAN: And what about me?
> ASLAN: For your loyalty, Susan, I shall string you along for a while, but in Book Seven you shall suffer a horrible tragedy, followed by eternal damnation.
> NEIL GAIMAN: Toldja you wouldn't like it.[37]

David Langford, perhaps best known to SF fandom as the editor of the United Kingdom fanzine *Ansible*, is both a fan and an author; he has written many parodies and works embedded in fandom. "The Spear of the Sun" is typically baroque; a complexly-nested and cross-connected story in which Langford appears as a "character," or more properly the author of a Father Brown fanfic framed within an article in an imaginary fanzine in an alternate universe. The imaginary fanzine, *G.K. Chesterton's Science Fiction Magazine*, lists Graham Greene, Jorge Luis Borges, and a stellar cast as contributors; it is dedicated to the work of G.K. Chesterton, whose definition of "Parody … as the worshipper's half-holiday"[38] might be taken as summing up Langford's work. The multiple parallels, contortions, and in-jokes of the framing story require a thorough steeping in fandom, but the Father Brown story within the frame stands on its own.[39] Neither could have been created except by one who inhabited the text in the spirit of admiration and even reverence Chesterton thought necessary for true parody.

---

37 Naill Renfro, Chronicles of Narnia: The Lion, the Witch, and the Wardrobe Movie Parody, December 13, 2005, http://naill-renfro.livejournal.com/506.html.

38 G.K. Chesterton, Varied Types 179 (Project Gutenberg, ed., Dodd, Mead & Company, 2004) (1905), available at http://infomotions.com/etexts/gutenberg/dirs/1/4/2/0/14203/14203.htm.

39 On nested stories of this type, see generally Brian McHale, Postmodernist Fiction 112 (1987). For some real Father Brown stories, see Gilbert Keith Chesterton, The Complete Father Brown Stories (1998); for darker yet equally playful GKC, try Gilbert Keith Chesterton, The Man Who Was Sunday: A Nightmare (1908).

Fan fiction and copyright law

Because they are ultimately the expression of an idea at least partly originated by another, fan works are always haunted by the specter of copyright. Analysis of this problem requires a two-step inquiry: first, whether the underlying work or element (such as a character) is protected by copyright and, second, if so, whether the fanfic or other fan work violates that copyright. The next two chapters explore these questions.

Chapter 2
The First Question: Are the Underlying Works or Characters Protected?

Copyright protects "original works of authorship fixed in any tangible medium of expression" including the literary, dramatic, graphic, and audiovisual works upon which so much fanfic is based.[1] Elements of the work that are not original, however, are not protected, nor is "any idea, procedure, process, system, method of operation, concept, principle, or discovery" incorporated therein.[2] Even those elements that are protected are protected only for a limited time; many still-popular works can be used in fanfic without raising copyright concerns because the copyrights have expired. But determining whether the copyright on a particular work or character has expired is not always simple.

The dramatic extensions of copyright law over the past century have made the duration of the average copyright term longer than that of the average human lifetime: most people will never see the copyright expire on any work published within their own lives. The Copyright Act of 1909[3] set the term of copyright protection in the United States at 28 years, renewable once.[4] The Copyright Act of 1976 extended the term for works created after January 1, 1978 yet further, to the lifetime of the author plus 50 years for most individually authored or co-authored works and 75 years for most other works.[5] The term was extended further—not without controversy[6]—by the Sonny Bono Copyright Term Extension Act of 1998 (CTEA), to the lifetime of the author plus 70 years and 95 years, respectively.[7]

The Copyright Amendment Act of 1992 retroactively granted an automatic copyright renewal for works published between 1964 and 1977 so long as those works were otherwise eligible for copyright renewal.[8] The length of this renewal term was extended by the CTEA to 67 years, so that works protected by the Act are

---

1 17 U.S.C. § 102(a) (2006).

2 17 U.S.C. § 102(b).

3 Copyright Act of 1909, ch. 320, 35 Stat. §§ 1075–1088 (1909).

4 The first U.S. copyright law, following the Statute of Anne, had set the term at 14 years, renewable once, and it had been gradually increased. 1 Stat. 124 (1790); see also Statute of Anne, 8 ANNE, c. 19 (1709) (14 years); 4 Stat. 436 (1831) (28 years); 16 Stat. 212 (1870) (28 years).

5 Copyright Act of 1976, Pub. L. No. 94-553, 90 Stat. 2541 (1976).

6 See, for example, *Eldred* v. *Ashcroft*, 537 U.S. 186 (2003).

7 Sonny Bono Copyright Term Extension Act, Pub. L. No. 105–298, 112 Stat. 2827 (1998) (codified as amended at 17 U.S.C. §§ 301–05).

8 Copyright Amendments Act of 1992, Pub. L. No. 102–307; 106 Stat. 266 (1992).

still in copyright. The 67-year extension also applies to works created in or before 1950 only if the copyright on those works was renewed or otherwise extended in some way after 1950; in other words, it does not apply to works created before 1923.[9] International law adds another layer of complexity: under the Uruguay Round Agreements Act of 1994, copyright is automatically extended for works originating in countries other than the United States that are parties to the World Trade Organization (WTO) or the Berne Convention,[10] even if copyright renewal formalities were not complied with.

Does this seem simple? At this point, if you're a copyright lawyer, you're mentally chiding me for oversimplification; if you're not, you may be a bit confused. It can often be difficult to determine whether a particular work is still in copyright; for the layperson, it can be effectively impossible. As a practical matter, though, the most active fandoms are for works still in copyright. It's also important to keep in mind that the international harmonization of copyright law is a recent and not entirely complete phenomenon; thus works out of copyright in one country may still be in copyright in another. This, taken with the frontierless nature of the Internet, means that a work that violates no copyright where it is posted may still violate copyright where it is downloaded.

A specific example may help. The worlds of Arthur Conan Doyle (especially the Sherlock Holmes stories and the Challenger stories, including *The Lost World*[11]) have provided story elements that have been effectively mined by generations of authors, in fanfic and in commercially published works. Arthur Conan Doyle published *The Lost World* in 1912 and died in 1930.

The Lost World's first U.S. copyright term expired in 1940; the renewed term expired in 1968, and the work entered the public domain in the United States. Because the work originated in the United Kingdom, a party to both the Berne Convention and the WTO, it is not necessary under U.S. law to determine whether the copyright renewal formalities were actually complied with. The 1998 CTEA did not affect the copyright because the work was first published before 1923. *The Lost World* is thus in the public domain in the U.S. and other authors may freely publish derivative works based upon it. Thus, in 1995 U.S. author Michael Crichton could publish a book with the same title and similar subject matter,[12] and in 1993 Brazilian author Marcio Souza could do the same with the U.S. publication of his

9 See generally U.S. Copyright Office, Circular 15a, Duration of Copyright: Provisions of the Law Dealing with the Length of Copyright Protection (2004), at 1–2, available at www.copyright.gov/circs/circ15a.pdf (providing a general summary for the statutory provisions under the Copyright Act of 1976).

10 Berne Convention for the Protection of Literary and Artistic Works, art. 7(1), September 9, 1886, as revised at Paris on July 24, 1971, and amended on September 29, 1979, 25 U.S.T. 1341, 821 U.N.T.S. 221 [hereinafter Berne Convention].

11 Arthur Conan Doyle, The Lost World (1912).

12 Michael Crichton, The Lost World (1995).

postmodern *Lost World II: The End of the Third World*,[13] which is simultaneously a postcolonial critique of the Conan Doyle original and an ironic appreciation of it. The original Portuguese-language publication of Souza's book in 1989 might have raised copyright concerns, though; under the Brazilian copyright statute in effect from 1973 through 1998, copyright endured for 60 years after the death of the author, a more generous term than the minimum term of 50 years after the death of the author mandated by the Berne Convention (to which Brazil has been a party since 1922).[14] Consequently, *The Lost World* might not have entered the public domain in Brazil until January 1, 1991—the first January 1 to fall 60 years after the death of Arthur Conan Doyle. However, in the United Kingdom at the time copyright endured for the life of the author plus 50 years, and *The Lost World* thus entered the public domain in the UK 10 years earlier. Under the "rule of the shorter term" contained in Art. 7(8) of the Berne Convention, Brazil could have applied the shorter UK term: "the term shall be governed by the legislation of the country where protection is claimed; however, unless the legislation of that country otherwise provides, the term shall not exceed the term fixed in the country of origin of the work."[15]

This does not mean that determining whether a work is in the public domain is a simple matter of counting and looking at a calendar. The existence of different terms for differently authored works and different types of works complicates matters, yet not as much as the many revisions in a country's copyright law that may occur over the duration of a single copyright—some with retroactive effect, some without. In the case of Sir Arthur, for example, a recent *New York Times* article makes, or at least quotes, the odd contention that "Sherlock Holmes remains

---

13 MARCIO SOUZA, LOST WORLD II: THE END OF THE THIRD WORLD (Lana Santamaria, trans., 1993), originally published as O FIM DO TERCEIRO MUNDO (Marco Zero, ed., 1989). Nor does Crichton's work infringe Souza's copyright, because the (few) elements Crichton's work has in common with Souza's are not original to Souza.

14 Lei No. 5.988/73, Art. 42, § 2 (granting protection for a period of 60 years from January 1 of the year following the author's death), repealed by Lei No. 9.610, February 19, 1998, available at www.wipo.int/clea/en/text_html.jsp?lang=EN&id=514#P144_15184 (English translation). Brazil's current copyright statute, Law No. 9610 on Copyright and Neighboring Rights, Art. 41, provides that "[t]he author's economic rights shall be protected for a period of 70 years as from the first of January of the year following his death, subject to observance of the order of succession under civil law."

15 Berne Convention, *supra* note 10, Art. 7(8). But see also generally *Land Hessen* v. *G. Ricordi & Co. Bühnen-und Musikverlag GmbH*, case C-360/00, June 6, 2002 (judgment of the court), available at http://eur-lex.europa.eu/LexUriServ/LexUriServ.do?uri=CELEX:62000J0360:EN:HTML; Directive 2006/116/EC of the European Parliament and of the Council of 12 December 2006 on the Term of Protection of Copyright and Certain Related Rights (codified version), OJ (L 372) 12–18, available at http://eur-lex.europa.eu/LexUriServ/LexUriServ.do?uri=OJ:L:2006:372:0012:0018:EN:PDF (effectively eliminating the rule of the shorter term as between EU member states).

under copyright protection in the United States through 2023."[16] This prompted immediate objections:

> [I]t's *not true.* All of the Sherlock Holmes books except one have now entered the public domain. And, yes, this creates quite a mess. But, in theory, anyone who created a work based solely on the public domain works, and which is not based on or derived from that last work, should, in fact, be legit without a license. That doesn't mean that [the copyright owners] wouldn't sue, but it's not correct to claim that Holmes is still completely covered by copyright.[17]

While it is true that some of the Holmes stories are still in copyright in the U.S., others are not; this makes the question of copyright in the character of Sherlock Holmes (and Doctor Watson, and Inspector Lestrade, and Mrs. Hudson) especially vexing. While those elements of a character that originated in stories now in the public domain are themselves in the public domain, it may take considerable work to pin down exactly when a character developed a particular trait, and even then reasonable persons might disagree. Nor is it clear who owns the copyrights; that, rather than the duration of the term, is the focus of the *New York Times* article, and it is not at all unusual, especially in the case of valuable older works, for there to be multiple claimants, any of whom might be ready to sue suspected infringers.

Copyright in characters

Can a fictional character be protected by copyright independently of the work in which it appears? Authors and fans alike often assume that fictional characters are protected, but the reality is less simple.[18] Does a fan work infringe copyright

16 Dave Itzkoff, *For the Heirs to Holmes, a Tangled Web*, N.Y. TIMES, January 18, 2010, www.nytimes.com/2010/01/19/books/19sherlock.html?pagewanted=all.

17 Mike Masnick, *NY Times Takes Up The Case Of Sherlock Holmes And The Lost Public Domain ... But Gets It Wrong*, TechDirt: Legal Issues, www.techdirt.com/articles/20100119/2318397826.shtml (January 20, 2010, 8:10 A.M.); see also Mike Masnick, *Elementary My Dear Watson ... It's Called The Public Domain ... Or Is It?*, TechDirt: Legal Issues, www.techdirt.com/articles/20091223/1120407488.shtml (December 24, 2009, 5:06 P.M.).

18 For further discussion, see, for example, Francis M. Nevins, Jr., *Copyright + Character = Catastrophe*, 39 J. COPYRIGHT SOC'Y U.S.A. 303, 304 (1992); Kathryn M. Foley, *Protecting Fictional Characters: Defining the Elusive Trademark-Copyright Divide*, 41 CONN. L. REV. 921 (2009); Michael Todd Helfand, *When Mickey Mouse Is as Strong as Superman: The Convergence of Intellectual Property Laws to Protect Fictional Literary and Pictorial Characters*, 44 STAN. L. REV. 623 (1992); Steven L. Nemetz, *Copyright Protection of Fictional Characters*, 14 INTELL. PROP. J. 59 (1999–2000); Dean D. Niro, *Protecting Characters Through Copyright Law: Paving a New Road Upon Which Literary, Graphic, and Motion Picture Characters Can All Travel*, 41 DEPAUL L. REV. 359 (1992);

if it is wholly original, aside from the appearance of boy wizard Harry Potter or starship captain James T. Kirk? If a story sends Harry Potter to visit India—modern, real-world India or a magical world inhabited by well-known figures from Indian mythology and literature—is the appearance of the character alone enough to render the work a copyright violation? Warner Brothers, owner of the copyright for the Harry Potter movies, seems to think so; it has brought actions to suppress commercial publication of works in the "Harry Potter Goes to India" and "Harry Potter Goes to China" vein. Content owners are no less confused on this issue than fans; lack of clarity in the law is partly to blame, although increased education might help as well.

Pictorial representations of characters, whether the universally recognized Mickey Mouse or the more recherché Belkar Bitterleaf, are protected.[19] This seems fairly straightforward: to copy the character in another pictorial work necessarily requires a fairly close copy of the original work. (This does not mean all such copies are infringing, however; fair use still applies.) But the law on copyright of fictional characters described in text rather than artwork is not so clear, although recent events may be swinging Warner Brothers' way. In the U.S., courts have applied two tests to determine whether a character described in text is protected. The first, and more widely applied, protects characters that are "sufficiently delineated" independently of the works in which they appear. The second, applied, although not consistently, in the Ninth Circuit, asks whether the character "constitutes the story being told."

The "sufficiently delineated" test

Under the "sufficiently delineated" test the literary Tarzan (as well as, but as distinct from, the cartoon or movie character Tarzan) is, while his copyright endures, protected. (The question of how long copyright in a character occurs will have to be revisited after we have explored the underlying copyrightability of characters.) The original work in which Tarzan appeared, *Tarzan of the Apes*, introduced the character fully delineated, as we know him today: the feral, orphaned Lord Greystoke, raised in the jungle by apes, who learned French as his first human language yet feels more at home in the trees, away from the humans who so often disappoint him.

When Edgar Rice Burroughs published *Tarzan of the Apes* in 1912 he unwittingly plugged into an archetype, as Bram Stoker had done just 15 years earlier with Dracula. Tarzan immediately found a place in the collective consciousness of the English-speaking world. Although the original Tarzan of the 1912 work was more introspective and contemplative than the silly superhero of the later movies

---

Catherine Seville, *Peter Pan's Rights: "To Die Will Be an Awfully Big Adventure,"* 51 J. Copyright Soc'y U.S.A. 1 (2003).

19 See, for example, *Walt Disney Prod.* v. *Air Pirates*, 345 F. Supp. 108 (N.D. Cal. 1972); *Gaiman* v. *McFarlane*, 360 F.3d 644, 660 (7th Cir. 2004).

and comics, "the delineation was complete upon the 1912 appearance of the first Tarzan title *Tarzan of the Apes*."[20] Burroughs' original Tarzan entered human society as an adult only to find it far more brutal than the "savagery" of the jungle, and at the end of the first book renounced his claim to humanity, claiming kinship only with the apes. Tarzan and his hold on the popular imagination provide endless material for researchers in psychology, literature, and colonial history, and cultural studies. Tarzan himself, swinging through the trees in leopard-skin loincloth, Jane Porter at his side, remains instantly recognizable, present at some level in all of our memories.

But what, precisely, makes Tarzan "sufficiently delineated" to be protected by copyright? Even courts that find this delineation seem unsure how to express it, beyond knowing it when they see it. In finding the character of Tarzan, as distinct from the story of *Tarzan of the Apes*, to be protected by copyright, Judge Werker of the Southern District of New York declared rather confusingly:

> It is beyond cavil that the character "Tarzan" is delineated in a sufficiently distinctive fashion to be copyrightable … Tarzan is the ape-man. He is an individual closely in tune with his jungle environment, able to communicate with animals yet able to experience human emotions. He is athletic, innocent, youthful, gentle and strong. He is Tarzan.[21]

What, really, does that tell us about Tarzan? Perhaps a majority of the protagonists of popular adventure films, shows, and stories, from Aang to Zorro, are "athletic, innocent, youthful, gentle and strong." Nor is a character who lives in the jungle likely to inspire the sympathy or interest of the audience if he or she is not "in tune with his jungle environment." That leaves us with "Tarzan is the ape-man."

The myth of the feral child has been a literary staple since the days of Romulus and Remus. Tarzan, though, has founded no cities;[22] he bears more resemblance to another famous literary feral child, Rudyard Kipling's Mowgli. The *Jungle Book*, containing Kipling's Mowgli stories, had been published just 16 years before *Tarzan of the Apes*. The stories are similar not only for the superficial similarity of their characters—the one raised by wolves, the other by apes—but for a shared skeptical attitude toward the "benefits" of civilization. Both can be, and are, read on several levels; as straightforward children's tales, as allegorical treatments of colonialism (perhaps indictments, perhaps celebrations), as psychological myths.[23]

---

20 *Burroughs* v. *Metro-Goldwyn-Mayer, Inc.*, 683 F.2d 610, 631 (2d Cir. 1982) (Newman, J., concurring).

21 *Burroughs* v. *Metro-Goldwyn-Mayer, Inc.*, 519 F. Supp. 388, 391 (S.D.N.Y. 1981). Most internal citations are omitted from most of the quotes from judicial opinions in this book, except where especially relevant.

22 I fully expect someone more versed in Tarzan lore than I am to contradict me on this.

23 See, for example, David Cowart, *The Tarzan Myth and Jung's Genesis of the Self*, 2 J. American Culture 220 (2004).

Yet no one would mistake Tarzan for Mowgli; the Indian wolf-boy, created by a British author living in Vermont, is instantly recognizable as a completely different person from the American author's English ape-man. If anything, Tarzan bears a greater resemblance to Enkidu, the wild-man raised by beasts, from the *Epic of Gilgamesh*. (While the *Epic of Gilgamesh* is thousands of years old, it was first translated into English in the 1870s and 1880s, beginning with George Smith's partial translation in 1871, in time to provide inspiration for both Kipling and Burroughs.) Though Enkidu is Gilgamesh's sidekick, he is also the more interesting character, and the relationship between Tarzan and the French military officer Lieutenant Paul D'Arnot seems to reflect that between Enkidu and Gilgamesh. Again, though, the early-twentieth-century English ape-man is instantly distinguishable from the ancient Mesopotamian beast-man. The perceived "civilizing" affect of female sexuality and affection is represented in both stories as well, by the relationships between Enkidu and Shamhat in the one and Tarzan and Jane Porter in the other, but this is a commonplace, even cliché, of male-oriented[24] heroic fiction. (Famously, U.S. president Ronald Reagan inhabited this narrative: "I happen to be one who believes that if it wasn't for women, us [*sic*] men would still be walking around in skin suits carrying clubs."[25])

The copyright protection of fictional characters is narrow, though. Tarzan is not Enkidu, just as his blatant imitator, Marvel Comics' Ka-Zar, is not Tarzan. (If Ka-Zar is more Tarzan than Enkidu, Marvel's current big earner, Wolverine, is more Enkidu than Tarzan.) Tarzan is protected by copyright,[26] and perhaps Harry Potter and Captain Kirk are protected as well, but the dozens of imitators flooding the shelves of your local Barnes & Noble are not infringements on Tarzan's copyright, so long as they are identifiably separate characters.

This raises the question of how Tanya Grotter infringes on J.K. Rowling's copyright in Harry Potter. Tanya, described in more detail in the next chapter, is a Russian Harry Potter clone, the heroine of a series of books by Dmitry Yemets. Although her surname rhymes with Harry's, she shares neither gender nor nationality with him. She attends Tibidokhs School for Behaviorally-Challenged Young Witches and Wizards, not Hogwarts School of Witchcraft and Wizardry. She sleeps in the loggia of her foster family's apartment, not the cupboard under the stairs of her uncle's and aunt's house. She fights Chuma-del-tort, not Voldemort. Still, it may be that the similarities between the stories amount to infringement even if the similarity between the characters does not.

---

24 I'm avoiding the word "phallocentric" here, because this is a book about copyright law, not a work of literary criticism.

25 Ronald Reagan, Remarks to International Federation of Business and Professional Women, reported in Walter Isaacson et al., *Trying to Make Amends*, Time, August 15, 1983, available at www.time.com/time/magazine/article/0,9171,949711,00.html.

26 In addition to the cases cited at notes 20 and 21, *supra*, see also *Edgar Rice Burroughs, Inc.* v. *Manns Theatres*, 1976 WL 20994 (C.D. Cal. 1976).

Tarzan's Tanya Grotter—his best-known female imitator—is Sheena, Queen of the Jungle. Sheena first appeared as a comic book character in 1937; though always overshadowed in the marketplace by Tarzan, she has remained a minor fixture of popular culture ever since, appearing in at least two television series and a movie as well as countless comics, and even transformed into a punk rocker by the Ramones. Sheena can claim antecedents predating Tarzan: she bears a more than passing resemblance to Rima, The Jungle Girl, heroine of William Henry Hudson's 1904 novel *Green Mansions*.[27] Sheena's co-creator, William Eisner, claimed to have derived the first syllable of her name, as well as her African setting, from H. Rider Haggard's She, who first appeared in print in 1886.[28] Rima and She, like Sheena, have stayed alive in popular culture. (The fact that both of them apparently die in the original books in which they appear is a minor handicap, easily retconned away.) Both have appeared in movies of their own (three movies, in She's case, although Rima may outscore her on points for having been played by Audrey Hepburn) and in other media; each, like Tarzan, Mowgli, and Enkidu, remains part of the ongoing tradition of adventure fiction.

So finally we are left with nothing that makes Tarzan unique but Judge Werker's circular conclusion: "He is Tarzan." Perhaps, like Justice Potter Stewart in another context, we could never succeed in intelligibly explaining what makes Tarzan Tarzan. But we know him when we see him.[29]

The "story being told" test

Not all characters achieve this exalted copyright status—protection independent of the protection of the works in which they appear. And under the Ninth Circuit's alternative "story being told" test, fewer would. According to this line of judicial reasoning, apparently anyone can write and publish an original story about Sam Spade, the archetypal noir detective created by Dashiell Hammett for *The Maltese Falcon*. Unlike Tarzan or Sheena, Sam Spade has no unmistakable literary antecedents; he is a detective, but he is no Sherlock Holmes or C. Auguste Dupin. Hammett himself stressed this in the introduction to the 1934 edition:

> Spade has no original. He is a dream man in the sense that he is what most of the private detectives I worked with would like to have been and in their cockier moments thought they approached. For your private detective does not—or did

27 William Henry Hudson, Green Mansions: A Romance of the Tropical Forest (1904).

28 H. Rider Haggard, She (1887) (originally appeared as a serial in The Graphic magazine in 1886–1887).

29 *Jacobellis* v. *Ohio*, 378 U.S. 184 (1964) (Stewart, J., concurring): "I shall not today attempt further to define the kinds of material I understand to be embraced within that shorthand description, and perhaps I could never succeed in intelligibly doing so. But I know it when I see it."

> not ten years ago when he was my colleague—want to be an erudite solver of riddles in the Sherlock Holmes manner; he wants to be a hard and shifty fellow, able to take care of himself in any situation, able to get the best of anybody he comes in contact with, whether criminal, innocent by-stander or client.[30]

Sam Spade may have had no original, but he had many successors; he was prototype as well as archetype. The character, much-copied and much-parodied, eventually became a cliché. Yet for some reason courts have been unwilling to extend the world-weary detective the same protection afforded the unworldly ape-man. This apparent discrimination against hard-boiled private detectives owes more to the legal test applied by the Ninth Circuit than to any inherent difference in the characters, however. Sam Spade's originality might seem to enhance his copyrightability, but the Ninth Circuit's "story being told" test is harder to satisfy than the "sufficiently delineated" test used by the Second Circuit to protect Tarzan.

In order for Warner Brothers to film the story (building the film around Humphrey Bogart's iconic portrayal of Sam Spade), Hammett and his publisher, Alfred A. Knopf Inc., granted Warner Brothers "certain defined and detailed exclusive rights to the use of The Maltese Falcon 'writings' in moving pictures, radio, and television."[31] Hammett then wrote additional Sam Spade stories and authorized CBS to broadcast radio plays based on those stories. Warner Brothers sued, claiming its exclusive rights to broadcast Sam Spade stories were infringed upon by the agreement between Hammett and CBS.

The case, *Warner Brothers* v. *Columbia Broadcasting*, was decided on a fairly simple issue—"that the intention of the parties … was not that Hammett should be deprived of using the Falcon characters in subsequently written stories, and that the contract, properly construed, does not deprive Hammett of their use."[32] The rights granted by Hammett and Alfred A. Knopf were to *The Maltese Falcon* alone, and not to the use of the characters in sequels.

Having apparently resolved the issue, the court nonetheless went on to address the copyrightability of the characters. "If Congress had intended that the sale of the right to publish a copyrighted story would foreclose the author's use of its characters in subsequent works for the life of the copyright, it would seem Congress would have made specific provision therefor."[33] As a general rule, apparently, characters were not independently protected by copyright, although there might be exceptions: "It is conceivable that the character really constitutes the story being told, but if the character is only the chessman in the game of telling

30 Dashiell Hammett, *The Maltese Falcon* (intro) (1934), available at www.thrillingdetective.com/trivia/triv244.html (last visited October 20, 2009).

31 *Warner Bros. Pictures* v. *Columbia Broadcasting Sys.*, 216 F.2d 945, 948 (9th Cir. 1954), *cert. denied*, 348 U.S. 971 (1955).

32 *Warner Bros. Pictures*, 216 F.2d at 950.

33 Ibid.

the story he is not within the area of the protection afforded by the copyright."[34] Sam Spade, it turned out, was just such a chessman: "We conclude that even if the Owners assigned their complete rights in the copyright to the Falcon, such assignment did not prevent the author from using the characters used therein, in other stories. The characters were vehicles for the story told, and the vehicles did not go with the sale of the story."[35] The court's ruminations on this point seem to be dicta, and have been treated as such by several courts.[36]

Is this inconsistent with the Tarzan cases? Is Tarzan a chessman as well? Perhaps not. The outcomes for Tarzan and Sam Spade might have been the same under either test. *The Maltese Falcon* is a story driven by plot and atmosphere; Sam Spade is not so much a man as an attitude, and might not be "sufficiently delineated" for protection even under our alternate *Burroughs* v. *MGM* test. In contrast, Tarzan's stories are about Tarzan; the plots are unmemorable, the settings varied—although a jungle Eden always lurks in the background. The story being told in *Tarzan of the Apes* is the story of Tarzan; the story being told in *The Maltese Falcon* is a bitter reflection on the moral frailty of humanity, no more the story of Sam Spade than it is the story of its MacGuffin, the bird itself, "the stuff that dreams are made of."[37]

---

34 Ibid.

35 Ibid.

36 See, for example, *Columbia Broadcasting Sys., Inc.* v. *DeCosta*, 377 F.2d 315, 321 (1st Cir. 1967); *Goodis* v. *United Artists Television, Inc.*, 425 F.2d 397, 406 n.1 (2d Cir. 1970). But cf. *Columbia Pictures Corp.* v. *National Broadcasting Co.*, 137 F. Supp. 348, 353 (S.D. Cal. 1955); *Walt Disney Prods.* v. *Air Pirates*, 345 F. Supp. 108, 111–12 (N.D. Cal. 1972); *Hospital for Sick Children* v. *Melody Fare*, 516 F. Supp. 67, 72 (E.D. Va. 1980). On appeal in *Air Pirates* the Ninth Circuit specifically refused to address the question of whether the test in *Warner Bros. Pictures* v. *Columbia Broadcasting* was holding or dicta. *Walt Disney Prods.* v. *Air Pirates*, 581 F.2d 751, 755 n.10 (9th Cir. 1978). The Ninth Circuit again declined to address this question in *Olson* v. *National Broadcasting Co.*, 855 F.2d 1446, 1452 n.7: "We therefore need not resolve the issue left open in *Air Pirates*, 581 F.2d at 755 n. 10, whether the Warner Bros. statements should be considered dicta."

37 Sam is, of course, misquoting Prospero:

You do look, my son, in a moved sort,
As if you were dismay'd: be cheerful, sir.
Our revels now are ended. These our actors,
As I foretold you, were all spirits and
Are melted into air, into thin air:
And, like the baseless fabric of this vision,
The cloud-capp'd towers, the gorgeous palaces,
The solemn temples, the great globe itself,
Ye all which it inherit, shall dissolve
And, like this insubstantial pageant faded,
Leave not a rack behind. We are such stuff
As dreams are made on, and our little life
Is rounded with a sleep. Sir, I am vex'd;

Then again, the Sam Spade court may have allowed itself to be influenced by a non-economic factor, one which should hold little or no weight in a regime in which copyright is perfectly alienable, but far greater weight in a European-style moral rights regime: Dashiell Hammett was Sam Spade's creator. Rather than deprive Hammett of the right to write additional stories about his creation, the court went out of its way to create a test under which Hammett would win. Hammett was lucky in this; the history of popular culture is replete with characters, from Superman to Nancy Drew, whose creators have received pittances and lost all right to create independent stories based on the character, then watched them go on to make millions for others.[38]

But where does this leave our other protagonists? Like Tarzan before him, Harry Potter has his name on the books and movies in which he appears; is the story being told in *Harry Potter and the Philosopher's Stone* the story of Harry Potter? What of other characters in the work? The sinister, enigmatic Professor Snape might be sufficiently delineated for protection under *Burroughs* v. *MGM*, but the story being told in the books (with the exception of the seventh book) is not the story of Snape. The "story being told" test seems especially likely to discriminate against secondary characters, however well-delineated.

These two tests—the "sufficiently delineated" test and the "story being told" test—are bound to yield different results in some cases. This inconsistency further enhances the confusion surrounding the copyrightability of fictional characters. The tension between these two tests has done nothing to clarify the copyrightability and extent of copyright protection of fictional characters.

The "story being told" or Sam Spade test is the more restrictive of the two, and has found no general acceptance outside the Ninth Circuit, in which it was

---

Bear with my weakness; my brain is troubled:
Be not disturb'd with my infirmity:
If you be pleased, retire into my cell
And there repose: a turn or two I'll walk,
To still my beating mind.

William Shakespeare, *The Tempest*, Act IV, Scene 1.

38 Nancy Drew was invented, more or less, by publisher Edward Stratemeyer, but the first Nancy Drew novels were written by Mildred Wirt under the name Carolyn Keene. Wirt gave up the rights not only to the character Nancy Drew, but also to the pseudonym Carolyn Keene. See, for example, Emily Jenkins, *The Case of the Girl Detective: With the Passing of Nancy Drew's First Author, the Mystery of the Teenage Sleuth's True Identity Only Deepens*, Salon.com, June 10, 2002, www.salon.com/books/feature/2002/06/10/drew; Amy Benfer, *Who was Carolyn Keene? An Interview with Mildred Wirt Benson, the Original Ghostwriter for the Nancy Drew Mystery Novels*, Salon.com, October 8, 1999, www.salon.com/life/feature/1999/10/08/keene_q_a. See also generally *Franklin Mint Corp.* v. *National Wildlife Art Exchange*, 575 F.2d 65, 66 (3d Cir. 1978).

originally adopted; courts outside the Ninth Circuit have avoided the reasoning in *Warner Brothers* v. *Columbia Broadcasting*.[39]

---

39 See, for example, *Goodis* v. *United Artists Television, Inc.*, 425 F.2d 397, 406 n.1 (2d Cir. 1970): "Although the Ninth Circuit did not reach the question whether Warner Brothers could have used the characters of the Falcon in a new series even without an exclusive copyright—by asserting, in effect, that now the Falcon's characters were in the public domain—we think such a conclusion would be clearly untenable from the standpoint of public policy, for it would effectively permit the unrestrained pilfering of characters." See also *Ideal Toy Corp.* v. *Kenner Prods.*, 443 F. Supp. 291, 301 n.8 (S.D.N.Y. 1977): "The plaintiff relies on the 9th Circuit case of *Warner Bros. Pictures, Inc. v. Columbia Broadcasting System, Inc.*, 216 F.2d 945 (9th Cir. 1954), *cert. denied*, 348 U.S. 971, 75 S.Ct. 532, 99 L.Ed. 756 (1955), to support its argument that the three 'Star Wars' characters at issue here are not within the copyright protection granted to the movie itself. This case is not the law of this circuit, and this Court declines an invitation to follow it for the reasons set forth by Judge Wollenberg in *Walt Disney Prods. v. Air Pirates*, 345 F. Supp. 108, 111–13 (N.D. Cal. 1972)." See also generally *Lotus Dev. Co.* v. *Paperback Software, Int'l.*, 740 F. Supp. 37, 51 (D. Mass. 1990) (referring only to the Second Circuit test); *Herzog* v. *Castle Rock Entertainment*, 193 F.3d 1241, 1259 (11th Cir. 1999) (applying the Second Circuit test); *Trust Co. Bank* v. *MGM/UA Entertainment Co.*, 593 F. Supp. 580, 585–87 (N.D. Ga. 1984), *aff'd*, 772 F.2d 740 (11th Cir. 1985) (referring to the Ninth Circuit test); *Klinger* v. *Weekly World News, Inc.*, 747 F. Supp. 1477, 1481 (S.D. Fla. 1990) (referring to the Ninth Circuit test); *Tralins* v. *Kaiser Aluminum and Chem. Corp.*, 160 F. Supp. 511, 516 (D. Md. 1958); *Columbia Broadcasting Sys.* v. *DeCosta*, 377 F.2d 315, 320 (1st Cir. 1967); *Siegel* v. *National Periodical Publishers, Inc.*, 508 F.2d 909 (2d Cir. 1974); *Atari, Inc.* v. *North Am. Philips Consumer Elecs. Corp.*, 672 F.2d 607 (7th Cir. 1982), *cert. denied*, 459 U.S. 880 (1982); *DC Comics, Inc.* v. *Reel Fantasy, Inc.*, 696 F.2d 24 (2d Cir. 1982); *Burroughs* v. *Metro-Goldwyn-Mayer, Inc.*, 519 F. Supp 388 (S.D.N.Y. 1981); *Filmvideo Releasing Corp.* v. *Hastings*, 509 F. Supp. 60 (S.D.N.Y. 1981), *aff'd*, 668 F.2d 91 (2d Cir. 1981); *Frye* v. *Young Men's Christian Ass'n of Lincoln, Nebraska*, No. 4:98CV3105, slip op. at 2 (D.Neb. July 20, 2009) ("As in *Nichols*, the characters in Kastleland are skeletal archetypes and the plot is largely composed of *scènes à faire*"; the District of Nebraska, within the Eighth Circuit, applying the Second Circuit test); *Gaiman* v. *McFarlane*, 360 F.3d 644 (7th Cir. 2004) (discussed in the text accompanying notes 60 and 61, *infra*; *United Feature Syndicate, Inc.* v. *Sunrise Mold Co.*, 569 F. Supp. 1475 (S.D. Fla. 1983); *Universal City Studios, Inc.* v. *Kamar Indus., Inc.*, 217 U.S.P.Q. 1162, 1166 (S.D. Tex. 1982) (stating "[t]he defendant's contention that copyright protection for a motion picture does not extend to characters or their names is not well taken in a situation involving a distinctive and well developed character such as 'E.T.'," and then citing, oddly, *Nichols* and *Warner Bros.* v. *CBS*, without further explanation); *Warner Bros., Inc.* v. *American Broadcasting Cos.*, 530 F. Supp. 1187 (S.D.N.Y. 1982), *aff'd*, 720 F.2d 231 (2d Cir. 1983) (discussing the copyrightability of Superman). But cf. from a court within the Fourth Circuit, *Hospital for Sick Children* v. *Melody Fare Dinner Theatre*, 516 F.Supp. 67, 72 (E.D. Va. 1980): "While characters alone may not be copyrightable [pursuant to *Warner Bros. v. CBS*], the amalgamation of the characters in the theme of Peter Pan was done by Barrie." *Herzog* v. *Castle Rock Entertainment*, 193 F.3d 1241, 1259 (11th Cir. 1999) (applying the Second Circuit test); *Trust Co. Bank* v. *MGM/UA Entertainment Co.*, 593 F. Supp. 580, 585–87 (N.D. Ga. 1984), *aff'd*, 772 F.2d 740 (11th Cir. 1985) (referring to the

Even within the Ninth Circuit, the "story being told" test is now viewed warily. In *Air Pirates*, the court, while refusing to characterize that part of the *Warner Brothers* v. *Columbia Broadcasting* decision containing the test as holding or dicta, explained that the logic of the "story being told" test was at most applicable only to purely literary characters, not characters accompanied by graphic representations:

> It is true that this Court's opinion in Warner Brothers Pictures v. Columbia Broadcasting System lends some support to the position that characters ordinarily are not copyrightable.
>
> * * *
>
> Judge Stephens' opinion considered "whether it was ever intended by the copyright statute that characters with their names should be under its protection." In that context he concluded that such a restriction on Hammett's future use of a character was unreasonable, at least when the characters were merely vehicles for the story and did not "really constitute" the story being told … In reasoning that characters "are always limited and always fall into limited patterns," Judge Stephens recognized that it is difficult to delineate distinctively a literary character. When the author can add a visual image, however, the difficulty is reduced. Put another way, while many literary characters may embody little more than an unprotected idea, a comic book character, which has physical as well as conceptual qualities, is more likely to contain some unique elements of expression. Because comic book characters therefore are distinguishable from literary characters, the Warner Brothers language does not preclude protection of Disney's characters.[40]

This, if anything, makes matters worse. What of a book with illustrations? Do cover illustrations count? What if the cover illustration is actually a photograph? What of a story with a well-known cartoon character, if the character is described only in text, without illustrations?[41]

But the difference in the approaches may be less dramatic than it appears. In the words of the leading U.S. copyright treatise:

Ninth Circuit test); *Klinger* v. *Weekly World News, Inc.*, 747 F. Supp. 1477, 1481 (S.D. Fla. 1990) (referring to the Ninth Circuit test).

40 *Walt Disney Productions* v. *Air Pirates*, 581 F.2d 751 (9th Cir. 1978), *cert. denied sub nom O'Neill* v. *Walt Disney Productions*, 439 U.S. 1132 (1979) (citations omitted).

41 See, for example, Frederic Tuten, Tintin in the New World (Baltimore: Black Classic Press, 1993). Not a perfect example, perhaps; the cover illustration is an original drawing of the characters used with permission of Hergé's estate, and the frontispiece by Roy Lichtenstein is also used by permission.

> Those cases which have denied such protection are more reconcileable [*sic*] with those which have recognized such protection than the language in some of the opinions would seem to indicate. That is, in those cases recognizing such protection, the character appropriated was distinctively delineated in the plaintiff's work, and such delineation was copied in the defendant's work. In the non-protection cases, the similarity generally was only of character type and not of a distinctively delineated character.[42]

In Nimmer's opinion, *Air Pirates* represents a distancing from the "story being told" test:

> From this it would seem to follow that a literary character may achieve separate copyrightability even if it does not meet "the story being told standard" provided the character is sufficiently developed and finely drawn so as to cross the line from "idea" to "expression." This would seem to portend a recognition by the Ninth Circuit of the generally accepted ["sufficiently delineated"] standard.[43]

While the "story being told" test is by no means defunct, it seems safe to say that in the future it will be applied cautiously, even in the Ninth Circuit. This is not the best possible news for fanfic writers: the "story being told" test is the more restrictive of the two, and thus protects fewer characters.

The Ninth Circuit backs away from the "story being told" test

While the Ninth Circuit has not yet overtly abandoned the "story being told" test, district courts within it seem to be taking Nimmer's view, or at least acknowledging that the current state of protection of characters created only in text is unclear:

> *Air Pirates* can be interpreted as either attempting to harmonize granting copyright protection to graphic characters with the "story being told" test enunciated in the Sam Spade case or narrowing the "story being told" test to characters in literary works. If *Air Pirates* is construed as holding that the graphic characters in question constituted the story being told, it does little to alter the Sam Spade opinion. However, it is equally as plausible to interpret *Air Pirates* as applying a less stringent test for protectability of graphic characters.
>
> Professor Nimmer has adopted the latter reading as he interprets Air Pirates as limiting the story being told requirement to word portraits. Further, Professor Nimmer finds that the reasoning of the Sam Spade case is undermined by the Air Pirates opinion, even as it relates to word portraits … This is true because

42 Melville B. Nimmer & David Nimmer, Nimmer on Copyright § 2–12 (LexisNexis, 2008).

43 Ibid.

> the use of a less stringent test for protection of characters in the graphic medium casts doubt on the vitality of the more stringent story being told test for graphic characters. As a practical matter, a graphically depicted character is much more likely than a literary character to be fleshed out in sufficient detail so as to warrant copyright protection. But this fact does not warrant the creation of separate analytical paradigms for protection of characters in the two mediums.[44]

Similarly, in *Toho* v. *William Morrow & Co.*, the Central District of California applied the "sufficiently delineated" test rather than the "story being told" test to Toho Films' copyright in its best-known character, Godzilla. While Godzilla has changed size, shape and other characteristics frequently over the course of his (or, in at least one case, her) existence, and often over the course of a single film, the court found that "Godzilla is always a pre-historic, fire-breathing, gigantic dinosaur alive and well in the modern world" and is thus sufficiently delineated to be protected by copyright:

> Morrow argues that the Godzilla character is not delineated enough to merit copyright protection. Only those characters that are highly delineated with constant traits qualify for protection separate from the works in which they appear. [*Nichols*] ("[T]he less developed the characters the less they can be copyrighted, that is the penalty an author must bear for marking them too indistinctly.") [*Olson*]. Morrow contends that because the Godzilla character has assumed many shapes and personalities over the course of the films, it has no constant traits and therefore cannot acquire copyright protection apart from the film in which it appears.
>
> Toho contends that where a character is visually depicted, and contains the requisite attributes of originality, a character is sufficiently delineated to receive copyright protection. [*Air Pirates*]. Moreover, Toho argues that [*MGM* v. *Honda*] is instructive. In that case, the court held that the James Bond character was protected by copyright, even though the character had changed "from year to year and film to film." The court further held that the James Bond character was copyrightable because of an identifiable set of traits that had developed over the course of the 16 James Bond films. In this case, Godzilla has likewise developed a constant set of traits that distinguish him/her/it from other fictional characters. While Godzilla may have shifted from evil to good, there remains an underlying set of attributes that remain in every film. Godzilla is always a pre-historic, fire-breathing, gigantic dinosaur alive and well in the modern world. This Court finds that Toho's Godzilla is a well-defined character with highly delineated

44 *Anderson* v. *Stallone*, No. 87-0592, 1989 WL 206431, at *6–7 (C.D. Cal. 1989) (citations omitted).

> consistent traits. Therefore, Toho has demonstrated prima facie ownership of copyrights in the Godzilla character apart from any film.[45]

Toho is especially disturbing for fan authors, as the work in question was a reference intended for Godzilla fans, "contain[ing] commentary, critique, and trivia[,] extensive detailed plot summaries of each Godzilla film[, and] numerous pictures from Toho's films[.]"[46] In other words, it was at least superficially similar to the Harry Potter Lexicon, discussed in detail in Chapter 4.

As the excerpt from *Toho* above makes clear, *MGM* v. *Honda* involved copyright in the James Bond character, apparently as represented in the 16 (to that date) "official" films rather than in the now largely unread stories by Ian Fleming. Like Godzilla, 007 has had many visually different onscreen incarnations, and his back-story and personality characteristics have undergone many changes. There is even a fan theory to account for this: "James Bond" and "007" refer not to any individual person, but are code names assigned to new agents as their predecessors in the position retire or are killed.[47]

American Honda Motor Co.'s advertising agency, Ruben Postauer, created an advertisement in which, according to the court:

> [A] young, well-dressed couple in a Honda del Sol [is] being chased by a high-tech helicopter. A grotesque villain with metal-encased arms jumps out of the helicopter onto the car's roof, threatening harm. With a flirtatious turn to his companion, the male driver deftly releases the Honda's detachable roof (which Defendants claim is the main feature allegedly highlighted by the commercial), sending the villain into space and effecting the couple's speedy get-away.[48]

The commercial can still be found online.[49] While the basic aspects—couple in a car, pursuing helicopter, weird villain, quip after casually defeating villain—can all be found in the James Bond movies, they can also be found throughout the action-movie genre. Nonetheless, the Central District of California found not only

---

45 *Toho* v. *William Morrow & Co., Inc.*, 33 F. Supp. 2d 1206, 1216 (C.D. Cal. 1998). As an aside, I'd just like to say what a delight it is to be part of a legal system in which the words "Godzilla is always a pre-historic, fire-breathing, gigantic dinosaur alive and well in the modern world" can appear in a judicial opinion.

46 *Toho*, 33 F. Supp. 2d at 1217.

47 See, for example, Derek James, *6 Insane Fan Theories that Actually Make Great Movies Even Better: #6. James Bond Is Not a Man, but a Code Name*, Cracked.com, January 11, 2010, www.cracked.com/article/18367_6-insane-fan-theories-that-actually-make-great-movies-better.

48 *Metro-Goldwyn-Mayer Inc.* v. *American Honda Motor Co. Inc.*, 900 F. Supp. 1287, 1291 (C.D. Cal. 1995).

49 See, for example, *Video: Honda US Del Sol Commercial ~ Classic!*, available at www.webridestv.com/videos/honda-us-del-sol-commercial--classic--32863 (visited January 12, 2010).

that the James Bond character was probably protected by copyright (which, in light of the other cases we've looked at, seems obvious under either the "sufficiently delineated" or "story being told" test) but that Honda's ad probably infringed on that copyright—at least, that MGM had established a sufficient likelihood of prevailing on the merits of the copyright claim to support the grant of a preliminary injunction. In finding the character protected, the court at first appeared to cling to the "story being told" test:

> Two subsequent Ninth Circuit decisions have cast doubt on the continued viability of the Sam Spade holding as applied to graphic characters … The [first of these,] *Air Pirates* … may be viewed as either: (1) following Sam Spade by implicitly holding that Disney's graphic characters constituted the story being told; or (2) applying a less stringent test for the protectability of graphic characters.
>
> * * *
>
> [The] second [of these, *Olson*] did little to clarify Air Pirates' impact on the Sam Spade test. In Olson … the court cited with approval the Sam Spade "story being told" test and declined to characterize this language as dicta. Later in the opinion, the court cited the *Air Pirates* decision along with Second Circuit precedent, recognizing that "cases subsequent to [the Sam Spade decision] have allowed copyright protection for characters who are especially distinctive." … However, later in the opinion, the court distanced itself from the character delineation test applied by these other cases, referring to it as "the more lenient standard[ ] adopted elsewhere."[50]

While the *MGM* v. *Honda* court leaned more unambiguously toward the "story being told" test than other recent decisions from courts within the Ninth Circuit, it recognized the confusion and, to be on the safe side, applied the Second Circuit's "sufficiently delineated" test as well.

> Reviewing the evidence and arguments, the Court believes that James Bond is more like Rocky than Sam Spade—in essence, that James Bond is a copyrightable character under either the Sam Spade "story being told test" or the Second Circuit's "character delineation" test. Like Rocky, Sherlock Holmes, Tarzan, and Superman, James Bond has certain character traits that have been developed over time through the sixteen films in which he appears. Contrary to Defendants' assertions, because many actors can play Bond is a testament to the fact that Bond is a unique character whose specific qualities remain constant despite the change in actors. See Pfeiffer and Lisa, *The Incredible World of 007*, at 8 ("[Despite the different actors who have played the part] James Bond is

50 *Metro-Goldwyn-Mayer Inc.*, 900 F. Supp. at 1295–96.

> like an old reliable friend."). Indeed, audiences do not watch Tarzan, Superman, Sherlock Holmes, or James Bond for the story, they watch these films to see their heroes at work. A James Bond film without James Bond is not a James Bond film. Moreover, as discussed more specifically below, the Honda Man's character, from his appearance to his grace under pressure, is substantially similar to Plaintiffs' Bond.
>
> Accordingly, the Court concludes that Plaintiffs will probably succeed on their claim that James Bond is a copyrightable character under either the "story being told" or the "character delineation" test.[51]

The court's references to Rocky and Superman are supported with footnotes to cases addressing the copyrightability of these characters.[52] Tarzan and Sherlock Holmes receive no footnotes, but we have already addressed Tarzan in some detail, and the passage of time has left Sherlock Holmes at least partially in the public domain.

The court's reasoning is disturbing, deeply disturbing. The name "James Bond" appears nowhere in the commercial, and in appearance the actor driving the car shares with James Bond (whose appearance, as noted, is ever changing) only the characteristics of being male and Caucasian, and perhaps fairly good-looking—not a rarity among movie leads. Honda argued that MGM was "simply trying to gain a monopoly over the 'action/spy/police hero' genre which is contrary to the purposes of copyright law."[53]

On this issue, with dueling expert testimony as to whether the James Bond film lay within a genre or were in fact the source of that genre, with all others in the genre as imitators, there would seem to be a triable issue of fact. Nonetheless, the court found that MGM had established a likelihood of prevailing on the merits—raising, though not answering, the question of where that leaves every arguably Bondesque action movie and television show of the past few decades.

The court relied to some extent on facts relating to the development of the commercial. Copyright infringement requires a valid copyright plus unauthorized copying. Granting the copyright in the character of James Bond and the lack of authorization, the question becomes whether Ruben-Postaer copied the character. Copying requires access to the protected work plus substantial similarity between the protected work and that allegedly infringing upon it. The court found evidence of access in:

> (1) [Ruben-Postaer vice-president] Yoshida's admission that he has at least viewed portions of the James Bond films on television; (2) the "Honda man's"

---

51 Ibid.

52 *Anderson* v. *Stallone*, No. 87-0592, 1989 WL 206431, at *6–7 (C.D. Cal. 1989); *Warner Bros. Inc.* v. *American Broadcasting Cos.*, 654 F.2d 204, 208–09 (2d Cir. 1981).

53 *Metro-Goldwyn-Mayer Inc.*, 900 F. Supp. at 1293.

> having been referred to as "James Bob"; and (3) the casting director's desire to cast "James Bond"-type actors and actresses, are factors sufficient to establish Defendants' access to Plaintiffs' work. Moreover, the sheer worldwide popularity and distribution of the Bond films allows the Court to indulge a presumption of access.[54]

Again, this seems obvious: everyone in the English-speaking world, and certainly everyone working in the media industry, has at least a passing familiarity with James Bond. This leaves only the question of substantial similarity, to which the court applied both an extrinsic test (looking at various elements of the commercial and comparing them to various elements of the Bond movies) and an intrinsic test (looking at "whether the 'total concept and feel' of the two works is also substantially similar"). The court found issues of material fact to preclude summary judgment. Overall, the court's language does seem to suggest, despite its protests, that entire genres can be preempted. If James Bond can own an entire genre, why can't Harry Potter, James T. Kirk, or Indiana Jones? And where would that leave the future of fiction?

Outside California's Central District (within which lies Hollywood), at least one district court has also applied both tests, but in this case with more emphasis on the Second Circuit's "sufficiently delineated" test. In *Bach* v. *Forever Living Products*, the Western District of Washington considered the copyrightability of proto-New-Age icon Jonathan Livingston Seagull. The defendant, a multi-level marketing company, used a seagull as its logo, which seems innocuous enough, but also referred to the logo as "Jonathan," which doesn't. The court, in what seems to be the current Ninth Circuit practice, waffled on which test to apply and ended up deciding the results would be the same under either:

> "While characters are ordinarily not afforded copyright protection … characters that are 'especially distinctive' or the 'story being told' receive protection apart from the copyrighted work." *Rice v. Fox Broad. Co.*, 330 F.3d 1170, 1175 (9th Cir.2003). Courts have given copyright protection to characters that are highly delineated or play a central role in an overall work. [See *Anderson* v. *Stallone*] (concluding that Rocky characters are both highly delineated and the "story being told" in the movies Rocky I, II, and III); [*Toho*] (Godzilla character protected); [*MGM* v. *Honda*] (James Bond character protected); Universal City Studios, Inc. v. Kamar Indus., Inc., 217 U.S.P.Q. 1162, 1165 (S.D.Tex.1982) (E.T. character protected) … But where the characters are not sufficiently delineated or are not the central focus of the work, courts decline to give the characters copyright protection.[55]

* * *

54 Ibid., at 1297.

55 *Bach* v. *Forever Living Products*, 473 F. Supp. 2d 1127, 1133 (W.D. Wash. 2007).

> [I]t is the unique combination of elements that makes up a protected character. The Court will therefore consider whether Jonathan Livingston Seagull is sufficiently delineated or "the story being told" considering the combination of all the elements of his character.
>
> Plaintiffs argue that like Rocky, James Bond, Godzilla, and others, Jonathan Livingston Seagull is a highly delineated character that warrants copyright protection. Plaintiffs contend that the Jonathan Livingston Seagull character is a "one-of-a-kind seagull—a thinking, talking, philosophizing, risk-taking, limit-testing seagull."
>
> * * *
>
> Every literary character has elements that are not original, but, as explained above, courts look to the combination of those elements to determine whether the character is protectable. Like other highly delineated literary and film characters, the Jonathan Livingston Seagull character is protected under copyright. Jonathan Livingston Seagull is a well-defined character—an ordinary seagull named Jonathan Livingston Seagull who is determined to fly higher and faster, who transcends his beginnings, and who teaches others to do the same. He is not a stock character and the fact that his character has not been delineated over time is inconsequential.[56]
>
> * * *
>
> In addition, to the extent that a character is protectable because it is the "story being told," Jonathan Livingston Seagull is protectable. He is the "story being told" and is not a mere "chessman in the game of telling the story." He is the title character in a book that is entirely about his development from an ordinary seagull to an extraordinary one. His character is protectable under this doctrine as well.[57]

In *Olson* v. *National Broadcasting Co.*,[58] the Ninth Circuit itself took a similar view, extending the protection of cartoon characters in *Air Pirates* to characters portrayed by live actors in movies and television shows:

> We recognize that cases subsequent to Warner Bros. have allowed copyright protection for characters who are especially distinctive. For example, cartoon characters may be afforded copyright protection notwithstanding Warner Bros. [See *Air Pirates*]. "[M]any literary characters may embody little more than

56 Ibid., at 1134–36.

57 Ibid., at 1136.

58 *Olson* v. *National Broadcasting Co.*, 855 F.2d 1446 (9th Cir. 1988).

> an unprotected idea [while] a comic book character, which has physical as well as conceptual qualities, is more likely to contain some unique elements of expression." For similar reasons, copyright protection may be afforded to characters visually depicted in a television series or in a movie.[59]

It might be worth noting that the *Olson/Air Pirates* reasoning might have been applied to *Bach* as well. *Jonathan Livingston Seagull* is illustrated, after a fashion, with photographs of seagulls, which might be said to be graphic representations of the character—though, the book's central thesis notwithstanding, one seagull looks very much like another to anyone who isn't a seagull.

The Seventh Circuit later took the view that with *Olson* and *Air Pirates* the Ninth Circuit had "killed" the "story being told" test:

> We are mindful that the Ninth Circuit denied copyrightability to Dashiell Hammett's famously distinctive detective character Sam Spade in [*Warner Bros. Pictures, Inc.* v. *Columbia Broadcasting System*]. That decision is wrong, though perhaps understandable on the "legal realist" ground that Hammett was not claiming copyright in Sam Spade—on the contrary, he wanted to reuse his own character but to be able to do so he had to overcome Warner Brothers' claim to own the copyright. The Ninth Circuit has killed the decision, see [Olson and Air Pirates], though without the usual obsequies[.][60]

The Seventh Circuit added an unnecessary but interesting rumination on the differing nature of purely textual fiction—novels and short stories—and graphic representations, whether through the use of drawings or live actors:

> The description of a character in prose leaves much to the imagination, even when the description is detailed-as in Dashiell Hammett's description of Sam Spade's physical appearance in the first paragraph of The Maltese Falcon. "Samuel Spade's jaw was long and bony, his chin a jutting v under the more flexible v of his mouth. His nostrils curved back to make another, smaller, v. His yellow-grey eyes were horizontal. The v motif was picked up again by thickish brows rising outward from twin creases above a hooked nose, and his pale brown hair grew down—from high flat temples—in a point on his forehead. He looked rather pleasantly like a blond satan." Even after all this, one hardly knows what Sam Spade looked like. But everyone knows what Humphrey Bogart looked like. A reader of unillustrated fiction completes the work in his mind; the reader of a comic book or the viewer of a movie is passive. That is why kids lose a lot when they don't read fiction, even when the movies and television that they watch are aesthetically superior.[61]

---

59 Ibid., at 1452.

60 *Gaiman* v. *McFarlane*, 360 F.3d 644, 660 (7th Cir. 2004).

61 Ibid., at 660–61.

This provides another reason for treating copyright in purely-textual characters differently: the very appearance of these characters is the product not purely of the author's imagination but of a joint effort of imagination on the part of the author and the reader.[62] All forms of storytelling necessarily leave some parts of the story untold; to tell every detail of the life of a single character would take a lifetime. Each viewer of a movie or a television series, or the reader of a comic book, may create a back-story in his or her mind, or imagine what happens in the interstices between scenes, just as the reader of a novel. But to the watcher of a Harry Potter movie, Harry looks and sounds like Daniel Radcliffe; while to each reader of a Harry Potter novel, Harry looks and sounds uniquely individual—with the proviso, of course, that his hair should remain as black as a blackboard, and his eyes as green as a fresh-pickled toad. By helping to create the character, the reader or viewer gains a stake in the character. Perhaps the different degrees of copyright protection extended to purely textual and graphically-represented characters reflect the opinion expressed by Judge Posner above—correct or otherwise—that the stake of a "reader of unillustrated fiction" is greater than the stake of "the reader of a comic book or the viewer of a movie." (Problems are bound to arise, of course, when characters have reached large audiences via both text-only and graphic representations, as the Harry Potter or Lord of the Rings characters have done.)

The two tests and copyright protection of characters today

Just as the Ninth Circuit may be limiting the "story being told" test, the Second Circuit has imposed limits on the protection afforded copyrighted characters under the "sufficiently delineated" test, also called the *Nichols* test after the first case to apply it, *Nichols* v. *Universal Pictures Corporation*.[63] From the outset, courts addressing the copyrightability of characters have recognized that the protection granted must be narrow. Without specifically invoking the *scènes à faire* doctrine, they have recognized that certain characters are stock. The first case to contemplate the copyrightability of "the characters, quite independently of the 'plot' proper" acknowledges this:

> If Twelfth Night were copyrighted it is quite possible that a second comer might so closely imitate Sir Toby Belch or Malvolio as to infringe, but it would not be enough that for one of his characters he cast a riotous knight who kept wassail to the discomfort of the household, or a vain and foppish steward who became amorous of his mistress. These would be no more than Shakespeare's "ideas" in the play, as little capable of monopoly as Einstein's doctrine of Relativity or Darwin's theory of the Origin of the Species. It follows that the less developed

62 See generally Roland Barthes, The Death of the Author, in Image—Music—Text 142 (Stephen Heath, trans., New York: Hill and Wang, 1977) and its innumerable ripples.

63 *Nichols* v. *Universal Pictures Corporation*, 45 F.2d 119 (2d Cir. 1930), *cert. denied*, 282 U.S. 902 (1931).

> the characters, the less they can be copyrighted; that is the penalty an author must bear for making them too indistinct.[64]

A year later, the Southern District of New York made this point more explicitly in a case against playwright Eugene O'Neill by Gladys Adelina Selma Lewis, who wrote under the name Georges Lewys. Often, when a work is successful, an unknown author emerges with a claim of plagiarism. In this case the successful work was O'Neill's play *Strange Interlude* and the unknown author was Lewys, whose poem "Verdun" was, or was planned to be, "placed in a crystal casket on a marble base at the entrance to the great Memorial Tower at Verdun."[65] Lewys claimed O'Neill had plagiarized her privately published (and, by the standards of the time, "obscene," although that seems silly now) novel, *The Temple of Pallas-Athenae*. O'Neill's play, *Strange Interlude*, was eventually filmed by MGM, starring Nina Shearer and Clark Gable (and with *Tarzan* star Maureen O'Sullivan in a minor role). O'Neill, who was not unbiased in the matter, thought the claim baseless: "A lady nut, who properly ought to be put in an asylum, is at present suing me for filching *Strange Interlude* from some unknown privately-printed bit of junk she wrote."[66]

Dismissing the idea that O'Neill's work or characters infringed on Lewys', Judge Woolsey also hinted, perhaps, that objectively *The Temple of Pallas-Athenae* (written, according to Lewys, when she was 19) was, like much online fanfic today, not very good:

> It is true that there are old and young people in both plots. It is true that there are fathers and mothers and daughters and sons. But, after having carefully read both books more than once, I think it is fair to say that in the plaintiff's book the characters are merely types—the socially ambitious mother and daughter, the obtuse but successful American business man, the dissipated foreign nobleman, the middle aged English philanderer, and the fabulously rich Russian princess. None of these types is individualized sufficiently to make the characters of the defendant any possible infringement of the plaintiff's copyright.
>
> In the defendant's book, on the other hand, the characters are individualized and are perceptible in the round, as it seems to me, to a very extraordinary degree.
>
> The plaintiff cannot copyright a type any more than could Miss Nichols in the case of Abie's Irish Rose [the case referred to in the text accompanying note 64, *supra*], by taking for her characters stock figures, such as a low comedy

64 Ibid., at 120.

65 *FRANCE: O, the Birds! O, the Birds!*, Time, January 28, 1929, www.time.com/time/magazine/article/0,9171,723584,00.html.

66 Madeline Smith & Richard Eaton, Eugene O'Neill in Court, preface (New York: Peter Lang Pub., 1993).

> Jew or a low comedy Irishman. We may, therefore, dismiss the question of any possibility of infringement of the plaintiff's types in The Temple by the defendant's characters in *Strange Interlude*.[67]

While *types* of characters are thus not copyrightable, individual characters, to the extent that they are recognizably individual, are. The "sufficiently delineated" or *Nichols* test seems inherently more sensible than the "story being told" test, as its wider adoption indicates.[68] While determining whether a character is sufficiently delineated to qualify for copyright protection presents its own problems, requiring judges and perhaps jurors to determine whether a particularly character constitutes the story being told requires them to become literary critics: on the most superficial level, perhaps, the story being told in *Magic Mountain* is the story of Hans Castorp, but few readers see the story so simply.[69] Generations of readers and critics have disagreed on what story *Moby Dick* is telling: how, then, can a court be certain which of the characters constitute that story? Harry Potter's name appears on the cover of each volume of his adventures, but to a greater or lesser extent, especially in the early books, he is something of an Everyman, designed to allow the readers to view his world from within. Is the story being told in *Mrs. Dalloway* the story of the titular character, or of her counterweight Septimus? Both, surely, but is there a limit to how many characters in one work can constitute the story being told?

Even taking the *Nichols* test as the general rule and leading trend, the place where the line is drawn between those characters that are protected and those that are not remains unclear. Clearly delineated central characters—Harry Potter and Captain Kirk—are probably off-limits for use as main characters in non-parody commercial works, although walk-ons might still be okay.[70] The protection

67 *Lewys* v. *O'Neill*, 49 F.2d 603, 612 (S.D.N.Y. 1931).

68 See, for example, *Caruthers* v. *R.K.O. Radio Pictures*, 20 F. Supp. 906 (S.D.N.Y. 1937); *Lone Ranger Inc.* v. *Cox*, 39 F. Supp. 487, 490 (W.D.S.C. 1941), *rev'd on other grounds*, 124 F.2d 650 (4th Cir. 1942); *Burns* v. *Twentieth Century Fox Film Corp.*, 75 F. Supp. 986 (D. Mass. 1948); *Burtis* v. *Universal Pictures Co., Inc.*, 40 Cal. 2d 823, 256 P.2d 933 (1953); *Giangrosso* v. *Columbia Broadcasting Sys., Inc.*, 534 F. Supp. 472 (E.D.N.Y. 1982); *Warner Bros., Inc.* v. *American Broadcasting Cos.*, 530 F. Supp. 1187, 1193 (S.D.N.Y. 1982), *aff'd*, 720 F.2d 231 (2d Cir. 1983); *Smith* v. *Weinstein*, 578 F. Supp. 1297, 1303 (S.D.N.Y.), *aff'd mem.*, 738 F.2d 419 (2d Cir. 1984); *Zambito* v. *Paramount Pictures*, 613 F. Supp. 1107 (E.D.N.Y. 1985). On limitations to copyright protection of characters see also generally *Echevarria* v. *Warner Bros. Pictures*, 12 F. Supp. 632, 635 (S.D. Cal. 1935); *Bevan* v. *Columbia Broadcasting Sys.*, 329 F. Supp. 601, 606 (S.D.N.Y. 1971); *Midas Prods.* v. *Baer*, 437 F. Supp. 1388, 1390 (C.D. Cal. 1977); *Rokeach* v. *Avco Embassy Pictures Corp.*, 3 Med. L. Rep. (BNA) 1774, 1779 (S.D.N.Y. 1978).

69 Hans Castorp, too, has his fan fiction: see, for example, Paweł Huelle, Castorp (Antonia Lloyd-Junes, trans., London: Serpent's Tail, 2007).

70 But see, for example, Julie Cromer Young, *Harry Potter and The Three-Second Crime: Are We Vanishing the De Minimis Defense From Copyright Law?* 36 N.M. L. Rev. 1 (2006).

of secondary, tertiary and minor characters is less clear: are Harry's sidekicks Hermione Granger and Ron Weasley, and Kirk's sidekicks "Bones" McCoy and Mr. Spock, also copyrighted? Again, it seems likely that they are; Spock, for example, is an original creation with an extensively developed personality, physiology, and back-story. (In fact, he's the only member of the original crew to have both his parents appear on the show.) We still can't be certain where that leaves minor characters—the acne-scarred teenage wizard Stan Shunpike or recurring Klingons Kang, Koloth, and Kor. Minor characters are often stock types, or have personalities and backgrounds only briefly hinted at; often they capture a fanfic writer's interest, earning them a place in the foreground of a story. But the *Anderson* v. *Stallone* court found many secondary and perhaps tertiary characters in the Rocky movies protected under both tests:

> All three Rocky movies focused on the development and relationships of the various characters. The movies did not revolve around intricate plots or story lines. Instead, the focus of these movies was the development of the Rocky characters. The same evidence which supports the finding of delineation above is so extensive that it also warrants a finding that the Rocky characters—Rocky, Adrian, Apollo Creed, Clubber Lang, and Paulie—"constituted the story being told" in the first three Rocky movies.[71]

Perhaps, in fact, a story is the sum of its characters.

Historical figures as fictional characters

An analogy to stories based on real persons may be useful. Few figures in early American history have been more thoroughly documented and researched than Thomas Jefferson; nonetheless, at least one author has claimed some of the facts of his life as her own creation. In 1979, Barbara Chase-Riboud wrote *Sally Hemings: A Novel*, a fictional account of the relationship between Jefferson and his slave Sally Hemings.[72] In 1982 Granville Burgess wrote *Dusky Sally*, a play on the same topic.[73] In 1988, shortly before the play was to be produced in Philadelphia, "Chase-Riboud, through her publisher, her agent, and her law firm, sent what Burgess describe[d] as 'a flurry of letters' alleging that *Dusky Sally* infringed on Chase-Riboud's copyright of *Sally Hemings*."[74]

Unsurprisingly the parties ended up suing each other, and somewhat more surprisingly the federal district court for the Eastern District of Pennsylvania agreed with Chase-Riboud that her copyright had been infringed. This may seem alarming at first: Thomas Jefferson and Sally Hemings were real people. About

71 *Anderson* v. *Stallone*, No. 87-0592, 1989 WL 206431, at *6–7 (C.D. Cal. 1989).

72 Barbara Chase-Riboud, Sally Hemings: A Novel (New York: Viking Press, 1979).

73 Granville Burgess, Dusky Sally (New York: Broadway Play Publishing, 1987).

74 *Burgess* v. *Chase-Riboud*, 765 F. Supp. 233, 234 (E.D. Penn. 1991).

Jefferson, thanks in part to his excessive self-documentation, a tremendous amount is known. Sally Hemings is considerably less well-documented, yet a great deal is still known—far more than about most individual slaves, or about most other people, of the time: her dates of birth and death, the identities of her parents, grandparents, children, and brother, the dates at which she traveled to and returned from France, some facts about her physical appearance, and more. Even more has been speculated upon by historians building on this information. In particular, Chase-Riboud and Burgess relied on Fawn Brodie's in-depth speculative study of the relationship between Jefferson and Hemings.[75] And historical fact, or even historical speculation presented as non-fiction, is of course not copyrightable; no one owns facts.[76] A "historical" character of whom nothing is known but a name (as in another lawsuit by Chase-Riboud, this time against DreamWorks for allegedly infringing on her novel *Echo of Lions* in the movie *Amistad*) may be a copyrightable fictional character. But Thomas Jefferson and Sally Hemings?

A second look at *Burgess* v. *Chase-Riboud*, though, reveals a somewhat less alarming reasoning. The court did not actually address Chase-Riboud's copyright in the characters; rather, it looked at scenes appearing in both Chase-Riboud's novel and Burgess' play with no support in the historical record. The most striking of these is Sally Hemings' dream, of which Judge Kelly wrote:

> *Sally Hemings' Nightmare.* Perhaps the single most glaring instance of "creative similarity" is the imagined slave auction. One of the climactic moments of Chase-Riboud's book is a scene in which Sally Hemings has a nightmare of Jefferson being sold at a slave auction. Needless to say, this is a completely imagined scene, yet it appears as a climax to *Dusky Sally* as well. Burgess argues that "dream sequences are an ancient literary device used to dramatize states of spiritual or emotional transcendence," and more imaginatively, that this too amounts to *scenes a faire*. I am inclined to agree with Chase-Riboud's contention that the glaring similarity in these scenes, standing alone, would arguably establish a valid copyright infringement.[77]

That does seem pretty convincing. There's no historical evidence for Hemings' dream, and Brodie includes no such speculation in her work; the dream seems to have been entirely Chase-Riboud's invention, and its appearance in Burgess' work seems to be copyright infringement.

The opinion does address the copyright in one character qua character, though: James Hemings, Sally's older brother. The real James Hemings also traveled to Paris, where Jefferson paid for him to study French and to be trained as a chef.

75 Fawn M. Brodie, Thomas Jefferson: An Intimate History (New York: Bantam, 1974).

76 See, for example, *Hoehling* v. *Universal City Studios, Inc.*, 618 F.2d 972 (2d Cir. 1980).

77 *Burgess*, 765 F. Supp. at 241.

At one point he apparently fought with his French tutor. He later traveled to Philadelphia with Jefferson, and after returning to Monticello trained his (and presumably Sally's) brother Peter to take his place as chef, after which Jefferson freed him. There's historical evidence that he traveled widely, was literate, and refused an offer from Jefferson to work at the White House. From concerns about his drinking expressed by Jefferson in a letter to his, Jefferson's, daughter, it appears that James may have been an alcoholic, and that alcoholism may have played a role in his eventual suicide.

This seems like quite a bit to go on; at this point most readers will have formed at least some mental sketch of James' character. And, of course, there was still more information on James Hemings' life available to Chase-Riboud and Burgess. Judge Kelly, though, found Burgess' James Hemings to be a copy of Chase-Riboud's character:

> Jimmy Hemings is a main character in both works, and his personality, adventures, and emotional highs and lows are depicted practically identically. In both works, Jimmy Hemings tells Sally they are free on French soil.[78]

So far this doesn't seem convincing; it all sounds a bit *scènes à faire*, or else simple historical fact. As for James and Sally being free on French soil, French abolitionists of the time made a point of informing visiting American slaves of the fact, encouraging them to petition to remain in France as free persons. Jefferson himself was not only aware of this but a party to it, having translated Condorcet's pamphlet on the subject into English so that it could be distributed to slaves who were literate and read (by someone who could speak English, more or less) to those who were not.[79] As the eldest, it seems probable James would have been the first to learn of this, and inconceivable[80] that he would not have told his sister.

Judge Kelly goes on to state:

> More significantly, in both works Jimmy Hemings is depicted as taking part in the attack on the Bastille[.]
>
> * * *
>
> Burgess asks, "What author worth his or her salt could resist working with the issue of how two relatively educated slaves—who knew they were free under French law—reacted to the storming of the Bastille? … Any author is free to

78 *Burgess*, 765 F. Supp. at 241.

79 See Brodie, *supra* note 75, at 300.

80 Yes, yes, I know: "You keep using that word. I do not think it means what you think it means."

> speculate that he participated in this colorful event, so long, of course, as he or she does not take substantially from someone else's treatment of the idea."
> This is the essence of Burgess' case. Yes, I took the "idea," but my "treatment" was different. How different? The Jimmy Hemings scenes are a good example. In both *Sally Hemings* and *Dusky Sally*, Jimmy Hemings excitedly narrates the story of his adventures at the Bastille to a group at Jefferson's home in Paris. In *Dusky Sally*, Jimmy enters Jefferson's home, "bloodied and dishevelled, carrying a pike and wearing the red, white and blue cockade of the Revolution." In Sally Hemings, Jimmy Hemings wore a cockade as well, but used a butcher's knife during the attack.[81]

Again, I'm unconvinced. It seems hard to imagine that any author writing a work set in Paris in July of 1789 could resist the urge to have a character be present at the storming of the Bastille. In the two competing works here, the weapons used are different. And the wearing of red, white, and blue cockades—the source of the colors of France's national flag—is historical fact; including a cockade in the description of James Hemings after storming the Bastille is surely protected by the *scènes à faire* doctrine.

The other similarities Judge Kelly sees between the characters are equally unconvincing:

> [I]n both works Jimmy Hemings, after being freed, returns to Monticello and tries to persuade Sally Hemings to escape; and in both works Jimmy Hemings thinks about killing Jefferson after he learns of his relationship with his sister.[82]

James Hemings did, in fact, return to Monticello for a time as a free man; history gives us no record of what he said to his sister there, but it's not unreasonable—especially in a novel or play—to assume that the topic of freedom would have arisen. As for thinking about killing Jefferson, even without the complications added by slavery, James would hardly have been the first, or last, older brother to contemplate such an action under the circumstances.[83] The thoughts of killing don't even happen at the same point in two narratives, nor are they expressed in the same way:

> In both *Sally Hemings* and *Dusky Sally*, Jimmy reacts angrily when Sally Hemings does not want to leave Monticello. In *Sally Hemings*, Jimmy contemplates killing Jefferson in Paris; in *Dusky Sally*, he actually charges Jefferson with a knife after Sally Hemings tells him she does not wish to leave Monticello.

81 *Burgess*, 765 F. Supp. at 241–42.

82 *Burgess*, 765 F. Supp. at 242.

83 In July 1789, Sally (1773–1835) would have been (about) 15, James (1765–1801) 24, and Jefferson (1743–1826) 46.

Perhaps most perplexingly, Judge Kelly states:

> [O]ther than a few references to James Hemings in some of Jefferson's papers, and Brodie's conclusion that the evidence suggested that "Jimmy Hemings was quick of temper and anything but the stereotype of the docile slave," there is practically no historical basis that Jimmy Hemings was "an angry young man" as Burgess contends. This view of his character was another invention of Chase-Riboud's which was copied, with very little modifications, by Burgess.[84]

The alcoholism and suicide alone suggest some inner demons, or at the very least a shortage of tranquility. And there are only a few ways a character in James' situation—educated, capable, with a clear view of the world denied to him by the glass walls of his prison, formed not only by slavery but by the bonds of family—might be expected to react; stoic acceptance and burning rage are two of the more likely, and stoic acceptance makes for a less interesting novel or play.

Judge Kelly's treatment of James Hemings, a historical character about whose life a fair amount is known, seems to extend copyright protection of characters to an extreme degree. James is a secondary character in both works. Much of the material in both depictions of James Hemings is based on the historical record; many of the parallels are really not all that parallel. Nonetheless, Judge Kelly seems to find Burgess' James Hemings an infringement on Chase-Riboud's, or at least seems to find the overlaps significant enough, taken with the other overlaps alleged by Chase-Riboud, that the play as a whole is an infringement on the novel:

> The real issue in this case is whether the largely cosmetic alterations Burgess made from Chase-Riboud's novel are enough to successfully avoid a copyright infringement action.[85]

And, Kelly finds, they are not. Fanfic authors can perhaps hope that Judge Kelly's treatment of the two James Hemings characters is dicta; the infringing nature of the entire work, rather than copyright in a particular character, was at issue here. And the dream sequence alone seems sufficient to establish infringement in this particular case.

It would be interesting to see how the case might be resolved today, now that the intertwined Jefferson and Hemings families have become fodder for far more novels, movies, and other works.[86]

---

84 *Burgess*, 765 F. Supp. at 242.

85 *Burgess*, 765 F. Supp. at 242.

86 See, for example, MAX BYRD, JEFFERSON: A NOVEL (1993); STEVE ERICKSON, ARC D'X (1993); BRUCE STERLING, WE SEE THINGS DIFFERENTLY, reprinted in GLOBALHEAD (1992); JEFFERSON IN PARIS (Merchant Ivory 1994) (movie); ANN RINALDI, WOLF BY THE EARS (New York: Scholastic, 1993); Sally Hemings: An American Scandal (CBS 2000) (TV miniseries). Perhaps the earliest such novel (although it describes a supposed relationship

Note: non-character story elements

Fanfic authors incorporate not only characters from the underlying works, but also non-character story elements. Sometimes, in fact, these elements are all that ties the fanfic to the underlying work: a Star Trek fanfic is still identifiable as such without Kirk or Spock or McCoy, or Picard or Riker or Worf, if it includes the *Enterprise*. Is the *Enterprise*, in all its various incarnations, protected by copyright? (Its visual representation can, of course, be protected by trademark; it is clearly capable of identifying a Star Trek show as distinct from other shows. Even the registry number NCC-1701 is probably capable of doing so.) If the *Enterprise* can be protected by copyright, how is it protected? Is it a character?

The Ninth Circuit seems to suggest that it is. In *Halicki Films, LLC* v. *Sanderson Sales and Marketing*, it seriously considered a claim of character copyright in a car named Eleanor appearing in the original and remake versions of the movie *Gone in Sixty Seconds*. In both movies, Eleanor is just a car (to be precise, a 1971 Fastback Ford Mustang in the 1974 original and a 1967 Shelby Mustang GT-500 in the 2000 Disney remake). Eleanor is not a car possessed by a demon, like Stephen King's Christine, nor more benignly animated, like Herbie the Volkswagen Beetle; nor does she have an onboard computer that speaks with a distinctive voice and even personality, like the *Enterprise*. She is just a car. She is an object in the story, not an actor. Nonetheless, she may be protected under, in typical latter-day Ninth Circuit fashion, either the "story being told" (Sam Spade) or "sufficiently delineated" (*Nichols*) test. First, the "story being told" test:

> This Court has stated that where a character "is only the chessman in the game of telling the story he is not within the area of the protection afforded by the copyright." *Warner Bros. Pictures, Inc. v. Columbia Broad. Sys., Inc.* Warner Bros. held that a character could only be granted copyright protection if it "constituted the story being told." The Defendants rely on this strict standard, arguing that Eleanor is not "the story being told" but is "simply a car." In deciding that Dashiel Hammet's "Sam Spade" character did not qualify for copyright protection, Warner Bros. reasoned that literary characters are difficult to delineate and may be based on nothing more than an unprotected idea. *Id.*; *see* [*Air Pirates*]. *Air Pirates*, however, distinguished cartoon characters from literary characters, reasoning that comic book characters have "physical as well as conceptual qualities, [and are] more likely to contain some unique elements of expression."[87]

not between Jefferson and Sally Hemings but between Jefferson and another slave, named Currer), predating Chase-Riboud's and Burgess' work by well over a century, was WILLIAM WELLS BROWN, CLOTEL; OR, THE PRESIDENT'S DAUGHTER: A NARRATIVE OF SLAVE LIFE IN THE UNITED STATES (London: Partridge & Oakey, 1853).

87 *Halicki Films* v. *Sanderson Sales & Marketing*, 547 F.3d 1213 (9th Cir. 2008) at 1224.

The implication is apparently that Eleanor, as a character in a movie rather than in a written work, may have those qualities. This is a bit disturbing because those qualities, aside from her name, were given to her not by the author of either film but by the Ford Motor Company, which sold similar cars to anyone willing to buy them. (Admittedly this is complicated a bit by the fact that Carroll Shelby, who designed the 1967 GT-500 for Ford, is a party to the action.) The court does not pause to address this first standard, though, but rushes directly to the second:

> This Court has also recognized copyright protection for characters that are especially distinctive, see [*Olson*], and has noted, consistent with Air Pirates, that copyright protection "may be afforded to characters visually depicted in a television series or a movie," *Olson* ... "Characters that have received copyright protection have displayed consistent, widely identifiable traits." The Defendants argue that, to the extent Eleanor can be regarded as a character, it is not sufficiently distinctive and therefore not deserving of copyright protection.[88]

The Ninth Circuit remanded the case to the district court (the Central District of California again) for determination of whether Eleanor was, in fact, a copyright-protected "character":

> The District Court did not directly examine the question of whether Eleanor is a character deserving of copyright protection. The court therefore never addressed the question of what the appropriate standard is for making such a determination. In examining the question whether Remake Eleanor was a derivative of Original Eleanor, however, the District Court implied that Eleanor is deserving of copyright protection-the court stated that, "[i]f the Remake Eleanor is deemed a derivative work of the Original Eleanor, Plaintiffs, as the author of the Original Eleanor, would also have the exclusive right to the Remake Eleanor."
>
> The Eleanor character can be seen as more akin to a comic book character than a literary character. Moreover, Eleanor "display[s] consistent, widely identifiable traits," [see] *Rice*, 330 F.3d at 1175, and is "especially distinctive," [see] *Olson*, 855 F.2d at 1452. In both films, the thefts of the other cars go largely as planned, but whenever the main human character tries to steal Eleanor, circumstances invariably become complicated. In the Original GSS, the main character says "I'm getting tired of stealing this Eleanor car." And in the Remake GSS, the main character refers to his history with Eleanor. Nevertheless, this fact-intensive issue must be remanded to the District Court for a finding in the first instance as to whether Eleanor is entitled to copyright protection. On remand the court should examine whether Eleanor's "physical as well as conceptual

88 Ibid.

> qualities [and] … unique elements of expression" qualify Eleanor for copyright protection.[89]

If Eleanor—not so much a character as a MacGuffin (and, though this is the Ninth Circuit, certainly not "the story being told")—is protected, then surely so are the *Enterprise*, the Klingon Bird of Prey that Kirk parks, invisibly, in Golden Gate Park, the Millennium Falcon, and Harry Potter's Firebolt, all of which are original creations rather than members of a class of real-world mass-produced consumer products. What of other, less original creations? Is James Bond's Aston Martin DB5 a "character"? What of his martinis, shaken, not stirred? His Walther PPK? We now know, at least, that Freddy Krueger's glove is, as an extension of the character of Freddy himself—a "component part of the character which significantly aids in identifying the character."[90]

Duration: characters partially in and partially out of copyright

Characters in series face a gradual phasing out of copyright: when the copyright on the oldest work in the series expires, other works featuring the character will still be in copyright. At what point does the character enter the public domain? While Harry Potter and James Bond are for the moment secure, there is, as we have seen, dispute about whether and to what extent Sherlock Holmes has entered into the public domain, and the question of whether the literary Tarzan is still in copyright is not a simple one. Tarzan first appeared in 1912; the copyright on that work expired at the end of 1968. But the author published many Tarzan stories after 1923, and died in 1950. Thus the later stories are still in copyright; the question becomes whether the later publication of stories about the same character can extend the copyright in the original. Common sense should dictate that it cannot; otherwise copyright in characters could be maintained perpetually by publishing a new authorized story every century or so, if not more often. Any new developments in Tarzan's character contained in works still in copyright would be protected, but those aspects of the character contained in works in the public domain would themselves be in the public domain. In the case of Tarzan, the character was fully formed after the first book (or, arguably, the first two books); after that he became the basis for a lucrative industry, which demanded from each new work in the series a sameness and commitment to the status quo worthy of a 1960s sitcom: Tarzan's character was no more likely to undergo further radical changes than Gilligan was to get off that island. (Copyright aside, the name Tarzan remains protected as a trademark, restricting commercial uses of the character.)

---

89 Ibid., at 1224–25.

90 *New Line Cinema Corp.* v. *Easter Unlimited Inc.*, 17 U.S.P.Q. 2d 1631, 1633 (E.D.N.Y. 1989) (citing *Dallas Cowboys Cheerleaders, Inc.* v. *Pussycat Cinema, Ltd.*, 604 F.2d 200, 204 (2d Cir. 1979)).

Nimmer addresses the problem similarly:

> Clearly anyone may copy such elements as have entered the public domain, and no one may copy such elements as remain protected by copyright. The more difficult question is this: may the character depicted in all of the works be appropriated for use in a new story created by the copier? … The better view … would appear to be that once the copyright in the first work that contained the character enters the public domain, then it is not copyright infringement for others to copy the character in works that are otherwise original with the copier, even though later works in the original series remain protected by copyright.[91]

This, Nimmer explains, is a consequence of the derivative nature of sequels:

> Subsequent works in a series (or sequels) are in a sense derivative works while the characters which appear throughout the series are a part of the underlying work upon which the later works are based. Just as the copyright in a derivative work will not protect public domain portions of an underlying work as incorporated in the derivative work, so copyright in a particular work in a series will not protect the character as contained in such series if the work in the series in which the character first appeared has entered the public domain.[92]

This logic works well enough with characters like Sherlock Holmes or Tarzan, who are introduced more or less fully formed in the first works in which they appear. With characters that develop significantly over the course of a series—Severus Snape, Willow Rosenberg, the Wizard of Oz—it becomes a bit more difficult to apply, although the earlier proviso that "no one may copy such elements as remain protected by copyright" should help to avoid confusion.

The medium makes no difference, according to Nimmer: "The same rule obviously applies to a character born in one medium who subsequently appears

---

91 Nimmer, *supra* note 42, § 2–12 (citing *National Comics Publishers, Inc.* v. *Fawcett Publications, Inc.*, 191 F.2d 594 (2d Cir. 1951); *Kurlan* v. *Columbia Broadcasting System, Inc.*, 256 P.2d 962 (Cal. 1953); *Gantz* v. *Hercules Publishing Corp.*, 182 N.Y.S.2d 450 (N.Y. Sup. Ct. 1959); *Grant* v. *Kellogg*, 58 F. Supp. 48 (S.D.N.Y. 1944), *aff'd*, 154 F.2d 59 (2d Cir. 1946); *Columbia Broadcasting Sys., Inc.* v. *DeCosta*, 377 F.2d 315 (1st Cir.), *cert. denied*, 389 U.S. 1007 (1967); *Harvey Cartoons* v. *Columbia Pictures Indus., Inc.*, 645 F. Supp. 1564, 1570–71 (S.D.N.Y. 1986) (using the Copyright Act of 1909); *DeCosta* v. *Columbia Broadcasting Sys., Inc.*, 520 F.2d 499 (1st Cir. 1975), *cert. denied*, 423 U.S. 1073 (1976); *National Comics Publishers, Inc.* v. *Fawcett Publications, Inc.*, 191 F.2d 594 (2d Cir. 1951)).

92 Nimmer, *supra* note 42, § 2–12 (citing *Micro Star* v. *Formgen Inc.*, 154 F.3d 1107, 1112 (9th Cir. 1998); *Burroughs* v. *Metro-Goldwyn-Mayer, Inc.*, 683 F.2d 610, 631 (2d Cir. 1982) (Newman, J., concurring)).

in derivative works in other media."[93] In other words, now that book-Tarzan has entered the public domain, there is no copyright preventing anyone who wishes from making a Tarzan movie, cartoon, or game—although, as noted above, the character is still protected by trademark for those uses. In addition, commercial works must tread carefully through an obstacle course of unfair competition, contract, and tort law; writers of noncommercial fanfic and similar noncommercial works, however, will be concerned mostly with copyright law.

The future of copyright protection of characters

The most recent U.S. case to address copyright in characters, *Salinger* v. *Colting*,[94] is not likely to reassure fanfic writers. The late J.D. Salinger, author of the perennial high-school English class assignment *Catcher in the Rye*, took objection to a work titled *60 Years Later: Coming Through the Rye*, written by Fredrik Colting under the name John David California. The protagonist of Colting's book is a character named Mr. C, who can be understood to be Holden Caulfield in his late seventies. Salinger himself also appears as a character. Most of the trial court's discussion dealt with the question of whether *60 Years Later: Coming through the Rye* was a parody or otherwise protected as fair use. (The Second Circuit Court of Appeals later vacated the trial court's judgment for procedural reasons.) The trial court directly addressed the copyrightability of Holden Caulfield. As a court within the Second Circuit, it applied the *Nichols* "sufficiently delineated" test, although curiously without citing *Nichols* itself:

> [T]he character of Holden Caulfield … is sufficiently delineated so that a claim for infringement will lie. 2 Nimmer on Copyright § 2.12 (2009) ("[I]n those cases recognizing such protection, the character appropriated was distinctively delineated in the plaintiff's work."). Additionally, for the reasons stated on the record of June 17, 2009, the Court found that the Plaintiff had access to Catcher and that there are similarities that are probative of copying between the works. [*Castle Rock Entertainment, Inc. v. Carol Pub. Group, Inc.*] Finally, the Court found that Plaintiff has shown that there is substantial similarity between *Catcher* and *60 Years*, as well as between the character Holden Caulfield from *Catcher*, and the character Mr. C from *60 Years*, such that it was an unauthorized infringement of Plaintiff's copyright. [*Suntrust Bank* v. *Houghton Mifflin Company*; *Castle Rock*].[95]

93 Nimmer, *supra* note 42, § 2–12 (citing *Silverman* v. *CBS Inc.*, 632 F. Supp. 1344 (S.D.N.Y. 1986), *rev'd on other grounds*, 870 F.2d 40 (2d Cir. 1989), *cert. denied*, 492 U.S. 907 (1989)).

94 641 F. Supp. 2d 250 (S.D.N.Y. 2009), *order vacated*, 607 F.3d 68 (2d Cir. 2010).

95 *Salinger*, 641 F. Supp. 2d at 254.

The trial court's conclusion that there was substantial similarity between the two works was reviewed de novo by the appellate court; nonetheless, despite this more stringent standard of review (as opposed to the "clearly erroneous") standard, it agreed that the two works were substantially similar.[96]

The court also rejected the related contention that the character of Mr. C was a protected parody of the character Holden Caulfield:

> To the extent Defendants contend that *60 Years* and the character of Mr. C direct parodic comment or criticism at *Catcher* or Holden Caulfield, as opposed to Salinger himself, the Court finds such contentions to be post-hoc rationalizations employed through vague generalizations about the alleged naïveté of the original, rather than reasonably perceivable parody.
>
> First, Colting's assertion that his purpose in writing *Catcher* [*sic*; presumably meant to be *60 Years*] was to "critically examin[e] the character Holden, and his presentation in *Catcher* as an authentic and admirable (maybe even heroic) figure" is problematic and lacking in credibility. [*See*] Woodmansee Decl., ¶ 13[:] ("Readers familiar with [*Catcher*] will anticipate the same laconic observations and reflections they associate with Holden Caulfield. What do they get from the 76 year old C? They get much the same kinds of observations and reflections, but coming from a 76 year old and applied to a world much changed in the 60 intervening years, such observations and reflections fall flat. They reveal a character whose development was arrested at 16, who instead of growing up could only grow old."); Woodmansee Decl., at ¶ 17 (stating that the observations and reflections of Mr. C evoke "[i]n style and content … vintage Holden Caulfield, and coming from a 16 year old, they seemed honest and endearing. Coming from the 76 year old C, however, they seem pathetic. Suggesting a life of isolated drifting, they evoke Aristotelian fear and pity—that is, they force readers to ask whether such anomie is all we fans of Holden may expect in old age. If this is where his rebellious independence leads, is it as attractive as we adoring fans of *CR* imagined?").[97]

This, unfortunately, is taking the court precisely where it ought not to go: into the realm of literary criticism. The problem with parodying a character whose original presentation is already complex enough that it might be said, if not to involve self-parody, at least to be critical of itself, is that it is difficult to know what part of the allegedly parodic content is in the later work, and which part is already present in the original. The court finds that no new parodic content or commentary on the character was added:

---

96 *Salinger* v. *Colting*, 607 F.3d 68, 83 (2d Cir. 2010).

97 *Salinger* v. *Colting*, 641 F. Supp. 2d 250, 258 (S.D.N.Y. 2009).

> However, Holden Caulfield as delineated by Salinger was already often "miserable" and "unconnected" as well as frequently "absurd[ ]" and "ridiculous," as Colting says of his elderly version of the character. In fact, it was these very characteristics that led Caulfield to leave or be expelled from three boarding schools, to wander the streets of New York City alone for several days, to lack any close friends other than his younger sister Phoebe, and ultimately to become a patient in a psychiatric hospital. Hence, to the extent Colting claims to augment the purported portrait of Caulfield as a "free-thinking, authentic and untainted youth" and "impeccable judge of the people around him" displayed in *Catcher* by "show[ing] the effects of Holden's uncompromising world view," those effects were already thoroughly depicted and apparent in Salinger's own narrative about Caulfield.[98]

The court then provides a long list of examples from Salinger's Complaint and from *Catcher in the Rye* itself, concluding:

> [T]he contrast between Holden's authentic but critical and rebellious nature and his tendency toward depressive alienation is one of the key themes of *Catcher*. That many readers and critics have apparently idolized Caulfield for the former, despite—or perhaps because of—the latter, does not change the fact that those elements were already apparent in *Catcher*.
>
> It is hardly parodic to repeat that same exercise in contrast, just because society and the characters have aged. *See* [Campbell], (Kennedy, J., concurring) ("Almost any revamped modern version of a familiar composition can be construed as a comment on the naïveté of the original because … it will be amusing to hear how the old tune sounds in the new genre.") *60 Years* attempts to contrast these two aspects of the Caulfield character in a manner that is nearly identical to that which Salinger did decades ago, and thus is anything but parodic in this regard.

This is disturbing for any fanfic author claiming, as so many do, that a character is being used parodically. Apparently a parody, at least of a character, is only a parody if the fanfic author's understanding of the character is as deep as the court's. A fanfic author who is naïve or obtuse and misses the irony written into the character by the original author may fail at parody.

The court is on firmer ground when it points out that the argument that Mr. C was a parody of Holden Caulfield did not emerge until after Salinger's lawsuit was filed, and that the original marketing of the book presented it as a sequel, not a parody or critical treatment:

> While it is true that an artist or author "need not label their whole [work] … a parody in order to claim fair use protection," [*Campbell*], it is equally true

98 Ibid., at 258–59.

> that "courts … must take care to ensure that not just any commercial takeoff is rationalized post hoc as a parody." [*Campbell*] (Kennedy, J., concurring).[99]

Rationalizing Mr. C as a parody post hoc was, to the court's eye, exactly what the defendant had done:

> Until the present lawsuit was filed, Defendants made no indication that *60 Years* was in any way a parody or critique of *Catcher*. Quite to the contrary, the original jacket of *60 Years* states that it is "… a marvelous *sequel* to one of our most beloved classics." (emphasis added). Additionally, when initially confronted with the similarities between the two works, rather than explaining that *60 Years* was a parody or critique of *Catcher*, Colting's literary agent, Mr. Sane contended that *60 Years* "is a completely freestanding novel that has nothing to do with the original *Catcher In The Rye*."
>
> Furthermore, in a number of public statements that were made prior to the filing of the present lawsuit, Colting himself made it clear that 60 Years was not a parody or critique of Catcher, but rather a tribute and sequel … ("'But this is no spoof,' said Windupbird's Fredrik Colting. 'We are not concerned about any legal issues. We think *60 Years Later* is a very original story that compliments *Catcher in the Rye*.'").[100]

In reviewing the trial court's rejection of Colting's post hoc rationalization of *60 Years* as a critical work, the appellate court applied the more lenient "clearly erroneous" standard, stating that the trial court's "finding is not clear error."[101] Interestingly, it added the dictum that "It may be that a court can find that the fair use factor favors a defendant even when the defendant and his work lack a transformative purpose. We need not decide that issue here, however."[102] It remains to be seen what, if anything, will grow from this in the Second Circuit in the future.

This alone—the apparently opportunistic attempt to recharacterize the work as a parody—might have been enough to dispose of the claim that Mr. C was a parody of Holden Caulfield, and it is far less worrisome than the court's earlier attempts to evaluate the merits of the parody. Most parodies, especially in fanfic, are sufficiently broad that they will be instantly recognizable as such, even when not specifically so labeled.

99 Ibid., at 260.
100 Ibid., at 260 n.3.
101 *Salinger*, 607 F.3d at 83.
102 Ibid.

Chapter 3
The Second Question: If the Underlying Works or Characters are Protected, does the Fan Work Infringe upon that Protection?

Copyright protects the text—that is, the expression—of a work of fiction, and under certain conditions may protect characters within the work. Fanfic rarely infringes by direct imitation of the work; that would defeat the purpose of fanfic. Instead, fanfic takes familiar story elements and combines them in unfamiliar ways. Doing so may nonetheless violate the copyright in the original work if the new work is a derivative work, because the copyright owner has the sole right to control the making and distribution of derivative works.[1] Certain uses that might seem infringing, even if they incorporate protected characters or are otherwise derivative, may be protected as fair use, as parody, or if the use is otherwise sufficiently transformative.

In a literary sense, fanfic is necessarily derivative; it cannot function otherwise. Tolkien pointed out that this was true of all fantasy, and perhaps of all fiction: "the Cauldron of Story[] has always been boiling, and to it have continually been added new bits."[2] Tolkien knew this as well as anyone; the Lord of the Rings trilogy draws heavily on a variety of sources, especially Beowulf and the Norse sagas but many others as well, possibly even including the Chinese classic *Journey to the West (西游记)*: Frodo and Sam provide ready analogues of the monk Xuánzàng and the loyal Friar Sand (Shā Wùjìng), utterly devoted to him, while Gandalf fills the role of Monkey (Sūn Wùkōng). Pig (Zhū Bājiè) is a bit harder to map, with his lighter aspects represented by Pippin and his darker aspects, perhaps, by Gollum. Even Xuánzàng's horse, Yùlóng Sāntàizǐ, finds his counterpart in Shadowfax.

Like Tolkien's work, Wu Cheng'en's sixteenth-century *Journey to the West* floats on its own cauldron of folklore and legend; in a sense much of it is a retelling of old stories. Tolkien, though, had a much closer source on which to draw: the four operas in Wagner's over-long and overwrought Ring Cycle. Tolkien himself denied the similarities; of his Ring and *Der Ring des Nibelungen*, Tolkien said "Both rings were round, and there the resemblance ceased."[3] Other similarities—a

1 17 U.S.C. § 106(2) (2006).

2 J.R.R. Tolkien, *Tree and Leaf*, in The Tolkien Reader 52 (1966).

3 Alex Ross, *The Ring and the Rings: Wagner v. Tolkien*, The New Yorker, December 22, 2003, www.newyorker.com/archive/2003/12/22/031222crat_atlarge?currentPage=1. There is no copyright issue; the dissimilarities in Wagner's and Tolkien's works aside, by

broken sword (Narsil/Nothung), shared characters (Mîm the Petty-Dwarf in *The Silmarillion* and *The Children of Hurin* and Mime the Dwarf in *Der Ring des Nibelungen*, both drawing their name but not really their characters from Mimir in the Poetic and Prose Eddas and the Ynglinga Saga)—can be explained away as derivations from the same underlying source material. Maybe.

Tolkien even put his ruminations on the nature of story into the mouth of Sam Gamgee, who muses on his own, and Gollum's, nature as narrative constructs: "Why, to think of it, we're in the same tale still! It's going on. Don't the great tales ever end?"[4] A change in viewpoint, Sam realizes, can completely transform a story: "Why, even Gollum might be good in a tale, better than he is to have by you, anyway. And he used to like tales himself once, by his own account. I wonder if he thinks he's the hero or the villain?"[5] In this Sam defends his author against possible charges of literary derivativeness.

So what makes a work legally derivative? The definition of "derivative work" in Section 101 of the Copyright Act, unfortunately, provides less illumination than it might:

> A "derivative work" is a work based upon one or more preexisting works, such as a translation, musical arrangement, dramatization, fictionalization, motion picture version, sound recording, art reproduction, abridgment, condensation, or any other form in which a work may be recast, transformed, or adapted. A work consisting of editorial revisions, annotations, elaborations, or other modifications which, as a whole, represent an original work of authorship, is a "derivative work."[6]

In essence, the first sentence tells us only that an adaptation from one medium, form, or language to another is a derivative work, as are shortened versions. "Fictionalization" is interesting, suggesting that a novel based on a historical account might be a derivative work, although, as we have seen, there is no

---

the time the Lord of the Rings was published, Wagner's copyright had expired. For an interesting case on the duration of copyright in an opera (La Bohème), see ECJ: *Land Hessen* v. *G. Ricordi & Co. Bühnen-und Musikverlag GmbH*, case C-360/00 (June 6, 2002) (judgment of the court), available at http://eur-lex.europa.eu/LexUriServ/LexUriServ.do?uri=CELEX:62000J0360:EN:HTML.

4 J.R.R. Tolkien, The Two Towers 408 (Ballantine Books: New York, 1965).

5 Ibid., at 409..

6 17 U.S.C. § 101. See also generally, for example, *M.H. Segan Ltd. Partnership* v. *Hasbro, Inc.*, 924 F. Supp. 512 (S.D.N.Y. 1996); *Moore Pub., Inc.* v. *Big Sky Marketing, Inc.*, 756 F. Supp. 1371 (D. Idaho 1990); *Pickett* v. *Prince*, 207 F.3d 402 (7th Cir. 2000); *Radji* v. *Khakbaz*, 607 F. Supp. 1296 (D.D.C. 1985) (copyright owner has exclusive right to make or authorize translation). But see Jaime E. Muscar, *A Winner is Who? Fair Use and the Online Distribution of Manga and Video Game Fan Translations*, 9 Vand. J. Ent. & Tech. L. 223 (2006) (arguing that in some cases—specifically fan translations of video games—a translation may be fair use).

copyright in historical facts or even theories. The U.S. Copyright Office is not necessarily in disagreement: "A fictionalization is a treatment of a factual work in which the elements are recast, transformed, or adapted to produce a work of fiction. A work which is only loosely based on the ideas or facts found in an earlier work, is not considered to be a derivative work."[7] Perhaps one that is closely based on a work of non-fiction may still be derivative.

The second sentence provides the additional information that a work can be derivative even though it is "an original work of authorship"—that is, even though the secondary work itself would otherwise be eligible for copyright protection under 17 U.S.C. § 102. It is this second sentence that most greatly expands the potential scope of the derivative works right, as far as fanfic and other fan works are concerned. While a certain amount of fan activity goes into, for example, preparing live performances of the underlying novels, short stories, or television episodes, most fanfic and other fan works are themselves original works of authorship rather than mere adaptations. The problem is that these original works incorporate characters, settings, and other story elements from the underlying works to a degree that may make the fan works derivative.

Once again, a visit to our three Lost Worlds may be instructive. Even if the original *Lost World* had still been in copyright at the time Crichton's novel of the same name was published, Crichton's version would not have infringed the copyright in the original, because Crichton's *Lost World* is not a derivative or copy of the original; rather, it is a sequel to (and thus derivative of) his earlier and wildly successful novel (and subsequent movie) *Jurassic Park*.[8] In fact, Crichton's *Lost World* is more a sequel to the movie than to the book: a central character in *Lost World* is mathematician Ian Malcolm (played by Jeff Goldblum in the movie) who was dead at the end of *Jurassic Park*, the novel, but alive at the end of *Jurassic Park*, the movie.[9] Crichton's *Lost World* is only tangentially fan fiction; by its title

---

7 U.S. Copyright Office, Compendium II of Copyright Office Practices §306.02(b), *Fictionalizations*.

8 Michael Crichton, Jurassic Park (1990); Jurassic Park (Universal Studios 1993).

9 This inconsistency is also noted by the court in a copyright infringement case brought against Crichton's *Jurassic Park*, not by the Conan Doyle estate, but by an author of children's books about a dinosaur theme park, partially set on an offshore island: "What seems to us a clear case of death is made more ambiguous by the sequel to *Jurassic Park*, a novel entitled *The Lost World*, where Malcolm is again a central character." *Williams* v. *Crichton*, 84 F.3d 581, 586 n.2 (2d Cir. 1996). While recognizing many similarities, the Second Circuit ultimately concluded that "the works are not substantially similar," dismissing many of the similarities as *scènes à faire* or simple coincidence. One of the distinctions—a hunting pack of Deinonychus in the plaintiff's work and of velociraptors in Crichton's—might have weighed differently had the court been informed that Crichton's "velociraptors" are not the (much smaller) dinosaurs usually known by that name, but in fact Deinonychus, following a classification since abandoned by most paleontologists. See Gregory S. Paul, Predatory Dinosaurs of the World: A Complete Illustrated Guide (New York: Simon & Schuster, 1988); see also *Williams*, 84 F.3d at 589–90.

and minor details (such as the reference to an absent character named John Roxton, also a character in Arthur Conan Doyle's original), it acknowledges a debt to the original work, but its major characters and specific setting are original to Crichton. Crichton's story is independent of the original and can be fully appreciated by those with no familiarity with the original. The major story elements that tie it to the original are dinosaurs and the general Latin American setting; Arthur Conan Doyle did not create dinosaurs or Latin America, and can claim no copyright in them. Shared story elements, even where created rather than drawn from the real world, do not make one story derivative of another: thus space-opera protagonists Honor Harrington and Miles Vorkosigan may be similar characters and inhabit similar SF universes operating according to similar rules of physics and with similar technology and political organization, but neither is derivative of the other. Any genre or subgenre of fiction is an ongoing conversation not only between authors and fans but between authors and authors; Honor's and Miles' authors, David Weber and Lois McMaster Bujold, use shared tropes from a particular genre.

Souza's *Lost World II*, on the other hand, is more clearly identifiable as fan fiction, and, had it not been sufficiently transformative, might have posed copyright problems had the original still been in copyright in the U.S. when the U.S. version of Souza's work was published.[10] While the story stands on its own, it is easier to understand—and much funnier—if the reader has also read the original or at least seen or heard one of the several film, television or radio adaptations of it; however, the fact that one work is in dialogue with another does not by itself render the later work legally derivative.[11] The novel's protagonist, Jane Challenger, is the granddaughter of Conan Doyle's protagonist, Professor George Challenger; the novel's central conceit is that she discovers, in the Brazilian Amazon, "reasonably healthy and well-fed species of capitalists considered extinct in England since the eighteenth century."[12] Classical capitalism and the economy of the author's own country are not the only dinosaurs in this story: the concepts inherent in Jane Challenger's journey—the idea of a "third world" that does not come into fully realized existence until it is "explored" and "discovered" by a representative of the world's "civilized peoples"—are dinosaurs as well: big, dangerous, and long past their time.[13]

The majority of fan fiction, though, is fanfic—informally published for the entertainment of the author and other fans, or for some other noncommercial reason. Even fan fiction like Souza's—formally and commercially published in

---

10 See, for example, *Suntrust Bank* v. *Houghton Mifflin Co.*, 268 F.3d 1257 (11th Cir. 2001) (vacating an injunction against the publication of *The Wind Done Gone*, a fictional work based on *Gone With the Wind*, discussed at 24–26, *infra*).

11 See, for example, The Lost World (First National Pictures 1925); The Lost World (Twentieth Century Fox 1960).

12 Marcio Souza, Lost World II: The End of the Third World (Lana Santamaria, trans., 1993), originally published as O Fim Do Terceiro Mundo (Marco Zero, ed., 1989).

13 Ibid..

order to make money for the author—may survive in the face of copyright if it is protected fair use. However, fair use will be harder to show for such works than for noncommercial works. Souza's novel would probably survive copyright scrutiny, because to the extent it borrows from the original, it does so as parody and commentary.

Fair use

At the heart of all arguments for the protection of fan works under U.S copyright law is the idea of "fair use." The term is often thrown about in fan forums, usually with little understanding of its meaning. There is, for example, a widespread but incorrect belief that noncommercial uses are presumptively fair uses. This may reflect the way things often work out in practice—there is a tendency on the part of many copyright owners to overlook noncommercial fan works, while fan works published for profit are often quick to attract legal action. But while the commercial or noncommercial nature of the use is weighed in determining whether a use is fair use under 17 U.S.C. § 107, it is not by itself determinative. A commercially published fan work may make fair use of the source material. Yet even in noncommercially published works, some fans may go overboard and engage in copying from the underlying works that exceeds the boundaries of fair use. The fact that one is a fan of the underlying work does not by itself render all of one's uses, or even all of one's noncommercial uses, of the work "fair."

Fair use, as somewhat vaguely and haphazardly defined by Congress, takes the commercial or noncommercial nature of a use into account, but does not make it the sole factor:

> Notwithstanding the provisions of sections 106 and 106A, the fair use of a copyrighted work, including such use by reproduction in copies or phonorecords or by any other means specified by that section, for purposes such as criticism, comment, news reporting, teaching (including multiple copies for classroom use), scholarship, or research, is not an infringement of copyright. In determining whether the use made of a work in any particular case is a fair use the factors to be considered shall include—
> **(1)** the purpose and character of the use, including whether such use is of a commercial nature or is for nonprofit educational purposes;
> **(2)** the nature of the copyrighted work;
> **(3)** the amount and substantiality of the portion used in relation to the copyrighted work as a whole; and
> **(4)** the effect of the use upon the potential market for or value of the copyrighted work.[14]

14 17 U.S.C. § 107 (2006). See also generally, for example, Jessica Elliott, *Copyright Fair Use and Private Ordering: Are Copyright Holders and the Copyright Law Fanatical*

These four factors have been much criticized for their nebulosity; it is difficult—often impossible—to determine in advance of litigation whether a particular use is "fair." The following discussion will attempt, by example, to give some guidance on the parameters of fair use through various examples, including an in-depth look at one fan video, "They're Taking the Hobbits to Isengard."

Derivative works and transformative uses

Section 106(2) of the Copyright Act grants the owner of a copyright the exclusive right to prepare or authorize the preparation of "derivative works based upon the copyrighted work[.]" This has been interpreted relatively narrowly, however, to mean only works where the amount of copying is substantial.[15] While any work incorporating characters, settings or story elements from an earlier work may be said to be "derivative" in a literary sense, not all such works will be "derivative" within the meaning of 17 U.S.C. § 106. In a legal sense the bar for finding a work to be derivative is set somewhat higher. The courts have long been aware of Tolkien's cauldron of story; 165 years ago, the aptly-named Justice Story wrote:

> In truth, in literature, in science and in art, there are, and can be, few, if any, things, which, in an abstract sense, are strictly new and original throughout. Every book in literature, science and art, borrows, and must necessarily borrow, and use much which was well known and used before … The thoughts of every man are, more or less, a combination of what other men have thought and expressed, although they may be modified, exalted, or improved by his own genius or reflection. If no book could be the subject of copy-right which was not new and original in the elements of which it is composed, there could be no ground for any copy-right in modern times, and we should be obliged to ascend very high, even in antiquity, to find a work entitled to such eminence. Virgil borrowed much from Homer; Bacon drew from earlier as well as contemporary minds; Coke exhausted all the known learning of his profession; and even Shakespeare and Milton, so justly and proudly our boast as the brightest originals would be found to have gathered much from the abundant stores of current knowledge and classical studies in their days. What is La Place's great work, but the combination of the processes and discoveries of the great mathematicians before his day, with his own extraordinary genius? What are all modern law books, but new combinations and arrangements of old materials, in which the skill and judgment of the author in the selection and exposition and accurate use

for Fansites?, 11 DePaul-LCA J. Art & Ent. L. & Pol'y 329 (2001); Nathaniel T. Noda, *When Holding On Means Letting Go: Why Fair Use Should Extend to Fan-Based Activities*, 5 U. Denver Sports & Ent. L.J. (2008).

15 See, for example, *Litchfield* v. *Spielberg*, 736 F.2d 1352 (9th Cir. 1984), *cert. denied*, 470 U.S. 1052 (copying must be substantial).

> of those materials, constitute the basis of his reputation, as well as of his copyright? Blackstone's Commentaries and Kent's Commentaries are but splendid examples of the merit and value of such achievements.[16]

Thus an adaptation of a work to a new medium or a translation to a new language, for example, is likely to be a derivative work: the English translation of the novel *Dr. Zhivago* is derivative of Boris Pasternak's original Russian text, while the 1965 film and the 2002 ITV television serial, both titled *Dr. Zhivago*, are derivative of both; the 1959 Brazilian film *Doutor Jivago* is derivative of the original novel, as is the 2006 Russian TV series *Дóктор Живáго*. All of these make some plot and character changes from the original, but are still recognizably the same work. The 2005 musical *Zhivago*, opening at San Diego's La Jolla Playhouse in 2005, is derivative as well, but is somewhat further toward the edge of section 106(2)'s coverage, because it contains original songs and the emphasis, as in any musical, is as much (or more) on the music as on the story. The 2007 Russian musical *Дóктор Живáго* and the forthcoming opera of the same name, each with their own original music, are similar. Had any of these adaptations of *Dr. Zhivago* been made without authorization, they would have violated Pasternak's copyright.

On the other hand, this exchange from the 1988 movie *Red Heat* is a passing reference, too trivial to render the entire movie derivative:

Arnold Schwarzenegger:	Tea, please.
James Belushi:	In a glass, with lemon, right?
Arnold Schwarzenegger (surprised):	Yes.
James Belushi:	Yeah. I saw *Dr. Zhivago*.

Red Heat is, in every possible way, not *Dr. Zhivago*. No one watching the former would be likely to see it as an adaptation of the latter. Belushi's reference to *Dr. Zhivago* (the 1965 movie, rather than the original text or one of the other derivative works) is a casual one, like the inclusion of a character named Strelnikov in the deplorable 1984 Cold War propaganda film *Red Dawn* (now, inexplicably, being remade, although this time as an exercise in jingoistic China-bashing rather than jingoistic Russia-bashing). Nor is the story element—a Russian drinking tea from a glass—unique or original to *Dr. Zhivago*; like images of World War II German soldiers wearing swastikas or Bastille-stormers wearing red, white, and blue cockades, its use is likely to be protected by the *scènes à faire* doctrine.

Somewhere between these two extremes—the casual reference and the adaptation of the entire story to a new medium—lies the borderline determining whether a work is "derivative" within the meaning of section 106(2).

Fan musicals: like the U.S. and Russian musical versions of *Dr. Zhivago*, a musical adaptation of a book or movie is probably derivative: a musical version

16 *Emerson* v. *Davies*, 8 F. Cas. 615, 619 (C.C.D. Mass. 1845) (No. 4,436).

of the book and movie *Gone with the Wind*, for example, even if intended to be humorous, is derivative:

> [A] non-parodic or non-satiric stage version of Gone With The Wind is a protected derivative use of the original works which only the holders of the valid, existing copyrights in such works have a right to exploit.[17]

Implicit in the court's statement is that a use that *is* parodic or satiric is, or might be, permissible. A parodic use, as we saw in the discussion of *60 Years Later: Coming Through the Rye* in Chapter 2, is fair use. This is good news for fans, as almost all fan musicals are played at least partly for laughs; they are intended to comment critically and humorously on the original, although the humor may be obscure to those outside the fandom. The musical format seems inherently to lend itself to comedy; "Harry Potter: The Musical" may not be that funny to non-fans, but to those in the fandom it is, as one fan put it, "a loving parody of Harry Potter, and to a degree, Harry Potter fandom."[18]

Somewhat less obviously, a book about and containing photographs of *The Nutcracker*, as choreographed by George Balanchine, is derivative of Balanchine's choreography. (Balanchine's 1954 choreography, and versions derived from it, are (along with Mikhail Baryshnikov's 1976 American Ballet Theater version) the most familiar to American audiences, who have been watching them at Christmastime every year since 1954. Tchaikovsky's original 1892 version, choreographed by Marius Petipa and/or Lev Ivanov (a subject for debate among ballet fans but outside the scope of this work), was already out of copyright at the time the allegedly infringing book was published.) The court explained that:

> [T]he standard for determining copyright infringement is not whether the original could be recreated from the allegedly infringing copy, but whether the latter is "substantially similar" to the former. The test, as stated by Judge Learned Hand in Peter Pan, is whether "the ordinary observer, unless he set out to detect the disparities, would be disposed to overlook them, and regard their aesthetic appeal as the same."[19]

In other words, a book that presents *The Nutcracker*, as choreographed by Balanchine, in pictures is telling essentially the same story Balanchine tells when the ballet is performed. This is bad news for a certain type of fan work—the documentary or tribute work, consisting of little more than stills from a favorite

17 *Metro-Goldwyn-Mayer, Inc.* v. *Showcase Atlanta Co-op.*, 479 F. Supp. 351 (N.D. Ga. 1979).

18 Comment posted June 26, 2009 by ClauClauClaudia on *The Harry Potter Musical In Its Entirety*, io9, http://io9.com/5303053/the-harry-potter-musical-in-its-entirety (last visited October 19, 2010).

19 *Horgan* v. *Macmillan, Inc.*, 789 F.2d 157 (2d Cir. 1986).

movie. Indeed, up until the time of the *Harry Potter Lexicon* case, courts had been fairly consistent in finding fan reference works heavily dependent on excerpts from the original works to be derivative.[20] The *Lexicon* case, though reaching a superficially similar result, provided long-awaited guidance to creators of such work on the limits of the exclusive right to prepare derivative works. Creators of other categories of works must still wait for guidance, however.[21]

The higher the degree of creativity in a fan work, the more likely the work is to be transformative and the less likely it is to be derivative. An analogy may be made here to the degree of creativity required for a derivative work to be independently copyrightable. While the Copyright Act makes no mention of a higher standard of originality for derivative works, courts have tended to set the bar for originality needed to make a derivative work copyrightable in its own right higher than that for a wholly original work.[22] Of course, where the use of the underlying work in a derivative work is unlawful to begin with, the derivative work is not eligible for copyright protection. Section 103(a) provides that "protection for a work employing preexisting material in which copyright subsists does not extend to any part of the work in which such material has been used unlawfully."[23] On the other hand, a work that is derivative in a literary sense but transformative in a legal sense is not "derivative" for copyright purposes.

Transformative works

Works that are transformative are not derivative within the meaning of section 106(2), even though their source is clear. A retelling of the events in *Gone with the Wind* from the point of view of a slave may be transformative, even though the characters, settings, and many of the events described are the same; the dramatic viewpoint shift, and the recasting of the relationships between the characters, make

20 *Warner Bros. Entertainment* v. *RDR Books*, 575 F.Supp.2d 513 (S.D.N.Y. September 8, 2008) (the Harry Potter Lexicon case, discussed in detail in Chapter 4); *Ty, Inc.* v. *Publ'ns Int'l*, 292 F.3d 512 (7th Cir. 2002); *Castle Rock Entertainment* v. *Carol Publ'g Group*, 150 F.3d 132 (2d Cir. 1998); *Twin Peaks Prods., Inc.* v. *Publ'ns Int'l, Ltd.*, 996 F.2d 1366 (2d Cir. 1993).

21 For example, while a guitar in the shape of the copyrighted symbol that for a while was the name of the artist formerly and once again known as Prince is derivative, what of a guitar incorporating Superman's red "S" logo? Does the fact that Prince (unlike the man from Krypton) is a musician and the symbol is used in its entirety render the use less transformative and thus an infringing derivative work? *Pickett* v. *Prince*, 207 F.3d 402 (7th Cir. 2000).

22 See, for example, *Gracen* v. *Bradford Exchange*, 698 F.2d 300 (7th Cir. 1983). On transformative works generally, see, for example, Jo-Na Williams, *The New Symbol of "Hope" for Fair Use:* Shepard Fairey v. The Associated Press, LANDSLIDE, September/October 2009, at 55.

23 17 U.S.C. § 103(a) (2006).

the retelling a new, original work, commenting on and critiquing the original.[24] The particular retelling at issue in *Suntrust Bank* v. *Houghton Mifflin Co.* was Alice Randall's novel *The Wind Done Gone*,[25] which, among other perceived transgressions, violated the Mitchell estate's peculiar prohibition on depictions of "miscegenation or homosexuality," prohibitions that had previously caused novelist Pat Conroy to decline the opportunity to write an "official" sequel to *Gone with the Wind*.[26] The original, with its overly sentimental view of life before the Civil War and its stubborn refusal to confront the realities of slavery, has, thanks to its cultural prominence, served as something of a stumbling block in American discourse for decades. Many find the movie unwatchable and the book unreadable for their willful blindness; a critical reexamination such as *The Wind Done Gone* may actually serve to rehabilitate and detoxify the original text, rendering it more palatable by bringing it in to the ongoing discourse rather than leaving it standing outside.

Note, by the way, that whether a work is transformative has nothing to do with the work's literary merit. A lot of fanfic is, sadly, not very good; this does not mean that it is not transformative. Similarly parodies need not be particularly funny in order to be protected as parodies:

> The threshold question when fair use is raised in defense of parody is whether a parodic character may reasonably be perceived. Whether, going beyond that, parody is in good taste or bad does not and should not matter to fair use. As Justice Holmes explained, "[i]t would be a dangerous undertaking for persons trained only to the law to constitute themselves final judges of the worth of [a work], outside of the narrowest and most obvious limits. At the one extreme some works of genius would be sure to miss appreciation. Their very novelty would make them repulsive until the public had learned the new language in which their author spoke." [*Bleistein* v. *Donaldson Lithographing Co.*] (circus posters have copyright protection); *cf. Yankee Publishing Inc. v. News America Publishing, Inc.*, 809 F.Supp. 267, 280 (S.D.N.Y. 1992) (Leval, J.) ("First Amendment protections do not apply only to those who speak clearly, whose jokes are funny, and whose parodies succeed").[27]

Transformative use and fair use

All fanfic is derivative in a literary sense; in order to be fanfic, it must include enough elements of the underlying original work to place the fanfic within the fandom. Most fanfic, however, is not derivative within the meaning of section

24 *Suntrust Bank* v. *Houghton Mifflin Co.*, 268 F.3d 1257 (11th Cir. 2001).

25 Alice Randall, The Wind Done Gone (New York: Houghton Mifflin, 2001).

26 *Suntrust Bank*, 268 F.3d at 1282 and n.6.

27 *Campbell* v. *Acuff-Rose Music, Inc.*, 510 U.S. 569, 582–83 (1994).

106(2). A steamy Harry/Draco romance, a trailer for a nonexistent "Lockhorns" movie, a video using original music and clips from the Lord of the Rings movies to show Gollum as a hip-hop star—all of these things actually exist, and all are substantial transformations of the original works. These transformative uses are more likely to be protected as fair use, even if they make use of copyrighted characters or other content:

> The first factor in a fair use enquiry is "the purpose and character of the use, including whether such use is of a commercial nature or is for nonprofit educational purposes." § 107(1) … The central purpose of this investigation is to see, in Justice Story's words, whether the new work merely "supersede[s] the objects" of the original creation, or instead adds something new, with a further purpose or different character, altering the first with new expression, meaning, or message; it asks, in other words, whether and to what extent the new work is "transformative." Although such transformative use is not absolutely necessary for a finding of fair use, the goal of copyright, to promote science and the arts, is generally furthered by the creation of transformative works. Such works thus lie at the heart of the fair use doctrine's guarantee of breathing space within the confines of copyright, and the more transformative the new work, the less will be the significance of other factors, like commercialism, that may weigh against a finding of fair use.[28]

As the court in *Campbell* points out, it is not necessary for a use to be transformative in order to be fair use—but it helps, a lot. The Harry/Draco romance (a slash genre with works numbering in the hundreds of thousands, at least), while it borrows characters and setting from J.K. Rowling's Harry Potter novels, transforms the basic personalities of the characters as well as the relationship between them and with other characters. The transformation occurs not because of the heteronormative expectations of some (though by no means all) readers; after all, there is no evidence in canon that either Harry or Draco is exclusively heterosexual, and considerable evidence in canon that each is attracted to other male characters.[29] It occurs because in canon Harry and Draco feel no emotion for each other warmer than intense dislike. Nor does this antagonism hide an underlying attraction, as does the constant bickering between Ron and Hermione; it is a genuine, rather than masking, mutual dislike. Harry is willing to save Draco's life out of recognition of their shared humanity, but with apologies to all the Drarry shippers out there,

28 Ibid., at 578–79.

29 In Harry's case, Ron Weasley, and to a lesser extent Cedric Diggory and possibly Oliver Wood; in Draco's, Crabbe and Goyle, although with the dysfunctional aspects one would expect of those three characters. I could offer pages of examples and argument here, but that's something for a fan forum.

that's as far as it goes.[30] A Harry and Draco who feel friendship, let alone romantic warmth, for each other are not the Harry and Draco of canon; they are transformed.

The Lockhorns movie trailer is less clearly transformative; it presents the characters, Leroy and Loretta Lockhorn, locked in the same dystopian, soul-destroying marriage portrayed in the long-running newspaper comic strip.[31] It is not the characters that are transformed, but the underlying nature of the work: the parodic humor comes from the utter unsuitability of the original, a one-panel comic strip without story arcs or other day-to-day continuity beyond the bitter, weary hatred of the titular couple for each other, to adaptation to a full-length motion picture format.

The hip-hop Gollum video, though it uses the character Gollum from the Lord of the Rings novels and movies, and images from the New Line movies, is the most clearly transformative: the song is original, and the images used are not entire clips, let alone entire movies, but pictures of Gollum, the towers of Barad-Dûr and Isengard, an Orc, the One Ring, and other miscellany, clipped from movie stills and crudely animated. And Gollum, of course, is not actually a hip-hop star.[32] He might, however, be a blues singer: one elaborately developed fan site has him surviving the fall into the lava at Sammath Naur and the destruction of the Ring to wander Middle Earth as Howling Wolf Gollum:

> We now know that H.W.G. is the very same Gollum of the Redbook of Westmarch. But nobody seems to hold that against him these days. Maybe it's because he brought the Blues to Middle Earth, maybe it's because they think that he suffered enough. And maybe it's because without him, the ring might never have been destroyed. Ask ten different folk and you will get ten different answers. But one thing pretty much everyone agrees on is that when it comes to singin' the blues, no one in Middle-Earth does it better, or has more of a reason to sing 'em than H.W.G.[33]

Transformative uses are not, as Justice Souter noted in *Campbell*, the only fair uses. But most fan works are transformative, and fan activists such as the Organization for Transformative Works focus on this in arguing that fanfic and other fan works are fair use.

---

30 As the author jokingly says, "you girls … must start to get past this." See Chapter 4, note 84, and accompanying text.

31 MaterialGirl850, The Lockhorns: The Movie (Trailer), October 27, 2006, www.youtube.com/watch?v=5Wla4TFEmpk.

32 Ned Evett & Paul Teharr, *Gollum Rap* (Towers Are the Players), available at www.albinoblacksheep.com/flash/gollum (last visited January 31, 2010).

33 The Runt, *The Legend of Howling Wolf Gollum*, www.stupidring.com/humor/hwg-legend.html (last visited January 31, 2010).

An additional note on parody

Even works that are not protected by fair use may be protected under the First Amendment. Section 107 is subject to change at the whim of Congress, but some uses protected under it, especially parody and criticism, are protected by the First Amendment's guarantee of freedom of expression. The First Amendment's protections are not necessarily coterminous with those of section 107; just as some material protected by section 107 is not constitutionally protected free expression, some constitutionally protected free expression lies outside the scope of section 107.

The U.S. Supreme Court addressed parody in *Campbell* v. *Acuff-Rose Music, Inc. Campbell* involved a parody of Roy Orbison's intensely irritating 1964 song "Oh, Pretty Woman." The song had been covered by several other musicians and served as the inspiration for the reprehensible movie *Pretty Woman* starring Julia Roberts and Richard Gere.[34] Luther Campbell, of the notorious early rap group 2 Live Crew, requested permission to perform a parody of the song; Acuff-Rose refused to give permission.[35] Despite the refusal, Campbell and 2 Live Crew recorded and distributed the parody, "Big Hairy Woman."[36] While relatively mild by comparison to some of 2 Live Crew's other works, the song could be considered shocking; the Supreme Court seemed to agree with the dissenting opinion of the appellate court's Judge Nelson that "Big Hairy Woman":

> "was clearly intended to ridicule the white-bread original" and "reminds us that sexual congress with nameless streetwalkers is not necessarily the stuff of romance and is not necessarily without its consequences. The singers (there are several) have the same thing on their minds as did the lonely man with the nasal voice, but here there is no hint of wine and roses."[37]

The Supreme Court agreed that the work was a parody, and that whether the parody was successful, let alone in good taste, was irrelevant: "having found [the element of parody] we will not take the further step of evaluating its quality. The threshold question when fair use is raised in defense of parody is whether a parodic character may reasonably be perceived. Whether, going beyond that, parody is in good taste or bad does not and should not matter to fair use."[38]

Parodies are a large part of the world of fanfic. Some fit clearly within the traditional boundaries of parody, like the numerous parodies of popular F/

---

34 PRETTY WOMAN (Touchstone Pictures 1990).
35 *Campbell* v. *Acuff-Rose Music, Inc.*, 510 U.S. 569, 572 (1994).
36 Ibid., at 572–73.
37 Ibid., at 582.
38 Ibid.

SF movies written as screenplays.[39] These parodies poke fun at the flaws and inconsistencies of the originals, but serve to enhance rather than reduce fans' enjoyment of the original. As a literary matter, some are "real parody, inseparable from admiration,"[40] while others, less fond, "yield to the spirit of contempt which destroys parody."[41] In the absence of any market for fan parodies, the incentive to create them can only come from admiration of the original, or from anger. The overwhelming majority of fan parodies and other fan works are probably labors of love; a few works, though, offend some in the audience sufficiently to inspire an anti-fandom devoted to heaping venom on the work. Many parodies of the comic strip *For Better or for Worse* probably fall into this category.[42] The "Big Hairy Woman" parody probably falls into the second category. Both types of parody, however, are equally protected under *Campbell*: "First Amendment protections do not apply only to those who speak clearly, whose jokes are funny, and whose parodies succeed."[43]

Here the literary and legal definitions part company. G.K. Chesterton would probably not have been comfortable with the idea of a "lethal parody" aimed at harming the market for the original work; nonetheless, "when a lethal parody, like a scathing theater review, kills demand for the original, it does not produce a harm cognizable under the Copyright Act."[44] But copyright law is concerned with the legal definition rather than a Chestertonian inquiry into the motives of the parodist;

39 See, for example, Cleolinda, *Memorable Movies in Fifteen Minutes Entries*, www.livejournal.com/tools/memories.bml?user=cleolinda&keyword=Movies+in+Fifteen+Minutes&filter=all; Evadne_noel, *Memorable Breadbox Editions Entries*, www.livejournal.com/tools/memories.bml?user=evadne_noel&keyword=Breadbox+Editions&filter=all; Mistful, *Memorable Entries*, www.livejournal.com/tools/memories.bml?user=mistful; Naill_renfro, *Memorable Parody Entries*, www.livejournal.com/tools/memories.bml?user=naill_renfro&keyword=parody&filter=all; Molly J. Ringwraith, *Memorable Entries*, www.livejournal.com/tools/memories.bml?user=mollyringwraith; Molly J. Ringwraith, *Harry Potter and the Deathly Hallows, Condensed Parody*, http://mollyringwraith.livejournal.com/66902.html (all sites last visited August 18, 2008); and the sadly-defunct *Jerry the Frog Productions*, available (via the Wayback Machine) at http://web.archive.org/web/20061130171850/www.jerrythefrogproductions.com/WhatsNew.html.

40 G.K. Chesterton, Varied Types 179 (Project Gutenberg, ed., Dodd, Mead & Company, 2004) (1905), available at http://infomotions.com/etexts/gutenberg/dirs/1/4/2/0/14203/14203.htm.

41 Ibid.

42 See, for example, beatonna, *Hark! A Vagrant, A Chilling Romance*, http://beatonna.livejournal.com/54383.html; Posting of Keogh, available at www.comixfan.com/xfan/forums/showthread.php?p=1442950#post1442950 (August 6, 2008) (*X-Parodies*); posting of yellojkt, available at http://livebythefoma.blogspot.com/2007/07/foobpocalypse-now.html (July 8, 2007) (*Foobocalypse Now*). The world of ironic *Mary Worth* fandom (the center of which can be found at www.joshreads.com) is more difficult to classify.

43 *Campbell* v. *Acuff-Rose Music, Inc.*, 510 U.S. 569, 583 (1994) (quoting *Yankee Publ'g Inc.* v. *News Am. Publ'g, Inc.*, 809 F. Supp. 267, 280 (S.D.N.Y. 1992)).

44 Ibid., at 591–92.

even if "Big Hairy Woman" is motivated by contempt rather than fondness for the original, it is still parody. Chesterton, no doubt, would have considered the song proof that Americans still laugh at things, not with them.

Campbell also draws a legal, rather than literary, distinction between parody and satire: "Parody needs to mimic an original to make its point, and so has some claim to use the creation of its victim's (or collective victims') imagination, whereas satire can stand on its own two feet and so requires justification for the very act of borrowing."[45] The court relies on dictionary definitions of satire as "a work 'in which prevalent follies or vices are assailed with ridicule…' or are 'attacked through irony, derision, or wit.'"[46] While this may serve to give an idea of satire to those who have not heard of it before, the distinction drawn between satire and parody may not be all that useful. (A perhaps better approach, eliminating the distinction, can be found in *Berlin* v. *E.C. Publications, Inc.*: "[A]s a general proposition, we believe that parody and satire are deserving of substantial freedom—both as entertainment and as a form of social and literary criticism."[47]) A work may parody a well-known original and simultaneously satirize the society of which that original is a part, and it is not always easy or even possible to draw a line between the two functions; Lewis Carroll's parodies (such as "You Are Old, Father William," itself often parodied) provide examples of works that do both, as do several of Weird Al Yankovic's music videos, the latter often with an added element of self-parody (or perhaps self-satire), as in "White & Nerdy."

Fanfic parodists are probably also on fairly solid ground, as long as they take heed of *Campbell*'s warning that works that copy more than necessary for parodic effect, to such an extent that they become substitutes for the original, may not be protected:

> The only further judgment, indeed, that a court may pass on a work goes to an assessment of whether the parodic element is slight or great, and the copying small or extensive in relation to the parodic element, for a work with slight parodic element and extensive copying will be more likely to merely "supersede the objects" of the original.[48]

Trademark

Character names and other story elements in a popular work of fiction may be protected by trademark law. Similar reasoning, specifically invoking the First Amendment, applies to parody and other fanfic uses of protected marks. Even fanfic that, perhaps by reason of advertising on the website on which it is posted, constitutes a use in commerce, may use otherwise protected marks as story elements:

45 Ibid., at 580–81.

46 Ibid., at 581 n.15.

47 *Berlin* v. *E.C. Publications, Inc.*, 329 F.2d 541 (2d Cir. 1964).

48 *Campbell*, 510 U.S. at 583 n.16 (1994).

> [W]hen unauthorized use of another's mark is part of a communicative message and not a source identifier, the First Amendment is implicated in opposition to the trademark right … [W]here the unauthorized use of a trademark is for expressive purposes of comedy, parody, allusion, criticism, news reporting, and commentary, the law requires a balancing of the rights of the trademark owner against the interests of free speech.[49]

The First Amendment interest of the fanfic author is thus balanced against the likelihood of confusion as to the source of the stories. Even without the disclaimers many fanfics contain, it seems highly unlikely that any readers will believe them to be created or authorized by the owners of the marks.[50] Here, too, is where those disclaimers—so meaningless for copyright purposes—actually have some use; they serve to reduce the likelihood of confusion yet further.

Other media and other fan works: fan art, filk, and fan videos

As many of the preceding examples show, fan-created content takes many forms in addition to all-text fanfic. Of these, original graphic art and videos pose fewer copyright problems. Art that imitates a protected graphic character poses somewhat more,[51] while work that combines copyrighted and original material may fall outside the scope of fair use even if intended as a parody. Although the court in *MGM* v. *Showcase Atlanta* seemed to equate "non-parodic" and "non-satiric," works that are satires, rather than parodies, may not enjoy the same level of protection. A great deal of fanfic borrows from one work to poke fun at another. When the humor is directed at both works, there is no problem. When one serves only as a vehicle, though,[52] or is copied substantially more than parody requires, there may be a problem. Song parodies and vidding are especially problematic.

Parodying songs, or simply setting new words to old tunes, is a universal human activity. Three-year-olds make up their own lyrics to "Happy Birthday to You" and "Twinkle, Twinkle, Twinkle Little Star." Both, incidentally, are themselves words set to tunes with which they were not originally paired; the English words

---

49 *Yankee Publ'g, Inc.*, 809 F. Supp. at 276.

50 See generally, for example, *Rogers* v. *Grimaldi*, 875 F.2d 994, 999 (2d Cir. 1989); *Cliffs Notes, Inc.* v. *Bantam Doubleday Dell Publ'g Group, Inc.*, 886 F.2d 490 (2d Cir. 1989); *Yankee Publ'g, Inc.*, 809 F. Supp. at 277–79.

51 See Leslie A. Kurtz, *The Independent Legal Lives of Fictional Characters*, 1986 Wis. L. Rev. 429, 445–51 (1986). See also generally Michael T. Helfand, *When Mickey Mouse is as Strong as Superman: The Convergence of Intellectual Property Laws to Protect Fictional Literary and Pictorial Characters*, 44 Stan. L. Rev. 623 (1992); Francis M. Nevins, *Copyright + Character = Catastrophe*, 39 J. Copyright Soc'y 303 (1992).

52 See, for example, *Dr. Seuss Enterprises, L.P.* v. *Penguin Books USA, Inc.*, 109 F.3d 1394 (9th Cir. 1997) (affirming an injunction against the publisher of a book about O.J. Simpson's murder trial imitating Dr. Seuss's style).

to "Twinkle, Twinkle" are from an 1806 poem by Jane Taylor, while the music was written by Mozart 25 years earlier. Nor was Mozart's music wholly original; it was an adaptation of the French folk song "Ah! vous dirai-je, Maman." The tune to "Happy Birthday to You" was originally published in 1893 by Patty and Mildred Hill as "Good Morning to All" (and the more familiar lyrics, whose copyright status is unclear, first appeared in print in 1912). Nor was the tune entirely original to the Hills; it resembles several earlier tunes. Horace Waters, founder of the piano company bearing his name and publisher of 30 of Stephen Foster's songs, published a similar tune, "Happy Greetings to All," in 1858. Everything, as Tolkien and Justice Story would have observed, is derivative.[53]

Putting new words to old tunes is also central to American culture—after all, our national anthem is set to the tune of "The Anacreontic Song," more often, if not correctly, called "To Anacreon in Heaven." In *Mason & Dixon*, Thomas Pynchon uses the tune for comic effect in post-revolutionary, pre-Star Spangled Banner America—Anacreon in Anachron. But "The Anacreontic Song" floated on a cauldron of story as well. The song drew its name from the Anacreontic Society, an eighteenth-century group of well-to-do London drinkers and partiers. The society in turn was inspired by Henri Estienne's sixteenth-century translations of the erotic poetry and drinking songs of the original Anacreon, who lived in Greece over 2,600 years ago.

Some of these parodies become established in their own right, living an outsider existence, often passed down from one year's kindergarteners to the next without passing through the adult world at all. These parody versions inform the "official" versions, so that most listeners are aware, on some level, that "Happy Birthday to You" is a song about the birthday person's visual and olfactory resemblance to a monkey, while "Jingle Bells" (words and lyrics published by James Lord Pierpont in 1857 under the title "One Horse Open Sleigh") is about the Batmobile (a name first used to describe Batman's car in *Detective Comics #48* in 1941) losing a wheel and the Joker (first appearance in *Batman #1* in 1940) getting away. In a neat bit of recursive homage, the 2008 Batman movie *The Dark Knight* lampshades the song: the Batmobile does lose a wheel, and the Joker gets away—at least for the moment.

Another tune that has taken on a life in the world outside the neat boundaries of copyright and commerce, best known from *Bridge on the River Kwai*, is actually the "Colonel Bogey March", written in 1914 by a British soldier, Marine Lieutenant (later Major) Fredrick Joseph Ricketts. Ricketts published the tune,

---

53 See Robert Brauneis, *Copyright and the World's Most Popular Song*, GWU Legal Studies Research Paper No. 1111624, http://ssrn.com/abstract=1111624, and, on Horace Waters' 1858 version, fn. 58 (citing Kembrew McLeod, Freedom of Expression®: Overzealous Copyright Bozos and Other Enemies of Creativity 16 (New York: Doubleday, 2005)); see also *Horace Waters, 1812–1893* [biography], PD Music, www.pdmusic.org/biographies/Waters%20Horace%20Waters.pdf (last visited March 10, 2010); *Eldred* v. *Ashcroft*, 537 U.S. 186 (2003).

and many others, under the name Kenneth Alford, because the military frowned on its soldiers making a profit in the outside world. It made a small fortune, to the presumed disgruntlement of his superiors: over a million copies of the sheet music were sold. The song's title comes from a fellow officer who, while golfing, instead of yelling "Fore!" used to whistle the two notes that became the intro to the first two lines.

The tune developed a complex independent life of its own. To Americans it is known, incorrectly, as the "Bridge on the River Kwai March." There is actually another tune in the movie *Bridge on the River Kwai* with that name, but no one remembers it. When the movie was released in 1957, however, the adults in the audience would all have had memories of World War II, and many would have been veterans. To anyone in the United Kingdom who was old enough to remember the war, and to any of the American or other soldiers (except, perhaps, Canadians—see below) who served alongside British troops in the war, the tune would have signified something quite different. It was known not as the "Colonel Bogey March" but as "Hitler Has Only Got One Ball." Among the less vulgar variations:

> Hitler has only got one ball,
> Göring has two but very small,
> Himmler is somewhat sim'lar,
> But poor Goebbels has no balls at all.

While the humor of the tune may be lost on modern audiences, it would have been instantly amusing to 1957 audiences, and its use in a Japanese POW camp not only amusing but also a symbol of defiance. But the value of the tune in the movie derives not from its "official" incarnation, but from the spin put upon it by outsiders to the licensed and recognized creative process: the British soldiers in World War II who used it as a vehicle for mocking their opponent. The tune itself is cheery and catchy enough that it might have been used in the movie, or a movie, anyway, but without the soldiers' parodic lyrics it wouldn't be funny, and its use in an Axis prisoner of war camp not especially brave.

Ricketts himself was still in the Marines during most of the war; he joined the military in 1895 (at the age of 14), became the Marines' Director of Music in 1927, and retired in 1944 at the age of 63, only to die the next year, a week after V-E Day. He would certainly have been familiar with the "Hitler Has Only Got One Ball" version of his tune; while his thoughts on the subject appear not to have been recorded, it seems safe to assume he would have approved.

Nor has the life of the tune ended there. To those who were in elementary school in the U.S. during the 1970s, it's also the "Comet-Vomit" tune:

> Comet, it makes your mouth turn green
> Comet, it tastes like Listerine

Comet, it makes you vomit
So get some Comet and vomit today!

Meanwhile, to Canadians, "The Colonel Bogey March" is the official march of The King's Own Calgary Regiment, an armored reconnaissance regiment deployed overseas in both world wars and more recently in Afghanistan.[54] A probably apocryphal tale relates that when Japan's Prime Minister arrived in Canada for a meeting of the then-G7 leaders in the 1970s, the Regiment's band caused a diplomatic embarrassment by playing its march.[55] Presumably in this instance any perceived insult to the Japanese Prime Minister came from the use of the song in the film, which portrays the Japanese military in an unflattering light, and not from the mockery of Nazi leaders—the World War II alliance with Germany being, by that point, an embarrassment best forgotten—nor from the tune, familiar in Japan from the children's music mini-show みんなのうた (*Minna No Uta*, a Japanese TV fixture since 1961, usually broadcast in five-minute filler segments)[56] and as the playground song "Saru, Gorira Chinpanji" ("猿, ゴリラ, チンパンジー"—"Monkey, Gorilla Chimpanzee"):

Saru, gorira chinpanji
Saru, gorira chinpanji
Saru, gorira saru
Gorira saru chinpanji.

The tune was also used in the 1986–1989 game show 風雲! たけし城 ("Turbulence! Takeshi's Castle," known in the U.S. as "Takeshi's Castle" and, in a dubbed spoof version, as "MXC: Most Extreme Challenge.")

The embarrassment occasioned by the song must either have been minor or have faded, as the U.S. Navy's Seventh Fleet Band was able to play the March in Yokosuka, Japan, in 2007.[57] In Germany itself the tune is more likely to be known, if at all, from its use in commercials for the revolting beverage Underberg.

The tune's appeal across a broad range of cultures and ages, and the diverse lyrics that have been put to it, reinforce the point: song parodies and other forms of setting one's own lyrics to a familiar tune is a universal and natural human activity. In the case of "The Colonel Bogey March," there is a cultural dimension

54 See King's Own Calgary Regiment, www.army.ca/wiki/index.php/King's_Own_Calgary_Regiment; The King's Own Calgary Regiment, www.kingsown.ca (both visited November 3, 2009).

55 It would have been funnier if it had been the German prime minister, though.

56 See generally みんなのうた, www.nhk.or.jp/minna (last visited November 3, 2009) (in Japanese).

57 Seventh Fleet Band: Colonel Bogey, October 21, 2007, www.youtube.com/watch?v=CtX8_2LViGA, posted by Gryphonette, October 22, 2007 (last visited November 10, 2008).

to this appropriation as well; a British military tune has been appropriated not only by Britain's allies (and former colonies), but by Britain's erstwhile enemies, against whom the tune was once aimed. This sort of cultural transformation is an essential tool of cultural survival in a global era; the appropriation of tunes, story elements, and other fragments of cultural exports and their adaptation to the importing culture helps to prevent the loudest cultures from drowning out the quieter ones.[58] This is not to suggest that Fredrick Ricketts' economic rights should be disrespected; Japanese television stations or German digestif manufacturers wishing to use the tune should (and presumably do) pay royalties. But any attempt to use copyright law to prevent the adaptation of the tune by U.S. or Japanese schoolchildren would be a use of copyright law in the cause of implementing a world monoculture; this is not something copyright law is intended to, or should, do. Fortunately no such thing has happened in the case of "The Colonel Bogey March." It would be nice to say that it has never happened at all, but as we shall see when we discuss Harry Potter, it may not be possible to say that.

Song parodies in fandom

Song parodies are an essential part of genre fandom. Fan song parodies are often called filks, although the two terms are not completely overlapping: filks can be original songs as well as contrafacta (new lyrics set to the tune of existing songs). Original songs are not only harder to compose, but also lack the instant appeal of a familiar tune; original filksongs that become well-known (even well-known within a particular fandom) are rare.[59] ("Star Trekkin'," by Rory Kehoe, John O'Connor, and Graham Lister, was commercially released became well-known in the world beyond fandom as a novelty recording, reaching #1 on the UK Singles Chart in 1987. However, it is not a completely original tune; it is a recognizable descendant of "The Music Man.") Original filksongs present no copyright problems; both words and music are the creations of the author(s) of the song. The majority of filks, though, are not original.

Just as medieval contrafacta bridged the gap between the secular and the sacred by setting religious words to popular tunes and/or secular words to the

58 See generally, for example, PASCAL ORY, Mickey, *go home!,* ou: D'un cas intéressant de désaméricanisation, in LA CULTURE COMME AVENTURE: TREIZE EXERCICES D'HISTOIRE CULTURELLE 227 (Paris: Editions Complexe, 2008).

59 The Star Trek filk "Banned from Argo" by Leslie Fish is perhaps the best-known example. A few other original songs have managed, like "Star Trekkin'," to cross over to the mainstream, also generally as novelty songs, including Jerry Buckner and Gary Garcia's 1982 song "Pac Man Fever." Then there are songs that, like several of the songs on the Led Zeppelin Runes album, can be seen as Tolkien fan music, although more of the "inspired by" variety. The phenomenon of wrock (wizard rock) within Harry Potter fandom has not yet produced mainstream crossovers. See generally, for example, Lacey Rose, *Media: Wizard Rock*, FORBES, July 13, 2005, www.forbes.com/2005/07/13/rowling-potter-band-cx_lr_0713harryband.html.

tunes of hymns, most filks bridge the gap between fandom and the mundane by setting fannish lyrics to mundane tunes. (The modern example of the traditional secular–religious bridging best known to copyright lawyers is the pairing of the George Harrison song "My Sweet Lord" and the Chiffons' "He's So Fine;"[60] the pairing, though with permission and tongue-in-cheek, of Mary Wells' "My Guy" and Whoopi Goldberg's "My God" provides another latter-day example.)

A filk can be set to the tune of a work out of copyright, such as the above-mentioned "The Music Man," avoiding copyright problems. Thus Gimli may safely express his admiration for Legolas to the tune of "The Yellow Rose of Texas."[61] Though many recordings of both songs are still in copyright, the music and lyrics of both are in the public domain. And sometimes a filk is set to a tune that has been parodied so frequently that it might reasonably be considered fair game, such as "My Favorite Things,"[62] a recording of which even appears, without copyright notice, on a U.S. government website.[63]

Most of the songs that are familiar to most people, though, are still in copyright. Thus many or most filks use the tunes of works still in copyright and still actively protected by the copyright owners.[64] Posting proposed alternate lyrics to a well-known tune should not, by itself, pose a copyright problem, as long as the lyrics are sufficiently original, because the music is not present in the text. The reader can imagine the tune while reading the lyrics—a tune played only in the reader's head is not (yet) a copyright violation. Such alternate lyrics, even when commercially published, have been found not to infringe copyright: use of "the titles" (in the "to be sung to the tune of" line), "the meter, and an occasional phrase from the original lyrics" where "it is clear that the parody has neither the intent nor the effect of fulfilling the demand for the original, and where the parodist does not appropriate a greater amount of the original work than is necessary to 'recall or conjure up' the object of his satire, a finding of infringement would be improper."[65]

---

60 See *Bright Tunes Music Corp.* v. *Harrisongs Music, Ltd.*, 420 F. Supp. 177 (S.D.N.Y. 1976), *aff'd sub nom*, *ABKCO Music, Inc.* v. *Harrisongs Music Ltd.*, 722 F.2d 988 (2d Cir. 1983).

61 See Robin Smallburrow, *The Yellow Rose of Rohan*, http://frogmorton4.tripod.com/filk/Yellow_Rose_of_Rohan.htm (last visited November 10, 2008).

62 Richard Rodgers & Oscar Hammerstein, *My Favorite Things* (1959) (song); see The Green Dragon, *My Favorite Things*, www.geocities.com/greendragon1420/MyFavoriteThings.htm (last visited November 10, 2008).

63 National Institutes of Health, Department of Health & Human Services, *My Favorite Things*, http://kids.niehs.nih.gov/lyrics/favorite.htm (last visited November 10, 2008).

64 See, for example, William H. Hsu, *Master Gandalf's Lowly Hobbit Band*, The Red Songbook of Westmarch, www.kddresearch.org/Tolkien/Humor/RedSOW (last visited November 10, 2008) (to the tune of the Beatles' *Sergeant Pepper's Lonely Hearts Club Band*).

65 *Berlin* v. *E.C. Publications, Inc.*, 329 F.2d 541, 543, 545 (2d Cir. 1964). Note, again, that the Second Circuit declines to draw a distinction between satire and parody. In words predictive of *Campbell*, the court stated "While brief phrases of the original lyrics

Songs that are recorded will attract a wider audience than lyrics alone, though, and while fan artists are not seeking an audience for commercial reasons, they nonetheless usually want to reach other fans. Thus the lyrics to "Hey There Cthulhu" are an original work of their creator, the Eben Brooks Band, but when set to the tune of The Plain White T's "Hey There Delilah" and recorded, copyright issues may arise.[66]

When original fan lyrics are set to tunes still in copyright and performed at conventions or posted online, both the copyright and the performance right in the music come into play. Non-recorded performances in the halls of the San Diego Convention Center during Comic-Con may skate by unnoticed or at least un-sued-upon; to date posted recordings of those performances have done so as well, but that is no guarantee they will continue to do so. The use of the copyrighted music is impermissible unless the song is being parodied or the use otherwise fits within the fair use exception.

Fan video works

A related category of fan work is the fan video (shortened to fanvid or vid). Some fan videos are wholly original, and thus need face only the problems also faced by fanfic: copyright in characters and the exclusive right to create derivative works. *The Hunt for Gollum*, a 40-minute original film describing a series of events described, at a remove, in Tolkien's original *Fellowship of the Ring* and mentioned briefly in passing in Peter Jackson's movie, uses no other author's video footage.[67] Most of the characters are original. It does, however, use a central character (Gollum) from Lord of the Rings, who is also, as the title makes clear, central to *The Hunt for Gollum*. The movie is not a parody, but the filling in of a part of the story Tolkien and Jackson both left undeveloped. It is probably a derivative work.

---

were occasionally injected into the parodies, this practice would seem necessary if the defendants' efforts were to 'recall or conjure up' the originals; the humorous effect achieved when a familiar line is interposed in a totally incongruous setting, traditionally a tool of parodists, scarcely amounts to a 'substantial' taking, if that standard is not to be woodenly applied." The court also dismissed as absurd the argument that imitation of the originals' rhyme scheme was in some way infringing: "[T]he fact that defendants' parodies were written in the same meter as plaintiffs' compositions would seem inevitable if the original was to be recognized, but such a justification is not even necessary; we doubt that even so eminent a composer as plaintiff Irving Berlin should be permitted to claim a property interest in iambic pentameter."

66 See Eben Brooks Band, *Hey There Cthulhu: The Photomontage Video*, www.youtube.com/watch?v=XxScTbIUvoA (last visited January 26, 2010).

67 See *The Hunt for Gollum*, www.thehuntforgollum.com (last visited January 26, 2010).

Similarly, the short fan movie *The Adventures of Batman and Robin ... and Jesus*[68] places the copyrighted (and trademarked) characters Batman, Robin and The Flash at Comic-Con in San Diego. The characters are portrayed by actors in costumes, except in the opening scene, when drawings are used. The story is original; the treatment of the characters and their relationship may be a critical or even parodic use.

On a smaller scale, the Potter Puppet Pals skits are also fan videos; like *The Hunt for Gollum*, they are both original (as video) and derivative (as stories), and use copyrighted characters. But because they are parodies, they are probably within the protection of *Campbell* v. *Acuff-Rose Music*.[69] Machinima—movies created using graphics rendering engines, usually although not always from copyrighted video games, are another special subcategory.[70]

These original video works are not the most common type of fan video, though, and are not what is usually meant when fans talk about fanvids and vidding. The terms are more often applied to fan videos using clips from existing movies and television shows, often combined with already-existing music. These clips and songs may be combined with each other for humorous or dramatic effect, as in the creation of fake movie trailers: scenes from the fourth and fifth Harry Potter movies can be combined with dialogue from the movie *Becoming Jane* to create a trailer for an imaginary movie, "Becoming Hermione," with Hermione Granger in the role of Jane Austen.[71] (The overlap between the casts of the underlying movies makes the voiceover particularly effective.) Or the creepy yet oddly unimpressive vampire Edward Cullen and vampire slayer Buffy Summers can meet in a six-minute mini-movie, with Buffy in the Bella Swan role. Predictably, after being stalked by Edward throughout the vid and pointing out to him (as she originally did to Angel) that "being stalked isn't really a big turn-on," Buffy ends up staking Edward.[72]

The uses in "Becoming Hermione" and "Edward Cullen Meets Buffy Summers" are transformative; they take small portions of the original to create something new. The end credits of "Edward Cullen Meets Buffy Summers" acknowledge the source material: the *Buffy the Vampire Slayer* television show, the *Twilight* movie

68 The Pine Oaks Lodge, *The Adventures of Batman and Robin ... and Jesus*, www.youtube.com/user/thepineoakslodge, or www.youtube.com/watch?v=R5I57uXkIFI (both last visited January 26, 2010).

69 *Campbell* v. *Acuff-Rose Music, Inc.*, 510 U.S. 569 (1994).

70 See generally, for example, Matthew Brett Freedman, *Machinima and Copyright Law*, 13 J. Intell. Property L. 235 (2005); Christina J. Hayes, Note, *Changing the Rules of the Game: How Video Game Publishers Are Embracing User-Generated Derivative Works*, 21 Harv. J.L. & Tech. 567 (2008); Christopher Reid, *Fair Game: The Application of Fair Use Doctrine to Machinima*, 19 Fordham Intell. Property, Media & Ent. L.J. 831 (2009).

71 *Becoming Hermione*, www.youtube.com/watch?v=k9O1zimYIBk (last visited January 26, 2010).

72 Jonathan McIntosh, *Edward Cullen Meets Buffy Summers*, www.youtube.com/watch?v=R_QEOwJ0pKA (last visited January 26, 2010).

and soundtrack, and the *Harry Potter and the Goblet of Fire* movie. The credits also speak directly to the transformative use issue, stating "This transformative work constitutes a 'fair use' of any copyrighted material as provided for in Section 107 of the US Copyright Law." None of this, of course, actually insulates the vidder; at best it is evidence of an intent not to infringe copyright. While in civil actions there may be liability for unintentional or even unconscious copyright infringement, criminal copyright infringement under 17 U.S.C. 506(a)(1) does include a *mens rea* requirement: "Any person who *willfully* infringes a copyright shall be punished" (emphasis added). Thus, for example, the deliberate recreation of movie trailers from the original films, when the copyright holder in the trailers has refused permission to reproduce those trailers in other media, would probably meet this requirement—and such a use would, in any event, be derivative.[73]

Section 506 goes on to include qualifications that would insulate most fan vidders from criminal copyright infringement charges in any event. The infringement is only criminal if committed:

> (A) for purposes of commercial advantage or private financial gain;
> (B) by the reproduction or distribution, including by electronic means, during any 180-day period, of 1 or more copies or phonorecords of 1 or more copyrighted works, which have a total retail value of more than $1,000; or
> (C) by the distribution of a work being prepared for commercial distribution, by making it available on a computer network accessible to members of the public, if such person knew or should have known that the work was intended for commercial distribution.[74]

Few fanvids are prepared "for purposes of commercial advantage or private financial gain," nor are they likely to fall within paragraph (C), which is aimed at

---

73 *Video Pipeline, Inc.* v. *Buena Vista Home Entertainment, Inc.*, 275 F. Supp.2d 543 (D.N.J. 2003). On unconscious and unintentional civil infringement, see *Bright Tunes Music Corp.* v. *Harrisongs Music, Ltd.*, 420 F. Supp. 177 (S.D.N.Y. 1976), *aff'd sub nom, ABKCO Music, Inc.* v. *Harrisongs Music Ltd.*, 722 F.2d 988 (2d Cir. 1983); see also generally 17 U.S.C. §501(a); Nimmer, *supra* Chapter 2, note 42, at § 13-08 *Characters*; Eric Goldman, *A Road to No Warez: The No Electronic Theft Act and Criminal Copyright Infringement*, 82 Oregon L. Rev. 369 (2003); on fanvids, see Sarah Trombley, *Visions and Revisions: Fanvids and Fair Use*, 25 Cardozo Arts & Ent. J. 647 (2008); Andrew S. Long, *Mashed Up Videos and Broken Down Copyright: Changing Copyright to Promote the First Amendment Values of Transformative Video*, 60 Okla. L. Rev. 317 (2007).

74 17 U.S.C. § 506(a)(1). Fair use has not-entirely-identical counterparts in the fair dealing doctrines of Canada, the UK, and many other mostly-Anglophone countries. See, for example, *CCH Canadian Ltd.* v. *Law Society of Upper Canada* [2004] 1 S.C.R. 339, 2004 SCC 13 (Can.); Giuseppina D'Agostino, *Comparative Copyright Analysis of Canada's Fair Dealing to U.K. Fair Dealing and U.S. Fair Use*, 53 McGill L.J. 309 (2008); Richard Peltz, *Global Warming Trend? The Creeping Indulgence of Fair Use in the International Copyright Law*, 17 Tex. Intell. Prop. L.J. 267 (2009).

"zero-day" and "negative-day" releases of pirated versions of commercial works. That leaves paragraph (B). If the film *Harry Potter and the Goblet of Fire* has a retail value of $10 and 101 viewers watch an unlicensed version posted on a website within 180 days, the operators of that website have distributed $1,010 worth of copyrighted works, bringing them within the scope of the paragraph. A zealous content-industry advocate might argue that this is what fan vidders have done. But it seems far more likely that the brief clips from *Harry Potter and the Goblet of Fire* appearing in "Becoming Hermione" and "Edward Cullen Meets Buffy Summers" have negligible value if taken separately. No one watches these videos for the chance to see a few seconds of video from the movie; after all, the content owners themselves make longer portions available as trailers online. The clips draw their entertainment value from the transformative use made of them by the vidders; fans watch "Becoming Hermione" to see Hermione Granger as Jane Austen, not Emma Watson as Hermione Granger.

Vidding

Another common type of fanvid is a vid that sets scenes from a familiar source to music; many fans use the terms "fanvid" and "vidding" to refer only to such videos and their making. A subset of this type of fanvid, the "anime music video" or "AMV" (constructed from anime clips set to music) has become sufficiently popular that the term AMV is often, if not correctly, used to describe all music fanvids.

Fanvids of this sort have less copyright leeway. They present a double problem: while fanfic involves mostly original material created by the fan author, and song parodies have original lyrics but not original music, fanvids have neither original artwork nor original music. All of the material used to create the fanvid was originally created by others, and all of it, typically, is protected by copyright. This problem is not unique to vidding; it is shared by mash-ups generally.[75] (Some fanvids use copyrighted video to showcase more or less original songs, as in the online videos of the fan-created *Goonies: The Musical* or Jon and Al Kaplan's *Conan the Barbarian: The Musical*.[76]) In addition to the copyright in the material used to construct the fanvid, the fanvid itself is a derivative work subject to all the concerns addressed above with regard to fanfic. That is, the work is potentially an infringement of the copyright in the original source video(s) as a derivative work under 17 U.S.C. §106(2), while simultaneously an infringement of the §106(1) reproduction right in the music to which the clips are set, and perhaps the §106(6) performance right as well.

---

75 See Robert S. Gerber, *Mixing It Up on The Web: Legal Issues Arising from Internet "Mashups,"* 18 INTELL. PROP. & TECH. L.J. 11 (2006).

76 Peter Sciretta, *Fan Created Goonies Musical*, /Film, January 4, 2010, www.slashfilm.com/2010/01/04/fan-created-goonies-musical; Jon & Al Kaplan, *Conan the Barbarian: The Musical* (2010), available from http://jonandal.com/index.html.

The 2010 DMCA rulemaking: good news for vidders?

To make a vid, a vidder must obtain video clips. These can be recorded from television or obtained from other vidders, but often the easiest way to obtain them is from a DVD. The problem with this is that nearly all commercially available DVDs are protected by a form of encryption called Content Scramble System (CSS). The encryption used in CSS is fairly weak and easily broken; a number of free and commercial programs are available for this purpose. However, copying CSS-encrypted DVDs is illegal under the anti-circumvention provisions of the DMCA. 17 U.S.C. §1201(a)(1)(A) provides that "No person shall circumvent a technological measure that effectively controls access to a work protected under this title." This prohibition is independent of any exceptions that might otherwise be allowed as fair use under section 107; Congress, in enacting §1201, chose to restrict certain rights that might previously have been protected as fair use.

Violation of §1201(a)(1)(A) can subject the violator to civil and criminal penalties under §1203 and §1204; a vidder might incur a greater penalty for the §1201(a)(1)(A) violation than for the vid itself—indeed, even if the vid were otherwise fair use, the penalties for circumventing CSS would still apply.

Fortunately for vidders, the DMCA included a provision, §1201(a)(1)(C), requiring the Librarian of Congress to periodically reexamine the effect of the anticircumvention provisions to determine "whether persons who are users of a copyrighted work are, or are likely to be in the succeeding 3-year period, adversely affected by the prohibition under subparagraph (A) in their ability to make noninfringing uses under this title of a particular class of copyrighted works" and to make appropriate rules to minimize that adverse impact.

In the most recent such rulemaking, in July 2010, the Librarian of Congress specifically exempted "Persons making noninfringing uses of … (1) Motion pictures on DVDs that are lawfully made and acquired and that are protected by the Content Scrambling System when circumvention is accomplished solely in order to accomplish the incorporation of short portions of motion pictures into new works for the purpose of criticism or comment, and where the person engaging in circumvention believes and has reasonable grounds for believing that circumvention is necessary to fulfill the purpose of the use in … (iii) Noncommercial videos."[77]

---

77 Exemption to Prohibition on Circumvention of Copyright Protection Systems for Access Control Technologies (Final Rule), 75 Fed. Reg. 43,825 (July 27, 2010), to be codified at 37 CFR Part 201. See also Recommendation of the Register of Copyrights in RM 2008-8; Rulemaking on Exemptions from Prohibition on Circumvention of Copyright Protection Systems for Access Control Technologies, Letter from Marybeth Peters (Register of Copyrights) to James H. Billington (Librarian of Congress), June 11, 2010; Statement of the Librarian of Congress Relating to Section 1201 Rulemaking, July 26, 2010, available at www.copyright.gov/1201. See also Fair Use and the DMCA Triennial Rulemaking, Copyright & Technology, July 29, 2010, http://copyrightandtechnology.com/2010/07/29/fair-use-and-the-dmca-triennial-rulemaking (last visited October 19, 2010). For the

In other words, decrypting and copying short clips from movies and TV shows on DVD for vidding purposes is now permissible, if the use of those clips in the underlying vid is itself noninfringing. As we have seen, the use of the video clips in a vid is likely to be transformative and protected under §107. Questions as to the permissibility of the use of any copyrighted music in the vid would appear to have no impact; the rule made by the Librarian of Congress addresses "noninfringing uses of … motion pictures" rather than uses which contain no infringement of any copyright whatsoever. So long as the use of the clips is noninfringing, vidders are now insulated from the anticircumvention provisions of §1201, and a major obstacle to the legality of vidding has been removed. (Note, however, that this has no effect on the permissibility of the use of copyrighted music in the vid.)

Drawing from a single source: "They're Taking the Hobbits to Isengard!"

A fanvid that draws all of its material from a single source has only one content owner to worry about; if that content owner is inclined to acquiesce, the fanvid author faces few problems. (Where more content owners are involved, the chance that one of them will be disinclined to acquiesce increases.) Erwin Beekveld's "They're Taking the Hobbits to Isengard,"[78] for example, draws entirely from a single source: the video is a comical remix of scenes and dialogue from the first two Lord of the Rings movies, *The Fellowship of the Ring* and *The Two Towers*, while the music is a cheery Euro-pop remix of Howard Shore's "Shire" and "Fellowship" themes from the soundtracks of those same movies.

Yet even a work apparently drawn from a single source may present complex problems of source. The use of the "Shire" and "Fellowship" themes in the movie underscores the difficulty of defining "originality" and "derivative work." The "Shire" theme was intended to evoke ideas associated with the Shire: nostalgia, a bucolic idyll, England. The "Shire" theme, heard in the song "In Dreams" and repeated throughout the movies, is recognizable to many as "This Is My Father's World," a hymn written by Maltbie Davenport, a Presbyterian pastor (and former Syracuse University Orangeman) from upstate New York, and set to a traditional English melody by Franklin L. Sheppard in 1915, for use in children's Sunday schools.[79] Thus either the hymn or the traditional melody to which it is set will evoke by association, as well as by its inherent nature, the qualities Shore sought, emphasizing the essential innocence of the Shire in contrast to the violent and sinister nature of much of the rest of Middle Earth.

---

situation just prior to the 2010 rulemaking, see Rebecca Tushnet, *I Put You There: User-Generated Content and Anticircumvention*, 12 Vanderbilt J. Ent. & Tech. L. 889 (2010).

78 Erwin Beekveld, *They're Taking the Hobbits to Isengard*, www.albinoblacksheep.com/flash/hobbits (last visited November 10, 2008).

79 See Franklin L. Sheppard, Alleluia (Baltimore: Presbyterian Board of Publications and Sabbath School Work, 1915), available at www.archive.org/stream/alleluiahymnalfo00pres#page/n7/mode/2up (last visited November 9, 2009).

Both the original tune and Sheppard's adaptation were long out of copyright by the time Shore wrote the "Shire" theme; Shore's borrowing may have been unconscious, or entirely coincidental. Beekveld could claim to be basing his electronic version of the tune on the earlier, out-of-copyright works, although in context and with the addition of the "Fellowship" theme that seems unlikely. In any event, as long as Beekveld's use remains noncommercial, New Line Cinema (the copyright holder in the Lord of the Rings movies, now owned by Warner Brothers) has seemed content to ignore it. Beekveld would like to "release an extended remix CD-Single of the above mentioned video. Permission of the copyright holder of the original works is required for that. If you think this would be a contribution to the progress of mankind, do not hesitate to drop New Line Cinema a line."[80] Beekveld's plea to the fans seems to show the widespread misperception, discussed previously, that the commercial or noncommercial nature of the use is determinative, with commercial works requiring permission while noncommercial fan works may not. But is Beekveld's use in fact a fair use? It is impossible to say without examining the four §107 factors:

> (1) the purpose and character of the use, including whether such use is of a commercial nature or is for nonprofit educational purposes;
> (2) the nature of the copyrighted work;
> (3) the amount and substantiality of the portion used in relation to the copyrighted work as a whole; and
> (4) the effect of the use upon the potential market for or value of the copyrighted work.

The first of these four factors, the purpose and character of the use, seems not to weigh on either side. The use is not commercial, except insofar as it increases traffic to Beekveld's website and enhances his professional reputation, but neither is it for a nonprofit educational purpose; like most fan works, it seems designed primarily to entertain fans of the underlying work, and to give its creator the pleasure of creating it.

The second factor, the nature of the copyrighted work, weighs against a finding of fair use; movies and music are traditionally accorded a high level of protection. Lord of the Rings is a work of fiction, and the story elements are not simply facts or ideas, but copyrightable expressions. There is no overriding public interest in having portions of the Lord of the Rings films be freely available to the public, as there might be with, for example, stills taken from a film of the assassination of President Kennedy.[81]

The third factor, the amount and substantiality of the portion used, weighs in Beekveld's favor. The three Lord of the Rings movies have a combined length of

80 Erwin Beekveld, www.beekveld.com (last visited September 29, 2009).

81 See *Time Inc.* v. *Bernard Geis Assocs.*, 293 F. Supp. 130 (S.D.N.Y. 1968).

over 11 hours.[82] Beekveld's video is one minute and 59 seconds long, and much of the video portion consists of a few seconds' worth of clips repeated several times. Nor are the clips that are used particularly crucial to the plot. Unlike, say, the crucial excerpt from President Gerald Ford's memoirs at issue in *Harper & Row*, Legolas saying "They're taking the Hobbits to Isengard!" reveals nothing the audience, or for that matter the other characters in the movie, don't already know; rather, it's one of the Captain Obvious moments for which Legolas is notorious.[83]

The fourth factor, market effect, is widely regarded as the most important and, in the opinion of many, should trump the other three. This factor also weighs in Beekveld's favor: the video of "They're Taking the Hobbits to Isengard" does not and cannot compete in the marketplace with the Lord of the Rings movie trilogy. No one will watch "They're Taking the Hobbits to Isengard" as a substitute for the movie; among other things, it lacks the plot and quite a few of the characters.

This is not as simple as it sounds, though; as we will see when discussing the Harry Potter Lexicon, factor four also covers effects on the market for possible future derivative works by the copyright holder. It is possible that New Line Cinema (or, now, Warner Brothers) might wish to make its own short comical music videos based on the film; Warner Brothers has shown its willingness to parody its own material with works such as the Looney Tunes short *Carrotblanca*.[84] It is rather less likely that New Line or Warner Brothers might wish to make such videos based upon the less than 1 percent of the movie represented in Beekveld's video. This possibility should be considered in assessing factor four. Even considering it, though, it seems likely that this factor weighs in Beekveld's favor.

So two factors weigh in favor of a finding of fair use, one against, and one is more or less evenly balanced. Shouldn't we be able to declare the use fair? Unfortunately, no. The factors are factors; despite the paramountcy often accorded to the fourth factor by the courts,[85] Congress has given no clear guidance on how the factors are to be weighted and applied. There is no way to know for sure whether this use, or a similar use of this sort, is fair until the parties go to court. This—the necessity of litigation in order to declare a use fair—is often criticized as having a chilling effect on uses that would otherwise be protected as fair use—for example, the use of the source material in "They're Taking the Hobbits to Isengard."

82 That's for the extended version DVDs; for the theatrical releases, it's a bit over nine hours.

83 For comparison, see *Harper & Row* v. *Nation Enterprises*, 471 U.S. 539 (1985).

84 Interestingly, Warner Brothers, which made *Casablanca* in 1942, no longer owned the copyright when it made *Carrotblanca* in 1995.

85 See, for example, *Harper & Row*, 471 U.S. at 566.

Drawing from multiple sources

The copyright situation of "They're Taking the Hobbits to Isengard" is simplified because the work is entirely derived from a single source (in this case, two closely related works) with a single copyright holder. The situation of most music fanvids is a bit more complicated. For example, "Aang Can't Wait to Be King"[86] sets scenes from the Nickelodeon series *Avatar: The Last Airbender* to Elton John's song "I Just Can't Wait to Be King" from Disney's *The Lion King*. Nickelodeon has little economic interest in suing or threatening to sue its fans—or, at least, that interest is outweighed by its interest in maintaining the fans' goodwill. And the use is probably transformative, so Nickelodeon is not assured of success even if it does sue. But Disney and Elton John have less to gain from the use of their song in a video based on another company's show, and the use is less likely to be protected. Disney, though, is every bit as dependent on the goodwill of fans as Nickelodeon is, and there is probably considerable overlap between the audiences of *Avatar* and *The Lion King*, so some disincentive to sue still exists. But the situation of a Kirk/Spock slash video, setting clips from the original Star Trek TV series to the song "Closer" by Nine Inch Nails,[87] is even more one-sided: the song is being used entirely for its effect when juxtaposed with the Star Trek characters, and there is no particular benefit to Trent Reznor (Nine Inch Nails) from allowing its use, other than the benefit of added exposure. Where the incongruity between the music and the images is greater, the humor is greater too—but the possibility that both content owners will take exception also increases. A fan video of the Archies playing the Sex Pistols' "God Save the Queen"[88] not only infringes on the copyright of the song, but may also be inconsistent with the "wholesome" image the Archie Comics company tries to market—although this is not an interest protected by copyright; nor, where the allegedly infringing use is noncommercial, is it protected by trademark. A fanvid may even combine copyrighted music with a multi-source transformative work along the lines of "Becoming Hermione" or "Edward Cullen Meets Buffy Summers." It might, for instance, be a femmeslash music vid featuring an imagined relationship between witches Willow Rosenberg (from the *Buffy the Vampire Slayer* television series) and Hermione Granger (from the Harry Potter movies), set to t.A.T.u.'s "All the Things She Said."[89] In the "Willow/Hermione—All The Things She Said" vid the use of the video clips is transformative, and has as strong a claim to being fair use as does the use of the

86 Aangi07, *Aang Can't Wait to Be King*, www.youtube.com/watch?v=3LC_FIvJc80.

87 Killa & T. Jonesy, *Closer (fan video)*, widely available, for example at www.youtube.com/watch?v=1PwpcUawjK0 (last visited November 10, 2008).

88 *God Save the Queen*, www.youtube.com/watch?v=sgnLL17QmTM; see also, for example, the more sentimental *Hey Ya Charlie Brown*, www.youtube.com/watch?v=KGnYw-OuCnI (both last visited November 10, 2008).

89 Sleepy Patty, Willow/Hermione—All The Things She Said, www.youtube.com/watch?v=kD2ZJH88GN4 (last visited January 26, 2010).

clips in "Becoming Hermione" or "Edward Cullen Meets Buffy Summers." The song "All the Things She Said," though, is presented substantially in its entirety and untransformed. While the argument might be made that the use of the video clips may make the use of the song transformative by causing viewers to see the song in a new light, this argument runs into the problem that the use of the entire song is not necessary to achieve the shift in perspective. The use of short clips from the song could accomplish the shift equally well; it is hard to see how the use of the song in its entirety can be fair use.

Even vids that do not use songs from a separate source, but incorporate clips including songs from a movie, are likely to face similar problems, because the music is separately copyrighted. Even where the songs are integral to the clip and thus part of the transformative use of the video, it may be hard to justify including an entire song if a short excerpt would serve. Thus a trailer for an imaginary movie, "The Jedi of Oz," is probably on fairly solid ground when it juxtaposes scenes from the Star Wars movies and *The Wizard of Oz* (the movie, naturally, not the book) to remark on the similarities between the two. These, after all, have been much commented on by fans and critics, and are presumably to some degree intentional: C3PO is the Tin Man (albeit with the Scarecrow's brain and the Cowardly Lion's courage), Chewbacca is the Cowardly Lion, Darth Vader is the Wicked Witch of the West, Ewoks are Munchkins, R2D2 is Toto, Uncle Owen and Aunt Beru are Uncle Henry and Auntie Em, and Luke, of course, is Dorothy.[90] Including the songs from the 1939 movie is a bit riskier, from a copyright perspective, but "The Jedi of Oz Trailer" limits itself to short excerpts, a few seconds long at most. This is probably just enough "to 'conjure up' at least enough of that original to make the object of its critical wit recognizable."[91] Other Star Wars/Wizard of Oz mash-ups can be found online, though, and some are less cautious, using entire songs.

Some fans see any use of a song in a vid as transformative on the theory that the images accompanying the music inform and transform the viewer's understanding of the song. For example, the website of the Organization for Transformative Works (OTW), a fanfic and fan works advocacy group, contains this opinion on a lawsuit by music content owners against video sharing site Vimeo:

> Here's a case that vidders might want to keep an eye on. Vimeo is being sued by a number of record companies—EMI, Capitol, Virgin—over audio tracks, which "are too often unlicensed copies of full songs." … While the suit seems to want to leave some space for transformative works—as the article notes, EMI is "careful to say that it is 'not seeking to stifle creativity or preclude members of the public from creating original, lawful audiovisual works,'" it also wants to stop usage of "the entire musical work deliberately and carefully synchronized into the video."

90 Mike Gilliland, *The Jedi of Oz Trailer*, www.youtube.com/watch?v=TvrrcAdm09E&feature=related (last visited January 26, 2010).

91 *Campbell* v. *Acuff-Rose Music, Inc.*, 510 U.S. 569, 588 (1994).

> Obviously we at the OTW disagree with the implication that the use of music "in careful synchronization" is automatically infringing. Music can be an interpretive tool, and vids are a form of speech: they show, they demonstrate, they make arguments. In a vid, music is not a "soundtrack"; it is an essential part of the argument and creates a new—intricate, and richly meaningful—whole.[92]

While the idea that "In a vid, music is not a 'soundtrack'; it is an essential part of the argument and creates a new—intricate, and richly meaningful—whole" is appealing to vidders and to fandom generally, this theory has yet to be tested in court and it is hard to be optimistic about its chances. It is possible that the current lawsuit brought by the music content industry against video-sharing site Vimeo will raise this question; the complaint alleges that among the user-generated content shared via Vimeo are:

> [A]udiovisual works which use copyrighted music in the foreground of the work, or synchronized with images such as animation, photographs, drawings, or other video footage. In all of these audiovisual works the music is not incidental; it generally is comprised of the entirety of a recording deliberately and carefully synchronized into the video in order to provide a focal point and appeal for the content. Many of these videos are equivalent to television programs or independent films, with recordings synchronized with the dialog or the visual material.[93]

Interestingly, this—at least the "focal point" part—comes close to acknowledging the OTW's point: the video is a new creation, of which the music is only a part; perhaps the use is transformative. There seems to be an error, though, at least as applied to fanvids. It may be true that in the "lip dub" videos complained of by Capital Records, the song is the focal point of the work and the video, if any, is just an excuse for posting the song. But with fanvids the video portion, rather than the music, is the focal point of the work. In fanvids, just as in movies, the music, while not incidental, provides support for (and, in many cases, humorous comment on) the main focus of the viewers' attention, the video.

The same paragraph also states, prior to the language quoted above, that:

> While Vimeo's materials tout its commitment to "original" content, its view of what is "original" is narrow and self-serving. While Vimeo claims to have no

---

92 Organization for Transformative Works, *News Roundup, Vimeo Sued Over Music Infringement*, submitted by fcoppa on December 31, 2009, 5:36 AM, http://transformativeworks.org/news (last visited January 26, 2010); see also generally, for example, Mike Riggs, *New YouTube Policy Heralds an end to Vidding, Mash-ups, Dancing Babies*, Reason, January 14, 2009, http://reason.com/blog/2009/01/14/new-youtube-policy-heralds-an (incl. comments) (last visited February 2, 2010).

93 Complaint, *Capital Records LLC* v. *Vimeo LLC*, 09-CV-10101, S.D.N.Y., December 10, 2009, at 9, para. 24.

> tolerance for the posting of pre-existing video content, it not only freely and readily permits, but actively encourages, its users to post audiovisual works that feature, contain, or even consist entirely of preexisting ***musical works***, including Plaintiffs' Recordings.[94]

A quick look at Vimeo.com shows that many fanvids are available there, some of them quite well done. A video of Xena, Gabrielle, and Genia from the *Xena: Warrior Princess* episode "Many Happy Returns" is set to the Madonna song "Like a Virgin," using clips from the television show arranged in a way that imitates—parodies, in fact—the music video for the original.[95] The use of the images to parody the original video is transformative, and the music industry plaintiffs do not seem overly concerned with the video in any event. Indeed, the complaint seems to seethe with rage at the idea that the defendant has somehow set video copyright interests above, or even against, music copyright interests: words alone proving insufficient, bolding and italics are brought into play—one senses a barely restrained urge to use the Caps Lock key as well.

While vidders and other fans would have much cause for rejoicing if a court were to examine the video and find its use of the song to be fair use as well, that seems less likely. Music fanvids, amusing as some of them are, are likely to remain something of a guerilla art form, and will probably eventually be chased from the well-lit public spaces of YouTube and Vimeo to some of the darker back alleys of the Internet. In particular, the music industry is notoriously diligent in enforcing its copyrights.

Why protect fan works?

Why should fan works be protected, or at least be any more protected than they already are? It is the position of the OTW that existing law already provides adequate protection: "While case law in this area is limited, we believe that current copyright law already supports our understanding of fanfiction as fair use."[96] While this may be true in the case of most noncommercially published fanfic, when extended to, for example, the use of entire copyrighted songs as the soundtrack for

---

94 Complaint, *Capital Records LLC* v. *Vimeo LLC*, 09-CV-10101, S.D.N.Y., December 10, 2009, at 9, para. 24 (emphasis in original). Paragraph 29 of a companion complaint, *EMI Blackwood Music Inc.* v. *Vimeo LLC*, 09-CV-10105, December 10, 1009, is essentially identical to para. 24 of the Capital Records complaint, save that the words "Musical Compositions" are substituted for "Recordings."

95 Given that the matter is currently being litigated, I will refrain from giving a cite; my apologies to the fan author.

96 Organization for Transformative Works, *Frequently Asked Questions, Legal: Is the OTW Trying to Change the Law?*, http://transformativeworks.org/faq-277 (last visited January 26, 2010).

vids, it seems to be wishful thinking. The OTW correctly points out that the current uncertain situation, in which neither fans nor content owners truly understand the boundaries of fair use in fan works, benefits neither: "We seek to broaden knowledge of fan creators' rights and reduce the confusion and uncertainty on both fan and pro creators' sides about fair use as it applies to fanworks."[97] The uneasy and unofficial accommodations that exist between many content owners and their fandoms are fragile; eventually a misunderstanding can lead to a lawsuit, and one lawsuit can turn a fandom against the content owner, causing financial damage. Clear rules, uniform across fandoms, would benefit everyone involved. The OTW suggests modeling such rules after the Documentary Filmmakers' Statement of Best Practices in Fair Use.[98] The presentation of the Statement as a rather lengthy and complex document may limit the incentive of the average fan to read it before spending a study break putting together a Naruto music video. Fans might benefit, however, from wider dissemination of the first two principles, reproduced in the Code of Best Practices in Fair Use for Online Video:[99] copying for purposes of "commenting on or critiquing of copyrighted material" and "using copyrighted material for illustration or example" may be fair use.

---

97 Ibid.

98 Documentary Filmmakers' Statement of Best Practices in Fair Use, http://centerforsocialmedia.org/rock/backgrounddocs/bestpractices.pdf (last visited January 26, 2010).

99 Code of Best Practices in Fair Use for Online Video, http://centerforsocialmedia.org/sites/default/files/online_best_practices_in_fair_use.pdf (last visited October 12, 2010).

Chapter 4
Three Interests of the Author in Conflict with Fanfic

There may be a limitless number of possible reasons for a content owner to object to fanfic, but the probable reasons fall into three general categories. First, the owner may object to the way in which the original material is used or depicted. U.S. copyright law recognizes only economic, not moral, rights in copyrighted works and characters, and provides no relief to the content owner in the absence of an actual infringement of copyright. (International copyright law does address moral rights, however,[1] and U.S. trademark law will protect famous trademarks from commercial uses that might dilute the mark by blurring or tarnishment.[2]) Second, the owner may object because the fanfic, by anticipating the author's future work, exposes the author to liability for copyright infringement in his or her future work. Third, the owner may object because the fanfic or other fan work borrows too extensively from his or her copyrighted work.

A look at an example of each may be instructive. First, the author's right to control the way in which his or her creations are used is at the core of the (unlitigated) dispute between Larry Niven and Elf Sternberg. Second, the author's right to use the derivative works right to protect his or her future works is at the core of the (also unlitigated) dispute between Marion Zimmer Bradley and Jean Lamb, and also forms part, though not the central part, of the third dispute. That third dispute, *J.K. Rowling* v. *Steven Vander Ark*, is the only one of the three to be litigated and has as its central focus a more traditional copyright claim: the author's right to prevent borrowing from his or her works.

Slash and related stories can be counted upon to raise the first objection. Every author has a personal squick threshold, and even before that is reached the author may object to an "unrealistic" portrayal of his or her characters or world, as happened with Larry Niven and his kzinti. For an example of the second objection and the possibly undesirable consequences of acting upon it, we'll visit the planet Darkover. After a Darkover fanfic made it impossible for her to publish her own work, author Marion Zimmer Bradley took the drastic step of curtailing

---

1 See Berne Convention, art. 6*bis*, 25 U.S.T. at 1349; see also Nolan, *supra* Chapter 1, note 14, 30 S. Ill. U. L.J. 533, 549–50, 562 (2006), on the idea of "copyright tarnishment." On moral rights of non-U.S. content creators under U.S. law, see, for example, Joshua M. Daniels, *"Lost in Translation": Anime, Moral Rights, and Market Failure*, 88 B.U. L. Rev. 709 (2008).

2 See 15 U.S.C. § 1125(c) (2006).

her own fandom. The third objection provides the only published opinion dealing specifically with fan writing, although not yet fanfic, to date. Harry Potter author J.K. Rowling took the surprising step of suing one of her most prominent fans for attempting to publish material commercially—even though the same material had long been available online, with Rowling's approval.

Larry Niven, Elf Sternberg, and Kzinslash

Larry Niven is a science fiction author best known for his Known Space series of stories, especially the novel *Ringworld*[3] and its sequels. The Known Space stories depict several alien species; one that features prominently is the kzinti (singular kzin). The kzinti are large and tiger-like in appearance and, to some extent, behavior: they are aggressive carnivores, warlike and prone to violence. Their saving grace is personal incorruptibility and adherence to a rigid code of honor. The kzinti also appeared in "The Slaver Weapon," an episode of the Star Trek animated series authored by Niven and based on an earlier Niven short story, and were subsequently referred to at several places in the sprawling agglomeration of materials that make up the Star Trek universe.[4]

Elf Sternberg describes himself as a writer of "science fiction, fantasy and erotica."[5] He has been posting slash and het fanfic online for at least two decades, since the days of Usenet. Sternberg wrote a slash story involving male kzinti and posted it in his online serial, *The Journal Entries*, from which it was later removed.

Niven had previously enjoyed a positive relationship with fandom. In the introduction to *The Ringworld Engineers*, published in 1980, he shows an attitude similar to Roddenberry's attitude toward Star Trek fandom:

> *Ringworld* is ten years old; and I have never stopped getting letters about it. People have been commenting on the assumptions, overt and hidden, and the mathematics and the ecology and the philosophical implications, precisely as if the Ringworld were a proposed engineering project and they were being paid for the work.

3 Larry Niven, Ringworld (1970).

4 *Star Trek: The Animated Series*, *The Slaver Weapon* (NBC television broadcast December 15, 1973). *The Slaver Weapon* is an adaptation of Niven's short story "The Soft Weapon," originally published in 1967 in Galaxy magazine. See Larry Niven, "The Soft Weapon," in Neutron Star 73 (New York: Ballantine Books, 1968). For a list of examples of kzinti elsewhere in the expanded Star Trek universe, see Memory Alpha, *Kzinti*, http://memory-alpha.org/en/wiki/Kzinti#Kzintis_in_the_Star_Fleet_Universe (last visited December 16, 2008).

5 Elf Sternberg, *Pendorwriting: Quality Science Fiction and Fantasy Erotica Since 1989*, http://pendorwright.com/about (last visited August 12, 2008).

* * *

> You who did all that work and wrote all those letters: be warned that this book would not exist without your unsolicited help. I hadn't the slightest intention of writing a sequel to *Ringworld*. I dedicate this book to you.[6]

The dedication is perhaps a deliberate echo of L. Frank Baum's prologue to *The Patchwork Girl of Oz*, thanking the fans of the Oz books for coming up with a way to learn more about happenings in Oz even after it had been permanently cut off from the rest of the world in the previous volume (which Baum had intended to be the last).[7] Niven has acknowledged *The Wonderful Wizard of Oz*[8] *as an influence on Ringworld*[9] and titled a novel *The Patchwork Girl*.[10]

Niven has always been aware of the close connection between the author and fandom; he has been receptive to those who point out scientific or continuity errors in his work, and cheerfully relates a tale of fans at an SF convention chanting "The Ringworld is unstable!" Nor is he a stranger to the fandom side of the partnership: he is the co-author of a *Divine Comedy* fan fiction novel that critically examines the theological assumptions underlying Dante's (long out of copyright, of course) original, and the author of a light-hearted homage to the Mars fiction of a more optimistic age, especially Edgar Rice Burroughs' Barsoom stories and C.S. Lewis' *Out of the Silent Planet*.[11]

Niven's and Sternberg's dispute never came to court, and the only sources for what happened, and what the participants thought about it, are their own published statements. Niven apparently sent Sternberg a cease-and-desist letter, and his attitude toward fandom and fanfic seems to have become a bit less idealistic; he later wrote:

> Last month a stranger in New Jersey asked permission to use the kzinti in his fanzine. (Fanzines, fan magazines, exist strictly for recreation). Gary Wells [the stranger in New Jersey] wanted nothing of Known Space, just the kzinti, embedded in a Star Trek background.
>
> I wrote: *I hereby refuse you permission to use the kzinti in any literary property. The last guy who did that involved the kzinti in a sadomasochistic homosexual*

6 Larry Niven, The Ringworld Engineers vii–viii (1980).

7 L. Frank Baum, *Prologue* to The Patchwork Girl of Oz 15–16 (1913).

8 L. Frank Baum, The Wonderful Wizard of Oz (1900).

9 Niven, Ringworld, *supra* note 3; Slashdot, *Ladies and Gentlemen, Dr. Larry Niven*, http://interviews.slashdot.org/article.pl?sid=03/03/10/167206&mode=thread&tid=134&tid=192 (March 10, 2003) [hereinafter Niven Slashdot Interview].

10 Larry Niven, The Patchwork Girl (1984).

11 Larry Niven & Jerry Pournelle, Inferno (New York: Pocket Books, 1976); Larry Niven, Rainbow Mars (New York: Tor Books, 1999).

> *gangbang, badly, and published it on a computer network. A friend alerted me, and we spoke the magic word and frightened him away.* ***(Lawsuit.)*** *I'm still a little twitchy on the subject, so don't take any of this too personally ...*
>
> Wells persisted. He sent me the Fleet bio for his kzin: a crewman aboard a federation battlewagon. He's got his format well worked out. It would have been fun to see what he might do with it; but I'm going to refuse him anyway. I don't want the playground getting too crowded. I hope the network bandit doesn't turn up again.[12]

At the time slash fiction was not a completely new phenomenon, but the wide reach it could attain via the Internet (at the time, through Usenet newsgroups) was. This may have been Niven's first encounter with slash based on his own work, and he may have been one of the first authors to have this experience.

Niven's reaction shows an awareness of the damage to his relationship with the fans; he seems distressed at the thought of having to expel the other kids from his "playground." Doing so may not have served him well; another phenomenon that was not yet fully understood was the power of the Internet to disseminate information and allow anyone and everyone to express an opinion. Niven was, and still occasionally is, mocked online by fans, sometimes viciously:

> Larry Niven actually had his lawyers send a cease-and-desist letter to the author (Elf Sternberg) for using his furry sapient felinoid aliens (think bipedal tigers), the Kzinti. Now they're called Felinzi. Niven lambasted Elf for bad writing, but the Journal Entries are a godzillion times better than the *crap* Niven is cranking out these days. Keep counting your money, Larry; at least Elf still has a soul.[13]

Other fans were less venomous, but still seemed to look askance: "One of the more infamous incidents is Larry Niven sending a 'cease and desist' letter to Elf Sternberg over the erotic fanfic 'The Only Fair Game.' There was no legal action beyond that, but Niven still gets needled about it occasionally."[14]

Niven's hope that the "bandit" would not turn up again was not to be realized, either. Apparently in response to Niven's mention of the incident in print, Sternberg posted an explicit slash story, "The Only Fair Game," claiming that the story was a parody protected under *Campbell*.[15]

---

12 Larry Niven, *Introduction* to Man-Kzin Wars IV (Larry Niven, ed., 1991). "The last guy who did that" and "the network bandit" are, presumably, Sternberg.

13 Ron's Links Page, http://ron.ludism.org/links.html (last visited August 12, 2008).

14 Posting of Darrin Bright to *Websnark: Protecting Gnomish Habitat Since 2008*, August 16, 2006, www.websnark.com/archives/2006/08/also_theres_a_g.html.

15 Elf Sternberg, *The Only Fair Game*, www.pendorwright.com/other/html/The_Only_Fair_Game.html (last visited August 12, 2008); *Campbell* v. *Acuff-Rose Music, Inc.*, 510 U.S. 569 (1994).

Twelve years after denouncing Sternberg's slash in print, Niven claimed not to remember it, though the question assumed that "The Only Fair Game" was the original story to which Niven objected, which may have confused the issue.[16] However, it is not entirely clear whether "The Only Fair Game" was in fact that original story. Sternberg describes it as "the infamous story that pissed off Larry Niven and started me down the career of infamy,"[17] but he also says he rewrote the original stories to:

> remove[e] anything about Kn*wn Sp*ce … And Larry said he'd drop the matter. He didn't. It showed up again, in [*Man-Kzin Wars IV*]. I understand the point he was addressing in MKW4, but rather than just say, "No, it's my work," he dragged the incident in. I decided to have one last laugh, and wrote one final story, which is absolutely a parody of Niven's universe—"The Only Fair Game," which is also on my home page and which is protected under US law (see: The Estate of Roy Orbison vs. Two Live Crew.)[18]

He answers the question "Is it true that Larry Niven hates you?" with:

> Yes, it's true. The story that aroused his ire no longer exists, as I deleted it and all references to it a long, long time ago, but every once in a while I see it reposted. Even though I have separated myself from the story a LONG time ago, it's hard to kill something once it's been released onto the 'net. :-)[19]

---

16 Niven Slashdot Interview (the questioner identified "The Only Fair Game" as the story giving rise to the cease-and-desist letter and Niven may have been confused). See Posting of LionMage to Slashdot, http://interviews.slashdot.org/article.pl?sid=03/03/10/16 7206&mode=thread&tid=134&tid=192 (last visited August 12, 2008): "What's interesting, though, is that Elf claims 'The Only Fair Game' is the original story where he ran afoul of Niven. I seem to recall an earlier work of Elf's that mentioned Kzinti, which was later edited so that the one Kzin character was changed to some sort of anthropomorphic tiger. (There have to be some early archives of the Usenet posts that contain the original version of the story.) I remember Niven's editorial in one of the Man Kzin Wars books, where he blasts Elf (though not by name) for writing a rather bad story involving a 'sadomasochistic homosexual gang-bang.' I'll never forget that line. Anyway, I assumed that Niven was speaking about this other, earlier story, and had no idea 'The Only Fair Game' even existed until today." (March 10, 2003, 1:54 P.M.).

17 *Mia's Index of Anthro Stories: Elf Sternberg*, www.furry.de/miavir/stories/sternberg_elf.html (last visited May 1, 2010).

18 Posting of Elf Sternberg to "What ever happened to Niven's Known Space?" http://groups.google.com/group/rec.arts.sf.written/browse_thread/thread/31365c23e529ee85/6eadf6478c3e30dd?#6eadf6478c3e30dd (December 14, 1995, 3:00 EST), the case referred to is apparently *Campbell.*

19 Elf Sternberg, *The Journal Entries FAQ*, http://everything2.com/e2node/the%2520Journal%2520Entries%2520FAQ (last visited August 12, 2008).

If there was no economic harm, why was Niven so upset?

There seems to be an implied value judgment in Niven's use of the words "sadomasochistic homosexual gangbang," making it easy to dismiss his apparent dismay as simple homophobia, and some have done so.[20] The actual objection is more complex, though. Niven complained that "[t]he bandit's kzin was ridiculous." Later he elaborated, "I don't buy its premise. An older species won't have human versatility in sex: sexual responses will be all hard wired."[21]

He seemed unconcerned about possible economic harm from the work; although claiming that the story "does [violate copyright], of course," he also observed wryly that "I notice the 'desist' had no effect."[22] What seemed to upset him the most was that the kzin in Sternberg's stories did not conform to the detailed biological and behavioral rules that he must have used considerable imagination and originality to create. The kzinti, as Niven has imagined and created them, are not human, and to make them act like humans is to disregard their basic nature. In copyright terms, this is closer to the assertion of a moral right than to any right recognized in U.S. law. It might conceivably make sense in trademark terms (the coined word "kzin," used in Niven's licensed-fanfic series, the Man-Kzin Wars, identifies those stories as works made or authorized by Niven, although it also identifies the species), save that Sternberg's work is not a commercial use.[23]

The Niven/Sternberg dispute highlights the gap between the expectations of content creators and the rights actually provided by U.S. law. Sternberg is as confused as Niven, if not more so, saying, "Niven, attempting to live off the sweat of his own brow, does have the right to control how his work is used." Niven, like all authors, has a right (albeit not an unlimited right) to control the products of his creativity—original works of authorship fixed in a tangible medium of

20 See, for example, Posting of Leslie R. (Member # 1599) to The Nice, Supermegatopia forum, http://nice.purrsia.com/cgi-bin/ultimatebb.cgi?ubb=print_topic;f=10;t=004414 (January 18, 2007, 3:29 A.M.). (Sternberg says "The Only Fair Game" "digs into Larry's well-rumored aversion to any sexuality that's even a little bit 'weird.' … Okay, so Larry doesn't like gays or leatherfolk … A lack of creativity in one department does not make Larry talentless. He's still one of my top five favorite fiction writers[.]")

21 Niven Slashdot Interview.

22 Ibid.

23 Because fanfic uses are generally not uses in commerce, issues of trademark infringement and dilution are unlikely to arise. There may be exceptions, of course. It is more difficult to say whether Sternberg's use is a use in commerce. "The Only Fair Game" is offered on Sternberg's website for free, not for sale. The website has neither banner ads nor pop-ups, although it is possible that some of the links on the site could be sponsored. The site does solicit and accept donations through two online payment services, PayPal and Amazon's Honor System. However, it appears to be a hobby site. See generally Joseph E. Edwards, *What constitutes "in commerce" within meaning of § 32(1)(a) of Lanham Trade-Mark Act (15 U.S.C.A. § 1114(1)) giving right of action for infringement of trademark "in commerce,"* 15 A.L.R. Fed. 368 (1973 & Supp. 2008).

expression—not the products of the sweat of his brow.[24] No matter how much sweat he expends, without originality there can be no copyright.

Copyrighting an alien species

Does Niven have a copyright in the kzinti, and did Sternberg infringe upon it? Copyright protects the expression of an idea; stories and, in some instances, characters in a work of fiction can be protected by copyright.[25] "The Only Fair Game" does not borrow its story or its characters from Niven's work, though; the plot and the characters are Sternberg's creations. The kzinti are not, but they are not a "character," either, and feline aliens are commonplace in SF universes; despite their coined name, the kzinti are unlikely to be protected by copyright.

English-language fandom is international enough, and cases of this sort are rare enough, that it may be instructive to look at the approaches taken in other Anglophone countries. The copyright treatment of species of imaginary creatures in Canada and the United Kingdom seems to lead to the same conclusion—that a fictional alien species (the only kind of alien species there is) is not, in itself, protected by copyright. In both countries, fictional species and alien races have been treated as non-copyrightable story elements. On the theory that there can be no copyright in a name or a single word, UK courts have refused to recognize copyrights in the names "Teenage Mutant Ninja Turtles," or "Ninja Turtles," and "Wombles."[26] The Teenage Mutant Ninja Turtles—Leonardo, Michelangelo, Donatello, and Raphael—are well-known to North American readers of a certain age. The Wombles may be more obscure. Those who were children in the UK in the 1970s will remember them as the environmentally conscious bandicoot-like protagonists of a series of children's novels by Elizabeth Beresford and the BBC animated television show *The Wombles*. As environmentally conscious and endearing as they may have been, however, the Wombles, or at least the name of their species, was not protected by copyright:

> It may be a defect in the law that, having invented the characters known as the "Wombles," the authoress has not a complete monopoly of the use of that

24 *Feist Publ'ns* v. *Rural Telephone Serv. Co.*, 499 U.S. 340 (1991); 17 U.S.C. § 102 (2006).

25 See *Nichols* v. *Universal Pictures Corp.*, 45 F.2d 119, 121 (2d Cir. 1930), *cert. denied*, 282 U.S. 902 (1931); see also generally Leslie A. Kurtz, *The Independent Legal Lives of Fictional Characters*, 1986 Wis. L. Rev. 429 (1986); but see *Warner Bros. Pictures* v. *Columbia Broad. Sys.*, 216 F.2d 945 (9th Cir. 1954), *cert. denied*, 348 U.S. 971 (1955) (no copyright in fictional detective Sam Spade).

26 *Mirage Studios* v. *Counter-Feat Clothing Co., Ltd.* [1991] F.S.R. 145 (Ch.) (Graham, J.) (Teenage Mutant Ninja Turtles, or Ninja Turtles); *Wombles, Ltd.* v. *Womble Skips, Ltd.* [1975] F.S.R. 488 (Ch.)(Wombles).

> invented word, which she could then assign to the plaintiffs, but such is the law and that being so it seems to me I must in fact dismiss this motion.[27]

Any remedy would have to lie in tort, for a claim of "passing off," and given the particular facts it seemed unlikely anyone would be misled:

> The Wombles have made their reputation by the fact that they are keen on cleaning up Wimbledon Common—although the only result of their mythical presence on Wimbledon Common has been to attract a very large number of people looking for them who are not so careful with their refuse as the Wombles themselves, so that our last state (speaking as a resident of Wimbledon) is somewhat worse than our first. But that is neither here nor there.
>
> [Defendant] provides these modern devices known as skips which litter the streets for the purpose of having rubbish and debris from demolished and repaired buildings put into them. Thinking of a name that might be used for the company one of the founders of the company chose—and chose quite deliberately because "Wombles" had the connection with cleaning up I have already mentioned—the word "Wombles," and so the name "Wombles Skips Limited" was chosen.
>
> The present action is an action claiming in substance that the defendant company, by using the word "Wombles" in connection with its name and also in connection with its skips (because "Wombles" is painted in very large characters indeed on its skips and underneath that, in smaller letters, just "Skips Limited") is in fact committing the tort of passing off.
>
> It seems to me that where what is alleged is that one person is passing off his goods or his business—and here it would be the business—as the business of somebody else, there must be a common field of activity.
>
> * * *
>
> I regret to say that in my opinion there is no such common field of activity. What the plaintiff is doing is to license people to use some of the copyright material comprised in and surrounding the Wombles. That in most cases, if indeed not in all of them, involves the use of a picture of one of the Wombles, whether it be a picture of Great Uncle Bulgaria, Tobermory, or one of the other well-known Wombles. But there is no such similar picture on any of the skips. Indeed Mr. Robin Jacob, appearing for the defendant, protested that he was the only real Womble because he was the only person really carrying on the business of clearing up rubbish, and it may be that hereafter the defendant company's skips will be illustrated accordingly. I have nothing to do with that at all.

27 *Wombles, Ltd.* [1975] F.S.R. at 491.

> It seems to me that the only conceivable ground for suggesting any business connection between the plaintiff and the defendant is that the characters, albeit mythical, are characters who clean up premises, but I do not think that anybody seeing a "Womble" skip, albeit in the road, albeit on one of the defendant's lorries, would think that there really was any connection between that and any business carried on by the plaintiff.[28]

Justice Walton, the author of the opinion, is obviously having fun with his Wombles. But his point is clear: while an individual Womble (Great Uncle Bulgaria, say) might be protected by copyright (an issue not before the court, but one we have already explored in some detail), the name "Womble" is not. In the words of commentator Francis M. Nevins, Jr., "It is universally recognized that protection for a character's name is not available in copyright law and must be sought elsewhere, primarily in the law of trademark and unfair competition."[29]

By the same reasoning the four Teenage Mutant Ninja Turtles may each be protected as characters, but the name and perhaps the concept of Teenage Mutant Ninja Turtles (or, as they were originally marketed in the UK, Teenage Mutant Hero Turtles[30]) are not. A small clothing manufacturer might even create a line of clothing aimed at cashing in on the popularity Ninja (or Hero) Turtles without violating copyright, where the turtles

> were humanoid to the extent that they were moving on what would in an ordinary turtle be the hind legs, they were muscular in human terms: there were four of them, but they didn't enjoy the artistic names of the plaintiff's turtles: they were renamed Trevor, Jake, Tony and I think, Totty. They wore coloured headgear in the form of caps, and on occasion bandanas, but not as masks. They had coloured pads on their knees and arms. In one of the designs, on a shop front one can detect the words, "ZZA," the inference being fairly clear that those letters indicate the end of the word "pizza," which [it] will be remembered is the one weakness of the Ninja Turtle. They are aggressive, though not carrying weapons, their aggression being directed more to the sporting field than the battlefield. On the three T-shirts that I have in front of me, though not in the designs … the

28 Ibid., at 489–91.

29 Francis M. Nevins, Jr., *Copyright + Character = Catastrophe*, 39 J. Copyright Soc'y U.S.A. 303, 304 (1992).

30 The name change apparently resulted from the Beeb's unflagging dedication to misunderstanding other cultures: "In January of this year BBC Television started putting out the videos under licence from the plaintiffs, though with this difference. The word 'Ninja' is an abbreviation of 'Ninjitsu,' meaning hired assassin. The BBC objected to the violent message involved in that. As a result on the BBC show they were known as Teenage Mutant Hero Turtles." *Mirage Studios* v. *Counter-Feat Clothing Co., Ltd.* [1991] F.S.R. 145, 148 (Ch.). The court is incorrect about the usage, at least; ninjitsu or ninjutsu (忍術) is a martial art, not a person, and a ninja is a practitioner, not an abbreviation, thereof.

> words "Ninja Turtle" appear on each. On the designs, on the whole the phrase used was "Hero Turtles," if they were described otherwise at all. However, the designs produced by Mr. Collins and largely reproduced on the T-shirts that I have seen were not exact copies of the plaintiff's caricature drawings. To the extent that one can tell the difference between one humanoid turtle and another they are not identical. The impact that one has is that what Mr. Collins has done is to copy the concept of the Ninja Turtle rather than the actual lines of the drawings themselves. Indeed, there is no question of that having occurred. The result is that one has a drawing of humanoid turtles, usually bearing the words "Ninja Turtles" on it, conveying the idea and concept behind the plaintiffs' Turtles but not in terms of line reproducing it as a copy.[31]

In other words, Collins' Turtles are apparently members of the same species as their more famous cousins Leonardo, Michelangelo, Donatello, and Raphael, but are separate individuals distinguishable even to a human, just as Sternberg's kzinti are separate individuals who share a species with Niven's kzinti. In the case of the Turtles, who are graphic characters, this apparently skirts the edges of copyright infringement:

> The difficulties surrounding any claim by the plaintiff based in copyright are primarily two. First, there is the rule in copyright that you can have no copyright in a name, and on that basis it is said that Teenage Mutant Ninja Turtles, or Ninja Turtles, are names and not subject to any copyright. The point seems to me not altogether easy to say whether a descriptive invented name is to be categorised as a name or as a description. The second and more fundamental difficulty in copyright is the saying that "there is no copyright in ideas." For myself, I find it difficult to determine what that phrase means in the present context. As I have said, although there are similarities in the graphic reproduction of the defendants' product to those in the plaintiffs' product, they are mainly reproductions of a concept, of the humanoid turtle of an aggressive nature. But whether that permits a claim in copyright or not seems to me to be a very open question; there is certainly an arguable case in copyright. I would not like to say what the final outcome of any case based in copyright would be.[32]

Even though Collins' Turtles might not infringe copyright, they might be actionable under other theories—in this case, the tort of "passing off" under UK law.[33] But the Ninja Turtles and the Wombles, unlike the kzinti, are graphic characters; the kzinti are a purely literary creation. (The Star Trek kzinti are another matter; the episode in which they appeared was authored, though not animated, by Niven, so he created the Star Trek kzinti as well—but those kzinti

31 *Mirage Studios* v. *Counter-Feat Clothing Co., Ltd.* [1991] F.S.R. 145, 150–51 (Ch.).

32 Ibid., at 154.

33 Ibid., at 156–60 (Ch.).

are not, strictly speaking, the kzinti at issue in the dispute between Niven and Sternberg. In addition, Sternberg's depiction of the kzinti, though perhaps "graphic," is not graphic.)

The Wombles and the Teenage Mutant Ninja Turtles, non-human though they may be, at least share our planet. But in Canada an extraterrestrial alien species has been found to skate on equally thin copyright ice. The Canadian court treated the Ewoks of *Return of the Jedi* (and elsewhere in the Star Wars universe) as a "character," using the "sufficiently delineated" *Nichols* test. Under the heading "The Ewok character in the script: a matter for copyright?" the court stated:

> 70. In essence the core of the plaintiff's argument is that the Ewok and its characteristics as developed in the script was copied without authorization by the defendants.
> 71. The name Ewok appears more than forty times in [Plaintiff Preston's] script Space Pets; as earlier noted it is not heard in the film and it appears only at the end with the printed list of credits to players and others.
> 72. While generally there cannot be copyright in a mere name where the name identifies a well known character copyright in the name and associated character may be recognized.[34]

So the name "Ewok" alone cannot be copyrighted, but if used as the name of a sufficiently delineated "character" or, in this case, extraterrestrial species, the entire species may be copyrighted, although the bar seems to be set fairly high:

> For such recognition it is said the character must be sufficiently clearly delineated in the work subject to copyright that it become widely known and recognized. In the words of Learned Hand J. "… the less developed the characters, the less they can be copyrighted; that is the penalty an author must bear for marking them too indistinctly".
> 73. If we review the character of the Ewok as developed in the script Space Pets we know that Ewoks are described in the following terms:
> - they are shorter than Olaks who stand a mere three feet tall;
> - like Olaks they are ape like and bipedestrian, apparently with hands;
> - their hair is darker and longer than the short haired Olaks who have light brown hair;
> - they have a face like a panda, with large white patches beneath their eyes and dark faces;
> - they are more warlike than Olaks and dress in heavier armour, of tree bark with skirt styled lower halves in pieces linked by tough vines, and they wear helmets of wood or hollowed skulls of larger animals;

34 *Preston* v. *20th Century Fox Canada, Ltd.*, 33 C.P.R. (3d) 242 (Fed. T.D. 1990), *aff'd*, 53 C.P.R. (3d) 407 (Fed. Ct. 1993).

- the Ewok chieftain has thinning hair hanging in long strings, is carried in a sedan chair, and wears a wardrobe like other Ewoks except that he also wears a metal crown;
- they have been at war for years against the Olaks, they use spears, a spinner type weapon thrown by hand and made from round pieces of wood with spikes sticking out around the edge, a large crossbow affair that takes several Ewoks to load and fire, and slings, with which they are very accurate;
- like Olaks, they live high off the ground in thatched houses slung between monstrous trees and access to these is by vines knotted for climbing, the houses are joined by platforms of tree limbs, bark and vines, and like Olaks they are very agile in their habitat;
- they speak the same basic language as the Olaks in a high, squeaky kind of dialogue that, when passed through the language interpreter (Langread) comes out sounding similar to the voices used by David Seville of Chipmonk [*sic*] fame which permits them to be understood by the human characters in the script and by the audience;
- they use a net trap made of vines which drops to trap intended quarry; in the one scene where their weapons are used they yell and "woop", rushing forward waving spears and whirling slings over their heads; in their habitat they swing by vines from one branch to another, while female Ewoks use the bridges; they beat drums and they use fire; and
- they appear to have many human characteristics, as do the Olaks.

These Ewoks are identifiably the Ewoks of *Return of the Jedi*. They are also, although neither the judge nor the parties mentions it, the Fuzzies of the late H. Beam Piper's novels *Little Fuzzy*, *The Other Human Race*, and the posthumously published *Fuzzies and Other People*.[35] (The third of these was published after the release of *Return of the Jedi* and thus could not have influenced either the film or Preston's script, but the character and characteristics of Piper's aliens were well established in the first two books.) The cover of the 1977 edition of *Fuzzy Sapiens* (the reissue title of *The Other Human Race*) shows a scene that could have come straight from Endor: tiny Ewok-like aliens carrying primitive weapons hide behind the stump of a giant tree, watching two humans in futuristic garb carrying weapons and instruments indicating advanced technology.

Piper aside, Preston's Ewoks were not sufficiently delineated to entitle him to a copyright on the species or exclusive use of the name:

> 74. In my view the characteristics set out in the script do not delineate the character of the Ewok sufficiently distinctly to warrant recognition as a character subject to copyright. Indeed, it is difficult to distinguish them from the Olaks in the script, in their general dress, their use of primitive weapons, their habitats

35 H. Beam Piper, Little Fuzzy (New York: Avon, 1962); The Other Human Race (1964) (republished as Fuzzy Sapiens; Fuzzies and Other People (1984)).

> and their respective roles which are essentially the same. Indeed, as suggested earlier, the plaintiff Preston and experts testifying in support of his case appeared to have difficulty in distinguishing between them in testimony which in part compared both primitive species from the script with Ewoks of the film.

Without mentioning Piper, George Lucas gave this derivation of the name Ewok:

> Well it started out I think working with the name Wookiee. It is a moving around the letters of Wookiee. I took the end of Wookiee, the "IE" off Wookiee and put it at the head, like Pig Latin, and then started, when I said it phonetically, it sounded like Ewok which is very similar to Miwok which is the indians that sort of inhabitated the area where I live and where my studio is. Matter of fact, there was a Miwok village just outside my office. So I thought that was a nice, nice sort of reverberation of the idea and eventually took the "I" and one of the "Os" out and it was Ewok.[36]

The obscurity of Preston's script was another problem; it was Lucas, not Preston, who made Ewoks famous. (This problem is unlikely to affect fanfic, as it is inherent in the nature of fanfic that the underlying works will be more famous than the fan works.)

> 75. Finally, in this case it cannot be said that the Ewok character as developed in the script is widely known by reason of the script in which Preston claims copyright. From his own evidence, Preston indicates that only he and Hurry would be aware of the contents of the script Space Pets, and aside from the allegations concerning the defendants, only one other person, a friend with whom he spent time in Alberta, was shown the script. He did talk about Ewoks with others, including the little people he encountered in Los Angeles in May 1982, the artist who prepared his logo design, and a friend through whom he made arrangements with two unnamed persons for auction sales of Ewok items of clothing. All of these activities together did not make well known the Ewok character as developed in the script. The process which made an Ewok well known, indeed famous, was the work under supervision of George Lucas and Lucasfilm Ltd. in production of the successful film, Return of the Jedi, and related distribution and promotional activities of the defendants.
> 76. In these circumstances, I conclude that the character of the Ewok as developed in the script Space Pets is not in itself subject to copyright.

If Ewoks described in text are not infringed upon by Ewoks in a motion picture, and graphic representations of Wombles are not infringed upon by the name of their species affixed to a rubbish skip, and graphic representations of four named Teenage Mutant Ninja Turtles are not infringed upon by graphic representations

---

36 *Preston*, 33 C.P.R. (3d) 242, para. 49 (Fed. T.D. 1990).

of four other named Teenage Mutant Ninja Turtles, it seems unlikely that Niven's kzinti described in text, or even graphically represented in a Star Trek animated episode, are infringed upon by Sternberg's kzinti described in text. Niven's individual kzinti are another matter; Niven has created several individual characters who are members of the kzin species, some of whom may be sufficiently delineated to be protected by copyright in their own right. Sternberg's work does not use any of these characters, so the question does not arise. But for fans wishing to write a fanfic featuring, say, the kzin from Niven's *Ringworld* series known first as Speaker to Animals and later as Chmee, the use must be transformative in order to be protected as fair use.

Is "The Only Fair Game" a derivative work?

Even if the kzinti themselves are not protected by copyright, does their inclusion in a story render that story derivative of Niven's Known Space series? If so, Sternberg's work may also violate copyright as an impermissible derivative work. As noted, fanfic is "derivative" in a literary sense, if not necessarily in a legal sense; it depends upon an appreciation of the original, shared between the author and the reader, for enjoyment and often for comprehensibility. And under section 106(2) of the Copyright Act Niven, as the owner of the copyrights in the Known Space stories, has the right to control works derived from those stories.

The bar for finding a work to be derivative is set relatively high. A translation of *Ringworld* into French[37] is a derivative work, as would be an adaptation of the story into some other form, such as a musical comedy.[38] But a work is not derivative unless the amount of copying from the original is substantial.[39] SF relies heavily on certain tropes, including, *inter alia*, space travel and feline aliens. The Wikipedia entry for "List of Fictional Cat-Like Aliens" lists 29 examples, many, including the kzinti, with their own Wikipedia entries.[40] The list is ever-changing—the kzinti were once the only species to be listed twice, in both their Known Space and Start Trek incarnations. Even a casual glance reveals that some fictional species—for example, the Catmen of Marion Zimmer Bradley's *Darkover* series—are omitted. So including feline aliens in his work, while not particularly original, does not

37 LARRY NIVEN, L'ANNEAU-MONDE (Fabrice Lamidey, trans., 2005).

38 See generally, for example, *Twin Peaks Prods., Inc.* v. *Publ'ns Int'l, Ltd.*, 996 F.2d 1366 (2d Cir. 1993).

39 *Litchfield* v. *Spielberg*, 736 F.2d 1352 (9th Cir. 1984), *cert. denied*, 470 U.S. 1052 (1985) (the mere fact that the movie E.T.: THE EXTRA-TERRESTRIAL and plaintiff's play LOKEY FROM MALDEMAR are both about aliens stranded on Earth and seeking to return home does not make the former derivative of the latter, even though the aliens in both stories have similar telekinetic powers and the stories end similarly).

40 Wikipedia, *List of Fictional Cat-Like Aliens*, http://en.wikipedia.org/wiki/List_of_fictional_cat-like_aliens (last visited May 1, 2010). And the felinity of some of the others, notably the Na'vi of James Cameron's *Avatar*, is debatable.

by itself make Sternberg's work derivative of Niven's. The fact that the aliens are called "kzinti," a word invented by Niven, and that they are intended to be understood by the reader as Niven's kzinti, is still probably not enough to render the work derivative. The kzinti are not a character, but a hypothetical alien species that has appeared in two widely-recognized but separate SF universes: Known Space and Star Trek. They are not so much an expression of an idea as an idea; the individual words "kzin" and "kzinti" are not, after all, themselves copyrightable, and standing alone they seem too slim a reed to support a claim that all works incorporating them are derivative.

Is "The Only Fair Game" protected as fair use?

Sternberg's use of the kzinti in "The Only Fair Game" is, as we have seen, almost certainly not copyright infringement. Indeed, the kzinti as a species (as distinct from individual kzinti characters) do not appear to be protected by copyright in the first place, while even the use of individual characters may be protected as fair use. And even if the kzin species is protected by copyright, Sternberg's use might be protected by the fair use exception to the exclusive rights of the copyright holder. It may be useful to restate the four fair use factors of section 107 here:

> **(1)** the purpose and character of the use, including whether such use is of a commercial nature or is for nonprofit educational purposes;
> **(2)** the nature of the copyrighted work;
> **(3)** the amount and substantiality of the portion used in relation to the copyrighted work as a whole; and
> **(4)** the effect of the use upon the potential market for or value of the copyrighted work.[41]

The first of these factors, the purpose and character of Sternberg's use, does not seem to weigh against Sternberg. While his work was not for the "nonprofit educational purposes" particularly favored by the statute, neither was it "of a commercial nature" and thus it was not particularly disfavored.[42] The original kzin slash story seems to have been written for the entertainment of Sternberg and other fans; "The Only Fair Game" for those same purposes and for criticism or comment as well. This does not mean, of course, that it succeeded. In the words of one fan:

> Not that I think Elf's stories are worth the electrons wasted in transmitting them. Those of us old enough to remember Elf's massive cross-posts of his fiction to a number of Usenet newsgroups (many of which were, in fact, inappropriate

41 17 U.S.C. § 107 (2006).

42 Indeed, "adding overt sexuality to a work could challenge our ideas about the original" and thus be both commentary and transformation. See Tushnet, *My Fair Ladies*, *supra* Chapter 1, note 14, at 275.

> venues for this sort of work) will remember the complaints about wasted bandwidth and so forth. At least now that this junk is all archived on the web, only people who want to see it can go seek it out, and the rest of us are spared.[43]

But the quality of the work is not a factor in determining fair use. To include quality as a criterion would inevitably require the courts to make judgments for which they are ill-qualified, and in many cases may be purely subjective: "It would be a dangerous undertaking for persons trained only to the law to constitute themselves final judges of the worth of [a work], outside of the narrowest and most obvious limits."[44]

The two extremes listed in Section 107(1) do not by themselves dispose of the "purpose and character" question:

> "Purpose" in fair use analysis is not an all-or-nothing matter. The issue is not simply whether a challenged work serves one of the non-exclusive purposes identified in section 107, such as comment or criticism, but whether it does so to an insignificant or a substantial extent. The weight ascribed to the "purpose" factor involves a more refined assessment than the initial, fairly easy decision that a work serves a purpose illustrated by the categories listed in section 107.[45]

"The Only Fair Game" takes a story element from Niven's work and presents it in a new way, apparently intended to be disconcerting. It seems to be a deliberate challenge to Niven's work; on balance, the first factor probably weighs somewhat in Sternberg's favor.

The Known Space stories (and for that matter the Star Trek stories, in various media) are creative and fictional works, so the second factor, the nature of the copyrighted work, favors Niven: "the second factor, if it favors anything, must favor a creative and fictional work, no matter how successful."[46]

---

43 Posting of LionMage (318500) to Niven Slashdot Interview, post by LionMage (318500)72 (March 10, 2003, 1:54 P.M.) (#5477971).

44 *Campbell* v. *Acuff-Rose Music, Inc.*, 510 U.S. at 582 (1994) (quoting *Bleistein* v. *Donaldson Lithographing Co.*, 188 U.S. 239, 251 (1903)). *Campbell* substitutes the more general "a work" for Bleistein's "pictorial illustrations." At issue in *Bleistein* was the ability to copyright circus posters, appreciated today, as they were not in their heyday, as an art form. See, for example, *Circus Posters in the Princeton University Library*, http://libweb5.princeton.edu/visual_materials/Circus/TC093.html (last visited August 15, 2008).

45 *Twin Peaks Prods., Inc.* v. *Publ'ns Int'l, Ltd.*, 996 F.2d 1366, 1374 (2d Cir. 1993).

46 Ibid., at 1376. See also *Brewer* v. *Hustler Magazine, Inc.*, 749 F.2d 527, 529 (9th Cir. 1984) ("The scope of the fair use defense is broader when informational works of general interest to the public are involved than when the works are creative products"); *Harper & Row Publishers, Inc.* v. *Nation Enter.*, 471 U.S. 539, 563 (1985) ("The law generally recognizes a greater need to disseminate factual works than works of fiction or fantasy"); *Stewart* v. *Abend*, 495 U.S. 207, 237–38 (1990); Nimmer, *supra* Chapter 2, note 42at § 13.05[A][2][a], p.9 (LexisNexis, 2008) ("copyright protection is narrower, and the

The third factor, "the amount and substantiality of the portion used in relation to the copyrighted work as a whole," favors Sternberg.[47] Almost nothing of Niven's work is used in "The Only Fair Game," other than the kzinti themselves.[48] To the extent that it is, as Sternberg claims, a parody, it must, to achieve its purpose, include enough elements of known space—in this case, the appearance and mannerism of the kzinti—to conjure up Niven's original in the mind of the reader.[49]

The fourth factor, "the effect of the use upon the potential market for or value of the copyrighted work," outweighs each and perhaps all of the other three in importance.[50] This also seems to weigh in Sternberg's favor. Parody and criticism generally do not compete with the author's own current or future work in the marketplace:

> Copyright holders rarely write parodies of their own works … or write reviews of them … and are even less likely to write new analyses of their underlying data from the opposite political perspective[.][51]

Parodies and, to a greater extent, critical reviews may impact sales by discouraging potential purchasers of the work, but this is not competition; it is the legitimate function of criticism.

While the list of factors is non-exclusive and the statute gives no specific formula for their application, three of the four factors, including the paramount fourth factor, favor Sternberg. Even if "The Only Fair Game" is otherwise an infringement on Niven's copyright, it is likely to be protected as fair use.

Sternberg seems to believe his work is protected as a parody:

---

corresponding application of the fair use defense greater, in the case of factual works than in the case of works of fiction or fantasy"); see also generally *Sony Corp.* v. *Universal City Studios, Inc.*, 464 U.S. 417, 455 n.40 (1984).

47 *Twin Peaks Prods., Inc.*, 996 F.2d at 1374 n.3 (citing 17 U.S.C. § 107 (1988)).

48 See generally *Twin Peaks Prods., Inc.*, 996 F.2d at 1376–77.

49 See *Campbell*, 510 U.S. at 588; *Columbia Pictures Corp.* v. *Nat'l Broad. Co.*, 137 F. Supp. 348, 354 (S.D. Cal. 1955); *Berlin* v. *E. C. Publ'ns, Inc.*, 329 F.2d 541, 545 (2d Cir. 1964).

50 17 U.S.C. §107 (2006); see, for example, *Twin Peaks Prods., Inc.*, 996 F.2d at 1376–77 ("The fourth factor, market effect, is 'undoubtedly the single most important element of fair use'") (quoting *Harper & Row Publishers*, 471 U.S. at 566).

51 *Twin Peaks Prods, Inc.*, 996 F.2d at 1377, citing *Warner Bros.* v. *Am. Broad. Cos., Inc.*, 720 F.2d 231, 242–43 (2d Cir. 1983); see also *Harper & Row Publishers, Inc.*, 471 U.S. at 584; and *Maxtone-Graham* v. *Burtchaell*, 803 F.2d 1253 (2d Cir. 1986). This is not to say that content owners never parody or spoof their own work; recent examples include the break-dancing Yoda Easter egg on the STAR WARS EPISODE III: REVENGE OF THE SITH DVD, and the three "Super-Deformed Shorts" (esp. *School Time Shipping*) on the *Avatar: The Last Airbender, Book Two: Earth* boxed set DVD.

LEGAL DISCLAIMER

> Concurrent with the United States Supreme Court decision regarding *Campbell v. Acuff-Rose Music, Inc (1994)* and the copyright laws of the United States, this is a work of *parody*. This work is posted freely without any request for renumeration [*sic*]; its only purpose is social commentary presented in an entertaining fashion.[52]

Whether it is actually is a parody, and if so whether it is protected under *Campbell*, is not so clear.[53] By the *Campbell* court's somewhat lenient definition, "The Only Fair Game" is probably a parody, mocking the machismo of the kzinti. (Niven might respond that machismo is a human characteristic, and anyone who perceives it in the kzinti is anthropomorphizing.[54]) "The Only Fair Game" may even meet the requirements of Chestertonian parody, "inseparable from admiration"; Sternberg has described Niven as "one of my top five favorite fiction writers." Niven seems content to let the matter lie. Other fanfic parody writers must await the eventual litigation of a similar case.

Marion Zimmer Bradley changes her mind

The late Marion Zimmer Bradley (universally known in fandom as MZB) is perhaps best known as the author of *The Mists of Avalon*,[55] a feminist retelling of Arthurian legends, and its sequels. Among genre SF fans, though, she is known as the author of the Darkover series of novels. Like *Star Trek* or Niven's Known Space series, the Darkover series involves multiple alien races in a distant future when travel between the stars is commonplace. Unlike the Known Space stories, almost all of the action takes place on a single planet, Darkover.

Even more so than Niven and Rowling, MZB was initially friendly to fanfic. In 1975 Darkover fans formed a fan group, The Friends of Darkover, which published Darkover fanfic in a letterzine and, from 1977, in a more formal fanzine, *Starstone*.[56] (Other Darkover fanzines included *Contes di Cottman IV* and *Moon Phases*.) MZB read the fanzine regularly and even published a few items in it.[57] In 1980 the first volume of Darkover fan fiction was commercially published, with MZB's approval. MZB wrote in the introduction "I have always encouraged young writers to write in my world; I think it's fun. Besides, how else can I get to

52 Sternberg, *supra* note 15.

53 *Campbell*, 510 U.S. 569.

54 If, in fact, the machismo was added by Sternberg, that too is transformation.

55 Marion Zimmer Bradley, The Mists of Avalon (1982).

56 Fabrice Rossi, *The History of Darkover Anthologies: The Friends of Darkover* (April 21, 1999), http://darkover.apiacoa.org/guide/short-stories/history.en.html.

57 Ibid.; Bradley, The Keeper's Price 7–8 (New York: Daw Books, 1980).

read Darkover stories without going to the trouble of writing them?"[58] The main goal and benefit, though, was not her own entertainment:

> I am awed and humbled at the notion that the very concept of Darkover could encourage so many young women, previously inarticulate, to try their voices at creating new characters and new situations in Darkover. In the jargon of feminism, one could say that Darkover gave them a "safe space in which to try creativity." Surrounded by a world ready-made for them, they could concentrate on character and incident, and not need to wake up a whole world of their own.[59]

She poured disapproval on authors who sought to suppress fanfic set in the worlds they had created:

> All the selfish exclusiveness of the Conan Doyle estate (which went so far as to demand that the late *Ellery Queen* anthology, *The Misadventures of Sherlock Holmes*, a very fine volume of Holmes pastiches, be withdrawn from sale and never reprinted, thus denying Holmes lovers a wonderful reading experience) has not stopped lovers of Sherlock from writing their own stories and secretly sharing them. Why should I deny myself the pleasure of seeing these young writers learning to do their thing by, for a little while, doing *my* thing with me?[60]

MZB addressed the excuses given by these authors: she did not "feel threatened by stories not consistent with [her] personal vision of Darkover."[61] Fanfic was as rewarding for the author as for the fans:

> When I was a little kid, I was a great lover of "pretend" games, but after I was nine or ten, I could never get anyone to play them with me … And now I have a lot of fans, and friends, who will come into my magic garden and play the old "pretend games" with me.[62]

It is interesting that MZB, like Niven, referred to her created world as a place to play. She concluded with an invitation to fans to write further fanfic:

> *Far, far away somewhere in the middle of the Galaxy, and about four thousand years from now, there is a world with a great red sun and four moons. Won't you come and play with me there?*[63]

---

58 Bradley, The Keeper's Price 7 (New York: Daw Books, 1980).
59 Ibid., at 12.
60 Ibid., at 14.
61 Ibid., at 14.
62 Ibid.
63 Ibid., at 15 (italics in original).

Most of all, MZB did not see any need to worry about the possibility that fanfic might preclude her from writing certain stories herself:

> Some critics have been disturbed by the possibility that I might exploit my dying fans, or steal their ideas, or use their work in my future novels …
>
> Of course, I get ideas from my young fans, just as I *give* them ideas. But as for stealing their ideas—I have *quite* enough ideas of my own …
>
> This is why I don't mind other writers writing about Darkover, and at the same time, I have no wish and no need to exploit their ideas. If I ever do make use of a fan's writing, it will be so altered and transmuted by its trip through my own personal dream-space that even the inventor would never recognize her idea, so alien would it be when I got through with it![64]

The Keeper's Price was followed by several similar volumes throughout the 1980s and early 1990s. The end of this idyll was not far off, however. Exactly what happened is even less clear than in the Niven/Sternberg dispute, but here are what appear to be the general outlines: in 1992, MZB was working on a novel, *Contraband.* A fan author, Jean Lamb, who had earlier published a short story in a commercially published Friends of Darkover collection,[65] published a Darkover fanfic, *Masks*, in *Moon Phases*. The various parties seem to agree that *Masks* was similar to *Contraband*, and that MZB had read or had the opportunity to read *Masks* while Lamb had not read or had the opportunity to read *Contraband.* In Lamb's words:

> I received a letter offering me a sum and a dedication for all rights to the text. I attempted at that point to _very politely_ negotiate a better deal. I was told that I had better take what I was offered, that much better authors than I had not been paid as much (we're talking a few hundred dollars here) and had gotten the same sort of "credit" (this was in the summer of 1992).
>
> At that point I did not threaten any sort of suit whatsoever; in fact, a few months later I received a letter from Ms. Bradley's lawyer threatening me with a suit should I be a bit too frank about Ms. Bradley's um, writing methods, and who her current collaborators were at the time (at least that is how I took the lawyer's phrasing). Needless to say, I could not afford to defend myself if sued. Winning with the truth could have bankrupted me (and probably still could).[66]

---

64 Ibid., at 13–14.

65 Jean Lamb, *Shut-In*, in RENUNCIATES OF DARKOVER (Marion Zimmer Bradley, ed., 1991). For more on the dispute and the uncertainties surrounding what actually happened and in what order, see Jim C. Hines, *Marion Zimmer Bradley vs. Fanfiction,* May 26, 2010, www.jimchines.com/2010/05/mzb-vs-fanfiction.

66 Post by Jean Lamb, Re: The infamous Marion Zimmer Bradley case, Usenet Newsgroup rec.arts.sf.written (March 19, 2001), http://groups.google.com/group/rec.arts.

A different perspective comes from Nina Boal, the editor of *Moon Phases*:

> People, I was right in the middle of this and discussed this with the parties involved first hand. The following was acknowledged by both sides. Marion did offer Jean a special dedication and also $500. Jean refused this, saying that she wanted a byline for the novel. Jean also became convinced (erroneously) that Marion intended to plagerize [*sic*] from her fan-written work about Danvan Hastur. Her actions made me positively sick. Jean was my good friend, but no more after what she did here and the unfounded accusations she made about Marion.[67]

In response to the incident, MZB backtracked on her earlier reasons for embracing fanfic:

> While in the past I have allowed fans to "play in my yard," I was forced to stop that practice last summer when one of the fans wrote a story, using my world and my characters, that overlapped the setting I was using for my next *Darkover* novel. Since she had sent me a copy of her fanzine, and I had read it, my publisher will not publish my novel set during that time period, and I am now out several years' work, as well as the cost of inconvenience of having a lawyer deal with this matter.
>
> Because this occurred just as I was starting to read for this year's *Darkover* anthology, that project was held up for more than a month while the lawyer drafted a release to accompany any submissions and a new contract, incorporating the release. I do not know at present if I shall be doing any more *Darkover* anthologies.
>
> Let this be a warning to other authors who might be tempted to be similarly generous with their universes, I know now why Arthur Conan Doyle refused to allow anyone to write about Sherlock Holmes. I wanted to be more accommodating, but I don't like where it has gotten me. It's enough to make anyone into a misanthrope.[68]

---

sf.written/msg/80c1db3e5e35c1f9?dmode=source&output=gplain.

67 Post by Nina Boal, mzb_newsletter—The Marion Zimmer Bradley Newsletter, Re: Contraband (March 19, 2001), http://groups.yahoo.com/group/mzb_newsletter/message/209?l=1; as reprinted in Darkover Wiki, Contraband (July 17, 2003), http://darkover.wikia.com/wiki/Contraband.

68 Marion Zimmer Bradley, Letter to the Editor, Writer's Digest, March 1993; see also Fan Works Inc., Fan Fiction Policies >> Bradley, Marion Zimmer, www.fanworks.org/writersresource/?action=define&authorid=53&tool=fanpolicy (last visited September 9, 2008); *Darkover Non-Guidelines* (April 21, 1999), http://darkover.apiacoa.org/guide/short-stories/non-guidelines.en.html (last visited October 19, 2010).

As the self-reference ("I now know why Arthur Conan Doyle refused …") makes clear, MZB was quite aware that she was backtracking. *Contraband* was never published. Lamb submitted *Masks* to DAW Books, the publishers of the Friends of Darkover anthologies:

> I can't use the book. A later submission to DAW of original work was returned in _incredibly_ short time with a preprinted slip. (this may have had more to do with the quality of the work than the byline, I hasten to add, though I've never seen them work quite that fast before).[69]

MZB responded by issuing the "Darkover Non-Guidelines." In dramatic contrast to her previous easygoing policy, the Non-Guidelines prohibited all fanfic:

> As things now stand, anyone writing a Darkover story, or using Mrs. Bradley's world or ANY of her characters, is violating her copyright. (Look up "derivative work" in the copyright law if you want the details.) She is NOT giving permission to do this. If she finds out that anyone is using her work in this fashion, she will turn the matter over to her lawyer.
>
> It's a shame, but the Darkover books are a large part of her livelihood, and she can't afford to have anyone compromise her copyright in them.
>
> Any Darkover stories sent to her are therefore returned or destroyed unread.
>
> If you see this notice and you have already written a Darkover story, please either destroy it or rewrite it so completely that it is not a derivative work of Mrs. Bradley's work.[70]

At least two of the statements in the first paragraph quoted above are untrue, or at least misleading. First, there is a widespread misconception that the author has the power to determine what is and is not copyright infringement. The decision of whether another work infringes copyright is not up to the author; it might have been more accurate to say "*may* violate her copyright." Second, copyright does not prohibit the use of "Mrs. Bradley's world or ANY of her characters." As we have seen, not all characters are protected by copyright, and even when characters are sufficiently developed or delineated to be copyrightable (or constitute the "story being told") the boundaries of that protection are not always clear.[71] Intertextuality is not necessarily copyright infringement. Even characters that might ordinarily be protected can make appearances in works unrelated to those from which they

69 Lamb, *supra* note 66.

70 *Darkover Non-Guidelines*, *supra* note 68.

71 See, for example, *Warner Bros. Pictures, Inc.* v. *Columbia Broad. Sys.*, 216 F.2d 945 (9th Cir. 1954); *Nichols* v. *Universal Pictures Corp.*, 45 F.2d 119 (2d Cir. 1930).

are derived without raising copyright concerns: Popeye the Sailor-Man can make a cameo appearance in Thomas Pynchon's *Mason & Dixon*, translating Hebrew for Dixon the surveyor.[72] Buffy Summers can fight out-of-copyright Dracula while making snide remarks about in-copyright Lestat.[73] The evil queen from Snow White can be merged with Jane Porter from the Tarzan series of stories and movies to serve as a major character in Donald Barthelme's *Snow White*.[74] (Snow White herself has probably long since entered into the public domain, even though Barthelme's character clearly derives at least as much from Disney's version—the last word of the book is "Heigh-ho"[75]—as from the now out-of-copyright Grimm version or earlier folktales.) Tarzan is protected as a character, or was at the time Barthelme wrote the novel.[76] Unlike "Tarzan," "Jane" is a fairly common given name, but Jane Porter, too, might be a sufficiently delineated character to be protected by copyright,[77] and Barthelme leaves no doubt (well, as little as possible, for him) which Jane he means: "Jane likes to swing from the lianas that dangle from the Meat Street trees."[78] But by 1967, when Barthelme wrote *Snow White*, Jane Porter had entered into the public domain in the United States (though not everywhere). This ability to make fair use of characters created by others is crucial to the many works that rely heavily or entirely on references to a large body of other works, from Barthelme's *Snow White* to Phillip C. Jennings' *The Buglife Chronicles*, Marvin Kaye's *The Incredible Umbrella*, and the Black Hole Travel Agency series by the late Brian Daley and still-active James Luceno.

Fanfic writers and fanzine editors are rarely in a position to challenge authors, though; in addition to the chilling effect of the threat of litigation,[79] there is the chilling effect of the threat of disapproval by the author and possible subsequent

72 THOMAS PYNCHON, MASON & DIXON 486 (New York: Henry Holt & Co. Publishers, 1997). Popeye's translation of "Eyer asher Eyeh" from Exodus 3:14 as a barely-modified version of his trademark (!) line, "I yam what I yam," is actually controversial, as another character hastens to point out. Popeye, if sufficiently delineated (as surely he is), is still in copyright; he first appeared in a Betty Boop cartoon in 1933, and took the lead in his own feature, *I Yam What I Yam*, in the same year. For Popeye's copyrightability in (UK) court, see *King Features Syndicate, Inc.* v. *Lechter* [1950] Ex. C.R. 297.

73 *Buffy the Vampire Slayer*: *Buffy v. Dracula* (WB television broadcast September 6, 2000).

74 DONALD BARTHELME, SNOW WHITE (1967).

75 Or is that two words? Ibid., at 181.

76 See *Burroughs* v. *Metro-Goldwyn-Mayer, Inc.*, 683 F.2d 610 (2d Cir. 1982); *Edgar Rice Burroughs, Inc.* v. *Manns Theatres*, 1976 WL 20994 (C.D. Cal. 1976); see also Kurtz, *supra* note 25, at 451–67.

77 See *Edgar Rice Burroughs, Inc.*, 1976 WL 20994 at ¶ 22–23.

78 BARTHELME, *supra* note 74 at 38.

79 On the inherently chilling effect of the threat of litigation, see Rebecca Tushnet, *Payment in Credit: Copyright Law and Subcultural Creativity*, 70 LAW & CONTEMP. PROBS. 135 (2007) ("As Jessica Litman points out, copyright owners find it incredibly useful to interpret current copyright doctrine to mean that the default is that any use of an existing

ostracism from fandom. The immediate effect of MZB's fanfic ban was to shut down the fanfic fanzines and to end the Friends of Darkover anthologies. Apparently three anthologies of stories already purchased were published, but the last came out in 1994.[80] By 1999 fan historian Patrice Rossi reported that the Friends of Darkover had "more or less stopped its activities."[81] The fanfic ban had killed Darkover fandom. Although there are several Darkover reference sites on the web, the fanfic ban has prevented the more active online life that many other fandoms enjoy. MZB died in 1999; Darkover novels continue to be published, with MZB listed as first author, but Darkover has faded from the prominence it enjoyed in genre fiction in the 1970s and 1980s.

Harry Potter and the unauthorized adaptations

Harry Potter is one of the world's most widely recognized fictional characters and the subject of numerous critical works, parodies, and works of fan fiction, formally published and otherwise.[82] Harry Potter fandom is one of the Big Fandoms, on a par with Star Trek, Lord of the Rings, and Star Wars fandom—and it has grown faster than the others, in large part because it came into being after the advent of the World Wide Web. Fans built thousands of websites with millions of pages, and in doing so built the global Harry Potter phenomenon. Most of these pages were small; some became enormous libraries of material, like Mugglenet, The Leaky Cauldron, Veritaserum, HPana, and the Harry Potter Lexicon. The Harry Potter Lexicon was, and is, the project of Steven Vander Ark. More of an encyclopedia than a dictionary, it contains entries on just about every character, place and object mentioned in the Harry Potter novels and associated materials. In 2004 J.K. Rowling, Harry Potter's author, chose it as one of her favorite fan sites, writing:

---

work infringes unless specifically excepted") (citing Jessica Litman, *Creative Reading*, 70 LAW & CONTEMP. PROBS. 175 (2007)).

80 SNOWS OF DARKOVER (Marion Zimmer Bradley, ed., 1980).

81 Rossi, *supra* note 56.

82 And even law review articles. See, for example, Aaron Schwabach, *Harry Potter and the Unforgivable Curses: Norm-formation, Inconsistency, and the Rule of Law in the Wizarding World*, 11 ROGER WILLIAMS U. L. REV. 309 (2006); Laura Spitz, *Wands Away (or Preaching to Infidels Who Wear Earplugs)*, 41 L. TEACHER 314 (2007); Benjamin H. Barton, *Harry Potter and the Half-Crazed Bureaucracy*, 104 MICH. L. REV. 1523 (2006); Paul R. Joseph & Lynn E. Wolf, *The Law In Harry Potter: A System Not Even a Muggle Could Love*, 34 U. TOL. L. REV. 193 (2003); William P. MacNeil, *"Kidlit" as "Law-and-Lit": Harry Potter and the Scales of Justice*, 14 L. & LITERATURE 545 (2002); Ruth Anne Robbins, *Harry Potter, Ruby Slippers and Merlin: Telling the Client's Story Using the Characters and Paradigm of the Archetypal Hero's Journey*, 29 SEATTLE U. L. REV. 767 (2006); Jeffrey Thomas et al., *Harry Potter and the Law*, 12 TEXAS WESLEYAN L. REV. 427 (2005); see also THE LAW & HARRY POTTER 67 (Jeffrey Thomas and Franklin Snyder, eds.; Durham, NC: Carolina Academic Press, 2010).

> This is such a great site that I have been known to sneak into an internet café while out writing and check a fact rather than go into a bookshop and buy a copy of Harry Potter (which is embarrassing). A website for the dangerously obsessive; my natural home.[83]

The text still appeared on Rowling's site in October 2010.

Like Niven, Rowling enjoyed a positive relationship with fandom and not only permitted, but encouraged fan fiction and other fan works. She actively engaged fandom and fanfic, at one point jokingly telling fans "Oh you girls and Draco Malfoy! You must start to get past this."[84] Later, after announcing, to prolonged applause, that she had "always thought of Dumbledore as gay,"[85] she added, "If I'd known it would make you so happy, I would have announced it years ago! … Oh, my god, the fan fiction now, eh?"[86] This may show a misunderstanding of the nature of fan fiction, or at least of slash: if Dumbledore is gay in canon, Dumbledore slash loses the transgressive quality that may be one of slash's essential components.[87] But setting that aside, it again shows Rowling's continuing engagement with fan writers.

J.K. Rowling and the commercially published fan fiction

While tolerant and even encouraging of amateur fanfic, Rowling and her publishers have had no tolerance for commercially published fan fiction. Rowling has said that she has read and enjoyed fanfic and has made no attempt to suppress it,[88] although Warner Brothers, which makes the Harry Potter movies:

83 J.K. Rowling, Official Site Section: Fan Sites, www.jkrowling.com/textonly/en/fansite_archive.cfm?year=2004 (last visited August 19, 2008).

84 Accio Quote!, J.K. Rowling, Steven King, and John Irving, Benefit Reading at Radio City Music Hall to Raise Money for Doctors without Borders and the Haven Foundation (August 1, 2006), www.accio-quote.org/articles/2006/0801-radiocityreading1partial.html (last visited August 19, 2008).

85 The Leaky Cauldron, J.K. Rowling at Carnegie Hall Reveals Dumbledore is Gay; Neville Marries Hannah Abbott, and Much More (October 19, 2007), http://the-leaky-cauldron.org/2007/10/20/j-k-rowling-at-carnegie-hall-reveals-dumbledore-is-gay-neville-marries-hannah-abbott-and-scores-more.

86 Ibid.

87 See, for example, Molly Ringle, *I Love the Smell of Fandom Rioting and Looting in the Morning*, October 27, 2007, http://lemonlye.livejournal.com/172557.html; Sonia Katyal, *Performance, Property, and the Slashing of Gender in Fan Fiction*, 14 Am. U. J. Gender Soc. Pol'y & L. 461 (2006), at 508–09.

88 Fan Works Inc., Fan Fiction Policies >> Harry Potter: J.K. Rowling & Harry Potter!, www.fanworks.org/writersresource/?tool=fanpolicy&action=define&authorid=108 (last visited August 19, 2008).

> [I]s not always as kind. They have gone after people who have used Harry Potter on their web sites and aggressively fought for the rights to domains related to Harry Potter. This has shut down a few Harry Potter fan sites with some fan fiction.[89]

Despite these occasional excesses, though, "[t]here has been no real effort on the part of Warner Brothers to seek to put an end to Harry Potter fan fiction."[90]

When movie copyrights are involved and an extra layer of administration is added between the author and the fans, tolerance tends to diminish. Thus Warner Brothers, the maker of the Harry Potter movies, has cracked down on fan sites that Rowling herself would most likely have left undisturbed. As seems to be the norm in such matters, Warner Brothers' enforcement efforts have been at times ludicrously ham-handed:

> [In December 2000] 15-year-old Claire Field received a letter from Warner Brothers' London legal department asking her to turn over the name www.harrypotterguide.co.uk. Like her dragon-defying idol, the British youth rebelled. She sent an e-mail message to a British tabloid, the Mirror, which ran a story about her. A U.K.-based online news site, the Register, picked up the story, which was soon posted on fan-related online newsgroups. Internet users from around world—youngsters and adults alike—are now urging Field to fight back.
>
> "I've just read the news that the Evil Dark Arts experts a.k.a. Warner Brothers are trying to cast some dark charms and shut down this site. GOLLY! What total ROT. We have got to get some good charms and wand waving to seriously sort them out," wrote a fellow Harry Potter fan on Field's Web site.
>
> * * *
>
> Its legal rights notwithstanding, Warner Brothers' crackdown has enraged many of Harry Potter's loyal fans. Hundreds of fan-site creators in addition to Field have been sent letters. Christie Chang, a 15-year-old from Singapore, has received two letters from Warner Brothers' lawyers. One says that the fan site, to which she devotes at least an hour a day, violates copyright laws by using various Harry Potter images. The other letter from the studio's lawyers demands back the domain name she has registered, www.harrypotternetwork.net, and insists she promptly contact them in Beverly Hills, California.[91]

---

89 Ibid.

90 Ibid.

91 Stephanie Grunier, *Warner Bros. Claims Harry Potter Sites*, ZDNet, December 21, 2000, http://news.zdnet.com/2100-9595_22-96323.html; see also Christina Z. Ranon, *Honor Among Thieves: Copyright Infringement in Internet Fandom*, 8 Vand. J. Ent. & Tech. L. 421 (2006) and accompanying text. The site at www.harrypotterguide.co.uk is still up, with a disclaimer: "This site is an unofficial Harry Potter site, and therefore should only

Such actions against noncommercial Harry Potter fandom seem shortsighted; they show a misunderstanding of where Harry's money comes from, and of the value of fandom as free advertising and marketing far more effective than any marketing campaign Warner Brothers could actually buy. This misunderstanding may be a temporary lapse, perhaps the result of overzealous employees incompletely socialized into the culture of genre works; that would explain why these actions seem to be more anomalous than not.

Commercial works are given far less leniency. Rowling and the other Harry Potter stakeholders have suppressed commercially published and distributed fan fiction, mostly in non-English-speaking countries. In Russia, Dmitry Yemets has done well with Tanya Grotter, who "rides a double bass, sports a mole instead of a bolt of lightning, and attends the Tibidokhs School of Magic."[92] Yemets describes Tanya as "cultural competition" and "a sort of Russian answer to Harry Potter."[93] Rowling, apparently, describes her as copyright infringement: in April 2003 she succeeded in blocking the distribution of Tanya Grotter's adventures in the Netherlands.[94] Tanya Grotter remains in print in Russia, where the 13 volumes of her adventures have sold three million copies.[95] The interest in the Tanya Grotter series outside of Russia seems to be generated by Rowling's attempt to suppress it and the subsequent notoriety; Yemets himself has "described the Tanya Grotter series as a purely Russian phenomenon, dependent on the language and culture, and commented that he would not place much faith in Tanya living a full life if she were brought to the playing field of Europe or America."[96]

---

be entered by people who fully understand that the site holds no connection to J.K Rowling, Bloomsbury, Scholastics or Warner Bros. It is however meant as an educational experience for all ages, and is non-profit." Claire Field, now 23, is still listed as the administrator. Claire Field, About the Webmistress, www.harrypotterguide.co.uk (last visited September 14, 2008). There is no site at www.harrypotternetwork.net. Christie Chang is apparently the administrator of The Harry Potter Network. Christie Chang, The Harry Potter Network, www.thehpn.com (last visited September 14, 2008).

92 Tim Wu, *Harry Potter and the International Order of Copyright: Should* Tanya Grotter and the Magic Double Bass *Be Banned?*, June 27, 2003, www.slate.com/id/2084960; see also Dennis S. Karjala, *Harry Potter, Tanya Grotter, and the Copyright Derivative Work*, 38 Ariz. St. L.J. 17 (2006).

93 Wu, *Harry Potter and the International Order of Copyright*.

94 Ibid.; *Rowling* v. *Uitgeverij Byblos BV*, 2003 WL 21729296, [2003] E.C.D.R. 23 (RB [Amsterdam] Arrondissementrechtbank, April 3, 2003); *affirmed*, 2003 WL 23192402, [2004] E.C.D.R. 7 (Hof [Amsterdam], November 6, 2003).

95 See generally Таня Гроттер, Новости, www.grotter.ru (last visited September 2, 2008).

96 Wikipedia, the Free Encyclopedia, Tanya Grotter, http://en.wikipedia.org/wiki/Tanya_Grotter#cite_note-7 (last visited September 2, 2008) (citing *The Russian Tanya Grotter—an Answer to Harry Potter*, Kiev Telegraph online edition, February 10–16, 2006 (no longer available online)).

Yemets tried, unsuccessfully, to defend the Tanya Grotter series as parody in the Netherlands lawsuit.[97] The trial court found that *Tanya Grotter and the Magic Double Bass* was "an adaptation of [Rowling's] book and was in competition with, rather than a parody of" it.[98] The appellate court agreed, adding that Yemets' book was not a parody, and "even if … viewed as a polemic, the writing of a fairy tale book was not the most appropriate manner to 'quote' from another works as part of such a polemic[.]"[99]

It may be that the Tanya Grotter books are not parodies; what they seem to be is inverse Mary Sue fanfic. "Mary Sue" refers to a subcategory of fanfic that places the author, or a character closely based on the author, into a fictional world. Yemets has done the opposite: he has taken Harry Potter, or a character very similar to him, and brought him from England to Russia. Because Harry and Tanya are creatures of text, this has meant a textual transplant; Harry has been removed from the narrative of John Donne and T.S. Eliot[100] and set down, after a quick change of gender and hair color, in the narrative of Pushkin and Baba Yaga. For example, the magic school Tanya attends is located on the island of Buyan, instantly recognizable to Russian readers, even very young ones, from Pushkin's *The Tale of Tsar Saltan*[101] and from Rimsky-Korsakov's opera of the same name.[102] (In yet another example of the inevitably derivative nature of all works in an ongoing literary tradition, Pushkin's poem in turn is based on a traditional Russian folk tale.) This sort of cultural Mary Sue tale has a long history in Russia; what Yemets is doing with Harry Potter is not dissimilar to what Alexander Volkov did with *The Wizard of Oz*. Volkov's first (unauthorized) translation is fairly close to L. Frank Baum's first Oz book, although there are some large changes. Volkov's later volumes are increasingly original, although they do incorporate some familiar story elements and settings.[103] Nor is this tradition of adaptation unknown in the

97 See, for example, JSBlog, *Tanya Grotter*, July 21, 2007, http://segalbooks.blogspot.com/2007/07/tanya-grotter.html; *Rowling* v. *Uitgeverij Byblos BV*, 2003 WL 21729296.

98 *Rowling* v. *Uitgeverij Byblos BV*, 2003 WL 21729296 (English-language summary).

99 Ibid., WL 23192402 (English-language summary of appeal).

100 See Schwabach, *supra* note 82, at 345–46.

101 Alexander Pushkin, Сказка о Царе Салтане, о сыне его славном и могучем богатыре Князе Гвидоне Салтановиче и о прекрасной царевне лебеди [The Tale of Tsar Saltan, of His Son the Renowned and Mighty Bogatyr Prince Gvidon Saltanovich, and of the Beautiful Princess-Swan] (1831), *available at* www.lib.ru/LITRA/PUSHKIN/saltan.txt; *see also* Alexander Pushkin, The Tale of Tsar Saltan (Louis Zellikoff, trans., Moscow: Progress Publishers, 1970), available at http://home.freeuk.com/russica4/books/salt/saltan.html.

102 Nikolai Rimsky-Korsakov, The Tale of Tsar Saltan (1900 opera, perhaps best known to most Americans for "Flight of the Bumblebee").

103 See Алекса́ндр Меле́нтьевич Во́лков [Alexander Melentyevich Volkov], Волшебник Изумрудного Города [The Wizard of the Emerald City] et seq. (1939),

U.S.—think, for example, how Disney's *The Little Mermaid* would have flopped had it remained true to the Danish original.

The Mary Sue subgenre of fanfic is accorded little respect among fans, but has its defenders, who see in it "the modern incarnation of an old and often celebrated phenomenon—retelling a canonical story to better represent oneself."[104] If Mary Sue can empower individual fanfic writers or the groups to which they belong,[105] Yemets may be empowering Russia, and through his retelling both protecting Russia's literary tradition and making a foreign character more accessible to a Russian audience.

In addition, Yemets is achieving what early observers (including Gene Roddenberry and the editors of *Star Trek: The New Voyages*) saw as one of the main benefits of fanfic: jump-starting his own career as a writer. And Yemets, who began with Tanya Grotter, is now focusing his attention on two new series—the Methodius Buslaev and Hooligan adventures.[106] Methodius Buslaev appears in the Tanya Grotter stories, but he is entirely Yemets' creation. In his own adventures Buslaev's world seems less Potteresque; like Volkov before him, Yemets started with an imported fictional world but, having grown confident from working with it, is taking it in a different direction from the one chosen by its original creator. Interestingly, Yemets explicitly encourages fanfic on the Buslaev website, urging readers to "write their own version of events" and answer the question "what happens after the book ends?"[107] At least one volume of these fan stories has been commercially published.[108]

---

available in English translation as Tales of Magic Land (Peter L. Blystone, trans, 2nd revised edition, Red Branch Press, 2010).

104 Anupam Chander & Madhavi Sunder, *Everyone's a Superhero: A Cultural Theory of "Mary Sue" Fan Fiction as Fair Use*, 95 Cal. L. Rev. 597, 598 (2007); see also, for example, Rebecca Tushnet, *Payment in Credit: Copyright Law and Subcultural Creativity*, 70 Law & Contemp. Probs. 135 (2007); Jacqueline Lai Chung, *Drawing Idea from Expression: Creating a Legal Space for Culturally Appropriated Literary Characters*, 49 Wm. & Mary L. Rev. 903 (2007).

105 Chander & Sunder, *supra* note 104, at 598.

106 See generally Мефодий Буслаев, www.buslaev.ru (last visited September 2, 2008) (Methodius Buslaev official website).

107 Фанаты Дмитрия Емца написали продолжение его книги, April 30, 2008, www.buslaev.ru/news/2305 ("Что происходит с героями, когда заканчивается книга? Что делает читатель, перевернув последнюю страницу? Читатель ждет продолжения любимого сериала и … пишет свою версию событий! И тогда герои начинают жить собственной жизнью").

108 Миры Тани Гроттер и Мефодия Буслаева, Фанаты Дмитрия Емца написали продолжение его книги, April 30, 2008, www.buslaev.ru/news/2305 (last visited September 2, 2008) (title translates to "Peace Tanya Grotter and Methodius Buslaeva"). A note on translations throughout this work: any translations from Portuguese or German, especially any errors, are my own. Any translations from Chinese are mine, too, with the indispensable help of Zhou Qienyuan—that is to say, the errors are mine and the parts that

Although Anupam Chander and Madhavi Sunder see noncommercial Mary Sue fanfic as fair use,[109] the Tanya Grotter novels might fail the fourth prong of the section 107 test. In July 2006, the best-selling children's book in Russia was *Таня Гроттер и перстень с жемчужиной* [*Tanya Grotter and the Pearl Ring*], the eleventh in the series.[110] *Harry Potter and the Half-Blood Prince*, published in Russian in December 2005,[111] was second.[112] It's hard to tell whether Tanya Grotter was actually displacing Harry Potter sales, or whether there was sufficient elasticity of demand for fantasy that all potential buyers of *Harry Potter and the Half-Blood Prince* or *Таня Гроттер и перстень с жемчужиной* would just as happily buy both works; for many fans, purchases are limited not by the cost of books but by the speed at which authors can produce works the fans want to read. On the same list, the translation of the fifth Harry Potter book, *Harry Potter and the Order of the Phoenix*, ranked sixth, while the fifth of Yemets' Methodius Buslaev adventures, *Мефодий Буслаев: Месть валькирий* [*Methodius Buslaev: Revenge of the Valkyries*], ranked tenth.[113]

Yemets is far from the only author to seek to bring Harry Potter into his own country's literary tradition. In neighboring Belarus, a Harry Potter clone—save that he is a technology-user in a world where most people use magic—rides a motorcycle and wields a grenade launcher in *Porri Gatter and the Stone Philosopher* and its sequels.[114] In China and India, with rich literary traditions and increasingly prominent positions in the world economy, the localization of Harry Potter is a form of empowerment. This empowerment may make good economic sense as well as good cultural sense. As Timothy Wu notes:

> [T]he argument for letting Potter crush his international competition is quite weak … [A]s trade economists will tell you, trade often works when countries imitate and improve the inventions of others … There is, in short, a secondary Potter market. Isn't this the international trading system at its best?

---

are correct are Dr. Zhou's. Any translations from Russian are by way of Google Language Tools, and I'm generously willing to give Google credit for the errors as well.

109 Chander & Sunder, *supra* note 104.

110 Elena Kitayeva, *Наши дети—это невыгодно*, Business Petersburg Online, September 13, 2006, www.dpgazeta.ru/article/104243.

111 News.RIN.ru, *Russian version of "Harry Potter and Half-Blood Prince" appeared in stores*, http://news.rin.ru/eng/news///3230 (last visited September 2, 2008).

112 Kitayeva, *supra* note 110.

113 Kitayeva, *supra* note 110.

114 Порри Гаттер и Каменный Философ [Porri Gatter and the Stone Philosopher] (Vremnya, 2002); Порри Гаттер: Личное дело Мергионы [Porri Gatter: Merlioniy's Personal File] (Vremnya, 2003); Порри Гаттер: 9 подвигов Сена Аесли [Porri Gatter: 9 Feats of Hay Aesli] (Vremnya, 2004); see generally *Порри Гаттер*, www.gatter.ru/main.asp; see also Wu, *supra* note 92, and Masterliness: Pori Gatter Porridge, www.masterliness.com/a/Porri.Gatter.htm (last visited September 8, 2008).

> Moreover, the writers of secondary Potters are probably better at creating versions of Potter suited to local conditions … Local writers do things to Harry that Rowling can't, like introducing him to local literary figures and putting him in local wars. It may be good and it may be bad, but it's a market failure to prevent it.[115]

In India, Harry Potter's broomstick takes him flying across Calcutta to meet characters from Bengali literature, Indian history, and cinema—or did, until he was grounded by a copyright lawsuit.[116] Rowling and Warner Brothers apparently retain the right to adapt Harry to other cultures—even if they never get around to it. While the character Harry Potter is protected by copyright and trademark, Warner Brothers, owner of the copyright in the Harry Potter movies, has even sought to prevent the use of sound-alike names in unrelated works, suing to enjoin the release of a movie with the title *Hari Puttar—A Comedy Of Terrors* about "a 10-year-old boy who moves to England with his parents and becomes embroiled in a battle over a secret microchip."[117] While this sort of *idem sonans* argument might make a certain amount of sense with Tanya Grotter, clearly intended as an imitation of Harry Potter, it seems a bit farfetched with a story that doesn't involve magic and a wizarding school; Harry Potter, after all, is a fairly ordinary English name—or at least it used to be. It seems unlikely that many parents with the surname Potter will be naming their sons "Harry" for the next few decades. Petunia Dursley thinks it's common in the British, as well as American, sense of the word: "[n]asty, common name, if you ask me."[118] In any event, a character's name alone is not copyrightable, whether it is a name real people might (and do) actually have, like Harry Potter, or a coined name like Tarzan. And "Hari" and "Puttar" are common names in India, and perhaps most significantly not the way "Harry Potter" is translated: In Hindi "Harry Potter" is "हैरी पॉटर." Meanwhile the title of "Hari Puttar," the movie, is "हरी पुत्तर," so the likelihood of confusion for the intended audience is reduced. (In any event, the movie is more like *Home Alone* than like Harry Potter). A Google image search for "हैरी पॉटर" turns up nothing but Harry Potter (at least on the first page), while a search for "हरी पुत्तर" turns up nothing but Hari Puttar. While the use was commercial, this absence of even initial interest confusion would seem to weaken any trademark argument as well.

---

115 Wu, *supra* note 92.

116 Chander & Sunder, *supra* note 104, at 610–11, nn.86, 90.

117 *Warner "Sues Over Puttar Movie,"* BBC News, August 25, 2008, http://news.bbc.co.uk/2/hi/entertainment/7580941.stm; see also Hari Puttar Official Website, www.hariputtarthefilm.com/index.html (no longer available as of June 4, 2010); Ramola Talwar Badam, *Bollywood's "Hari Putar" Wins "Harry Potter" Suit*, Associated Press, September 23, 2008, available at www.usatoday.com/life/movies/news/2008-09-23-hari-puttar_N.htm (last visited October 18, 2010); Anna Phillips, *Copyright or Trademark? Can One Boy Wizard Prevent Film Title Duplication?*, 11 San Diego Int'l L.J. 319 (2009).

118 J.K. Rowling, Harry Potter and the Sorcerer's Stone 7 (1997).

In China, Harry's unauthorized adventures have taken him through Chinese literature, into an outer space filled with magical fairylands, and, curiously, into the world of Tolkien's *The Hobbit*.[119] Chinese students have studied at Hogwarts, no doubt on a Mary Sue scholarship, in *Harry Potter and the Chinese Overseas Students at the Hogwarts School of Witchcraft and Wizardry*.[120] Some of these are low-grade attempts to cash in on the popularity of Harry Potter; the hobbit adventure, *Hali Bote yu Bao Zulong*, seems to be one of these.[121] Others are fanfic in the truest sense, like "Harry Potter and the Showdown":

> One … writer is a manager at a Shanghai textile factory named Li Jingsheng. "I bought Harry Potter 1 through 6 for my son a couple of years ago, and when he finished reading them, he kept asking me to tell him what happens next," he explained. "We couldn't wait, so I began making up my own story and in May last year, I typed it up on my computer. I had to get up early and go to bed late to write this novel, usually spending one hour, from 6 to 7 in the morning and 10 to 11 in the evening to write it."
>
> The result was "Harry Potter and the Showdown," a 250,000-word novel, the final version of which he placed recently on Websites, followed by a notice saying he was looking for publishers. The book quickly logged 150,000 readers on a popular Chinese site, Baidu.com's Harry Potter fan Web page.
>
> "This is fantastic," Gu Guaiguai, an admiring reader, wrote online about "Showdown." "I wonder if Rowling would bother to continue to write if she had read it."[122]

While *Showdown* is probably a better read than, say, *Bao Zulong*,[123] it was not written for profit—nonetheless, it has been sold in hard-copy form, without the

119 See generally Naill Renfro, *Pirate Naill Reads*, available at http://naill-renfro.livejournal.com/2074.html (last visited September 2, 2008).

120 Chris Walters, *Chinese Fake Harry Potter Is Awesome; Also A Dragon*, Consumerist, August 11, 2007, http://consumerist.com/consumer/fakes/chinese-fake-harry-potter-is-awesome-also-a-dragon-288542.php.

121 Renfro, *supra* note 119.

122 Howard W. French, *Chinese Market Awash in Fake Potter Books*, N.Y. Times, August 1, 2007, available at www.nytimes.com/2007/08/01/world/asia/01china.html?pagewanted=2&ei=5087&em&enF. For an English-language equivalent, see Cassandra Claire's novel-length fanfic, *Draco Dormiens*, and its sequels. The novels have been taken offline by their author following a fandom dispute too convoluted and arcane to describe here, but are still widely available. See, for example, *The Draco Trilogy*, http://web.archive.org/web/20061016094249/http://www.heidi8.com/dt (last visited September 15, 2008). Ms. Claire has gone on to become the author (as "Cassandra Clare") of the Mortal Instruments fantasy trilogy.

123 See *Harry Potter and the Showdown*, N.Y. Times, August 10, 2007, available at www.nytimes.com/2007/08/10/opinion/10potter8.html (last visited October 19, 2010).

consent or even knowledge of the author, Mr. Li.[124] This double piracy is, at least potentially, an infringement on both Rowling's copyright in the Harry Potter character and Li's copyright in the original elements of his work.

In general, the Harry Potter copyright machine has been tolerant of fanfic and parody, even commercially published parody such as the Belarusian adventures of Porri Gatter.[125] Commercially published parodies have also been tolerated in the Czech Republic,[126] France,[127] Hungary,[128] Indonesia,[129] and throughout the English-speaking world,[130] even though the fair use and First Amendment concerns underlying the U.S. Supreme Court's protection of parody in *Campbell* may have no counterparts in some countries. Works which are merely new adventures of Harry Potter, such as the Chinese and Indian examples discussed above, or that achieve substantial commercial success with a character based on Harry Potter—Tanya Grotter—have not been tolerated. Alternatively, commercially published works in certain large markets—China, India, and Russia—may inspire a stronger reaction because these countries are perceived, often incorrectly, as more prone to copyright violation.[131] India has been a particular target: in addition to the lawsuits against Harry's Bengali adventures[132] and his unrelated sound-alike Hari Puttar,[133] the Potter industry even sued the

124 French, *supra* note 122.

125 See *supra* note 114 and accompanying text; see also Kevin O'Flynn, *Potter Spawns Parody Part II*, St. Petersburg Times (Russia), November 29, 2002, available at www.sptimes.ru/index.php?action_id=2&story_id=8705 ("Natalya Dolgova of Rosmen, the Russian publishers of Harry Potter, said she had read portions of the Porri Gatter book and had no plans to sue. 'It's a parody,' she said").

126 See Peter Jolin, Harry Pouter and Phil O'dendron's Stone: Parody of Harry Potter and the Philosopher's Stone, Somewhere on the Edge of Good Taste (2005), and its sequels. The English-language version of the first book is notable for the intense hostility its spam e-mail marketing campaign aroused among English-speaking fans. See, for example, www.amazon.com/Harry-Pouter-Phil-Odendrons-Stone/dp/8086947033/ref=sr_1_1?ie=UTF8&s=books&qid=1220896574&sr=1-1 (last visited September 8, 2008).

127 See Pierre Veys, Harry Cover: L'ensorcelante parodie (2005); Pierre Veys, Harry Cover: Les mangeurs d'anglais (2007) (graphic novels).

128 See K.B. Rottring: Heri Kókler és az Epeköve (2005), and its many sequels.

129 See Happy Porter: Penyusup di Sekolah Sihir Homework (2007), available at www.bukukita.com/infodetailbuku.php?idBook=5259 (last visited September 8, 2008).

130 Far too many to list, but see, for example, Michael Gerber, Barry Trotter and the Unauthorized Parody (2001), and its sequels. The first in the series was originally published in the U.S. as Barry Trotter and the Shameless Parody (2001) (the change of title from the U.K. to the U.S. edition is itself a joke, playing on the "translation" of the original U.K. title of the first book, Harry Potter and the Philosopher's Stone to Harry Potter and the Sorcerer's Stone for the U.S. market).

131 See generally Aaron Schwabach, *Intellectual Property Piracy: Perception and Reality in China, the United States, and Elsewhere*, 2 J. Int'l Media & Ent. L. 65 (2007).

132 See *supra* note 116 and accompanying text.

133 See *supra* note 117 and accompanying text.

organizers of a Durga Puja festival in Kolkata for building a large papier-mâché castle intended to represent Hogwarts.[134]

The HP Lexicon takes one step too far

The HP Lexicon, praised by Rowling, eventually went beyond what she was willing to allow: in 2007 the site's author, Steven Vander Ark, and RDR Books, a small publisher in Muskegon, Michigan, agreed to publish much of the information in the HP Lexicon in book form.[135] While the book could not reproduce the entire content of the Lexicon website, with its detailed descriptions and excerpted text for just about every person, place and thing in the Potterverse, in its original form it still included extensive sample text and, inevitably, spoilers for those who had not yet read the entire series. Warner Brothers sued to stop publication of the book. Although Rowling had not written a guide to her own work, she stated that "[s] he had been planning to write her own definitive encyclopaedia, the proceeds of which she had intended to donate to charity."[136] At a dramatic trial Vander Ark, according to one reporter, "broke into sobs on the witness stand," and the judge suggested that the case should never have been brought:

> Judge Patterson … reminded the parties that in "Bleak House," the character Miss Flite faithfully attends every day of the trial and finally dies in her little attic.
>
> "A very sad story," Judge Patterson said. "Litigation isn't always the best way to solve things."[137]

At least one observer saw a parallel to the abusive proceedings of the Ministry of Magic:

---

134 *India Court Rejects Harry Potter Author's Claim*, available at AFP, October 12, 2007, http://afp.google.com/article/ALeqM5hZhGr-qlWfYdFig_iagNfYzU-l8w (last visited October 19, 2010).

135 See Tim Wu, *J.K. Rowling's Dark Mark: Why She Should Lose Her Copyright Lawsuit against the Harry Potter Lexicon*, Slate, January 10, 2008, available at www.slate.com/id/2181776 (last visited October 19, 2010); RDR Books, *Harry Potter Lexicon Update*, available at www.rdrbooks.com/books/lexicon.html (last visited October 19, 2010). See also, for example, Aaron Schwabach, *The Harry Potter Lexicon and the World of Fandom: Fan Fiction, Outsider Works, and Copyright*, 70 U. Pitt. L. Rev. 387 (2009); Shira Siskind, *Crossing the Fair Use Line: The Demise and Revival of the Harry Potter Lexicon and Its Implications for the Fair Use Doctrine in the Real World and on the Internet*, 27 Cardozo Arts & Ent. L.J. 291 (2009).

136 *Rowling Wins Book Copyright Claim*, BBC News, September 8, 2008, available at http://news.bbc.co.uk/2/hi/entertainment/7605142.stm (last visited October 19, 2010).

137 Anemona Hartocollis, *Trial Over Potter Lexicon Ends With an Olive Branch*, N.Y. Times, April 17, 2008, available at www.nytimes.com/2008/04/17/nyregion/17potter.html?_r=1&scp=5&sq=rowling&st=nyt&oref=slogin (last visited October 19, 2010).

> An expert witness for the plaintiffs, Jeri Johnson, an American expatriate who is a senior tutor at Oxford University, seemed to play the role of Dolores Umbridge, the Ministry of Magic's apparatchik at Hogwarts, as she testified.
>
> She dripped contempt as she referred to Mr. Vander Ark's work as "the so-called lexicon." She said she found Mr. Vander Ark's commentary in the book to be "weak waggishness."[138]

Rowling herself admitted that she did not think the HP Lexicon would displace sales of the Potter novels,[139] and said that she was not sure she had "the will or the heart" to write her own guide.[140] Also, she stated that she was motivated not by economic factors but by "outrage"; under U.S. law, copyright is meant to protect the author's economic rights, not to protect the author from feeling outraged.[141] Nonetheless, the court enjoined publication of Vander Ark's book.[142]

Although the injunction may have been bad news for Vander Ark and RDR, it was not necessarily bad news for fandom. Judge Patterson's opinion was at best lukewarm toward Rowling's arguments; he observed that "[i]ssuing an injunction in this case both benefits and harms the public interest."[143] Perhaps most importantly, the court found that the Lexicon was not a derivative work: "A work is not derivative, however, simply because it is 'based upon' the preexisting works."[144] The court reasoned that the very existence of exceptions for parody and critical commentary, which are of necessity based upon the works they parody or evaluate, requires that "derivative" mean something more than merely "based upon." The court adopted the reasoning of Judge Posner in *Ty, Inc.* that "ownership of copyright does not confer a legal right to control public evaluation of the copyrighted work."[145] In a footnote it highlighted the necessarily inverse relationship between derivativeness and transformativeness:

---

138 Ibid. The author may have been thinking of a parallel to the hearing of Mary Cattermole before Dolores Umbridge. See J.K. Rowling, Harry Potter and the Deathly Hallows 259–61 (Scholastic Books, 2007). See generally Schwabach, *supra* note 82; Thomas et al., *supra* note 82; Joseph & Wolf, *supra* note 82 for a discussion on the flaws in the Ministry of Magic's legal procedures.

139 See Hartocollis, *supra* note 137 ("Can you imagine anyone reading this lexicon for entertainment value?" the Judge asked. "Honestly, your Honor, no," Ms. Rowling replied).

140 *Rowling Wins Book Copyright Claim*, *supra* note 136.

141 Hartocollis, *supra* note 137.

142 *Warner Bros. Entertainment* v. *RDR Books*, 575 F.Supp.2d 513, 554 (S.D.N.Y. September 8, 2008). Many of the documents relating to the case are also collected in Robert S. Want, Harry Potter and the Order of the Court: The J.K. Rowling Copyright Case and the Question of Fair Use (2008).

143 *Warner Bros. Entertainment*, 575 F.Supp.2d at 553.

144 Ibid., at 538.

145 Ibid., at 538–39 (citing *Ty, Inc.* v. *Publ'ns Int'l*, 292 F.3d 512, 521 (7th Cir. 2002) (concluding that a collector's guide to Beanie Babies was not a derivative work); *Castle Rock Entertainment* v. *Carol Publ'g Group*, 150 F.3d 132, 137 (2d Cir. 1998) (finding that

> [t]he law in [the Second] Circuit has recognized that "even when one work is 'based upon' another, 'if the secondary work sufficiently transforms the expression of the original work such that the two works cease to be substantially similar, then the secondary work is not a derivative work and, for that matter, does not infringe the copyright of the original work.'"[146]

The version of the Lexicon considered by the court failed because it copied Rowling's text extensively in a way that was not a fair use of Rowling's material. Even so, some of the section 107 factors weighed in Vander Ark's and RDR's favor. The first factor, purpose and character of the use, weighed in the defendants' favor because the use was transformative[147]—that is, it altered the "expression, meaning, or message" of the original.[148] The Lexicon is a reference work; the seven Harry Potter novels tell a story. The use of material from the two School Books[149] presented a bit more of a problem, because they are partly reference works themselves.[150] However, "the Lexicon's use is slightly transformative in that it adds a productive purpose to the original material by synthesizing it within a complete reference guide that refers readers to where information can be found in a diversity of sources."[151] The best evidence of the transformative nature of the Lexicon is that it was widely relied on as a reference source, even by Warner Brothers, Electronic Arts (the makers of Harry Potter video games), and Rowling herself.[152] This was undercut only slightly by defendants' desire to make a profit by providing the first comprehensive Harry Potter reference guide on the market.[153]

---

a Seinfeld trivia book was derivative); *Twin Peaks Prods., Inc.*, 996 F. 2d at 1373 (stating that guide to Twin Peaks television series that set out detailed plot descriptions of first eight episodes was derivative)).

146 *Warner Bros. Entertainment*, 575 F.Supp.2d at 538 n. 17, quoting *Well-Made Toy Mfg. Corp.* v. *Goffa Int'l Corp.*, 354 F.3d 112, 117 (2d Cir. 2003), which in turn is quoting *Castle Rock*, 150 F.3d at 143 n. 9.

147 *Warner Bros. Entertainment*, 575 F.Supp.2d at 541.

148 See *Campbell* v. *Acuff-Rose Music, Inc.*, 510 U.S. 569, 579 (1994).

149 The School Books, referred to in the opinion as the "companion books," are two books used by Harry at school, with annotations in the margins by Harry and his friends. They are more in the nature of reference works than stories; they do not advance the plot or develop the characters significantly, but they do provide additional depth and illumination. See J.K. Rowling, Fantastic Beasts & Where to Find Them (2001) (a bestiary describing many species of magical creatures and beings, some very important to the stories and others that do not even appear; provides some insight into the tension between magical humans, non-humans, and Muggles); J.K. Rowling, Quidditch Through the Ages (2001) (a history of Quidditch, providing incidental glimpses of the Ministry of Magic and wizarding communities in other countries).

150 *Warner Bros. Entertainment*, 575 F.Supp.2d at 541–42.

151 *Warner Bros. Entertainment*, 575 F.Supp.2d at 542.

152 *Warner Bros. Entertainment*, 575 F.Supp.2d at 542.

153 *Warner Bros. Entertainment*, 575 F.Supp.2d at 545.

Rowling's and Warner Brothers' complaint draws a distinction that the court, and so far the law generally, do not formally acknowledge, but that may become important in assessing the legality of fanfic and other fan-generated content:

> [T]here is a significant difference between giving the innumerable Harry Potter fan sites latitude to discuss the *Harry Potter* Works in the context of free of charge, ephemeral websites and allowing a single fan site owner and his publisher to commercially exploit the *Harry Potter* Books in contravention of Ms. Rowlings' wishes and rights and to the detriment of other *Harry Potter* fan sites.[154]

The second factor, the nature of the underlying work, favored the plaintiffs, as will always be the case with complex literary worlds: "[i]n creating the Harry Potter novels and the companion books, Rowling has given life to a wholly original universe of people, creatures, places, and things ... Such highly imaginative and creative fictional works are close to the core of copyright protection, particularly where the character of the secondary work is not entirely transformative."[155]

The third factor, the amount and substantiality of the allegedly infringing use, was somewhat more difficult to assess. The court agreed with the defendants that "[t]o fulfill its purpose as a reference guide to the Harry Potter works, it is reasonably necessary for the Lexicon to make considerable use of the original works."[156] However, the Lexicon engaged in more verbatim copying of Rowling's exact turns of phrase than was strictly necessary for description: "[v]erbatim copying of this nature demonstrates Vander Ark's lack of restraint due to an enthusiastic admiration of Rowling's artistic expression, or perhaps haste and laziness as Rowling suggested[.]"[157]

The fourth and most important[158] factor, effect on the potential market for or value of the underlying work, seemed to weigh slightly in favor of the plaintiffs, largely because of the School Books. The fact that Rowling might plan to publish her own encyclopedia was irrelevant, because "the market for reference guides to the Harry Potter works is not exclusively hers to exploit or license, no matter the commercial success attributable to the popularity of the original works ... The market for reference guides does not become derivative

---

154 First Amended Complaint at 3, *Warner Bros. Entertainment, Inc.* v. *RDR Books* (2007) (No. 07 Civ 9667).

155 *Warner Bros. Entertainment*, 575 F.Supp.2d at 549 (citing *Castle Rock Entertainment* v. *Carol Publ'g Group*, 150 F.3d 132, 144 (2d Cir. 1998); *Twin Peaks Prods., Inc.*, 996 F. 2d at 1376; *Paramount Pictures Corp.* v. *Carol Publ'g Group*, 11 F.Supp.2d 329, 336 (S.D.N.Y. 1998)).

156 *Warner Bros. Entertainment*, 575 F.Supp.2d at 546.

157 *Warner Bros. Entertainment*, 575 F.Supp.2d at 548.

158 *Twin Peaks Prods., Inc.*, 996 F.2d at 1377 ("The fourth factor, market effect, is 'undoubtedly the single most important element of fair use'") (quoting *Harper & Row, Publ'rs* v. *Nation Enter.*, 471 U.S. 539, 566 (1985)).

simply because the copyright holder seeks to produce or license one."[159] With regard to the seven novels,

> there is no plausible basis to conclude that publication of the Lexicon would impair sales of the Harry Potter novels. Plaintiffs' expert Suzanne Murphy, vice president and publisher of trade publishing and marketing at Scholastic, testified that in her opinion a child who read the Lexicon would be discouraged from reading the Harry Potter series because the Lexicon discloses key plot points and does not contain "spoiler alerts." (Tr. (Murphy) at 409:12-411:7.) Children may be an elusive market for book publishers, but it is hard to believe that a child, having read the Lexicon, would lose interest in reading (and thus his or her parents' interest in purchasing) the Harry Potter series. Because the Lexicon uses the Harry Potter series for a transformative purpose (though inconsistently), reading the Lexicon cannot serve as a substitute for reading the original novels; they are enjoyed for different purposes. The Lexicon is thus unlikely to serve as a market substitute for the Harry Potter series and cause market harm.[160]

With regard to the two School Books, the picture was somewhat different:

> On the other hand, publication of the Lexicon could harm sales of Rowling's two companion books. Unless they sought to enjoy the companion books for their entertainment value alone, consumers who purchased the Lexicon would have scant incentive to purchase either of Rowling's companion books, as the information contained in these short works has been incorporated into the Lexicon almost wholesale. (Tr. (Murphy) at 419:10–19; *id.* (Rowling) at 104:2–11.) Because the Lexicon's use of the companion books is only marginally transformative, the Lexicon is likely to supplant the market for the companion books.[161]

The court also raised the possibility that the verbatim reproduction of the songs and poems in the novels could "impair the market for derivative works that Rowling is entitled or likely to license."[162]

On balance, the four statutory factors weighed against (though not, apparently, heavily against) a finding of fair use.[163] However, the opinion left plenty of room for RDR and Vander Ark to redesign the Lexicon around it, and they have done so. A revised Lexicon was released in January 2009, with the apparent consent of Rowling and Warner Brothers. According to Vander Ark, "We learned a lot at the trial about what was acceptable, what would follow the fair use guidelines[.] That was not clear before. There was no law on the books that made it clear what was

159 *Warner Bros. Entertainment*, 575 F.Supp.2d at 550.
160 *Warner Bros. Entertainment*, 575 F.Supp.2d at 550.
161 *Warner Bros. Entertainment*, 575 F.Supp.2d at 550–51.
162 *Warner Bros. Entertainment*, 575 F.Supp.2d at 551.
163 *Warner Bros. Entertainment*, 575 F.Supp.2d. at 551.

acceptable and what wasn't. So, coming out of the trial, I had a much better idea of what should go into the book."[164] The revised and now-released Lexicon bears this disclaimer on its cover:

> Harry Potter and the names of fictitious people and places in the Harry Potter novels are trademarks of Warner Bros. Entertainment, Inc. This book is not written, prepared, approved, or licensed by Warner Bros. Entertainment, Inc., Scholastic Corporation, Raincoast Books, Bloomsbury Publishing Plc, or J.K. Rowling, nor are the author, his staff members, www.HP-Lexicon.org, or the publisher in any way affiliated with Warner Bros. Entertainment, Inc., Scholastic Corporation, Raincoast Books, Bloomsbury Publishing Plc, J.K. Rowling, or any other person or company claiming an interest in the Harry Potter works.[165]

For fanfic authors generally, the opinion provides a certain reassurance. While numerous other opinions have addressed problems of copyright in characters, derivative works, and transformative works, the Lexicon case comes closer to the heart of modern fandom than these earlier decisions; it finally provides clear guidance, in a fandom context, for what fans can and cannot do.

For Vander Ark himself the eventual publication of the Lexicon comes at a high emotional cost. For Big Name Fans (BNFs) like Vander Ark, the fandom identity becomes an important part of overall identity, not least because of the thousands of hours of work required to create and maintain it. The Lexicon lawsuit not only presented the rare spectacle of an author turning on a BNF, but also divided fandom, subjecting Vander Ark to attacks from other fans and leaving him feeling "cast out of the 'Harry Potter community.'"[166] Vander Ark has said that he found the experience alienating and unpleasant in the extreme, although he has persevered in fandom and the eventual resolution of the controversy has brought about a gradual return to normal.[167]

---

164 See James Pritchard, *New Version of "Harry Potter" Guide to be Released*, www.thefreelibrary.com/New+version+of+'Harry+Potter'+guide+to+be+released-a01611735062 (visited October 18, 2010); see also "The Harry Potter Lexicon," e-mail from Steve Vander Ark to author, January 30, 2009; "Steve Vander Ark's Lexicon, Right to Write Center," e-mail from Roger D. Rapoport (RDR Books) to author, January 31, 2009 (copies on file with author); Steven Vander Ark, The Lexicon: An Unauthorized Guide to Harry Potter Fiction and Related Materials vii (2009).

165 Steve Vander Ark, The Lexicon: An Unauthorized Guide to Harry Potter Fiction and Related Materials (cover) (Muskegon, MI: RDR Books, 2009).

166 Hartocollis, *supra* note 137.

167 Conversation between Steve Vander Ark and author at Azkatraz (Harry Potter fan convention), San Francisco, July 19, 2009.

Chapter 5
Fanfic: The New Voyages

Fan v. fan: copyright in fanfic

Accusations by fans that other fans have plagiarized their fanfic are, sadly, not unknown. If the first, copied fanfic is itself an unlawful use of the underlying work—that is, an infringement on the copyright in the underlying work—that infringing fanfic is not itself protected by copyright.[1] Plagiarizing it may be unethical, but not illegal, although it may nonetheless have social consequences within the fandom.[2] If the first fanfic makes lawful use of the underlying work, however, it is copyrighted, as far as (but only as far as) any original contribution made by the fanfic author. Section 103(b) of the Copyright Act provides that:

> The copyright in a compilation or derivative work extends only to the material contributed by the author of such work, as distinguished from the preexisting material employed in the work, and does not imply any exclusive right in the preexisting material. The copyright in such work is independent of, and does not affect or enlarge the scope, duration, ownership, or subsistence of, any copyright protection in the preexisting material.[3]

Thus, where a fanfic is a parody or makes transformative or otherwise fair use of the underlying material, those elements of the fanfic that are the original work of the fan author are themselves protected, and, absent an assignment or transfer of copyright to a third party, that copyright is the property of the fan author. If, as sometimes happens, a second fan copies all or a substantial part of the fanfic and posts it online, claiming to be the author, that second fan has committed a legally actionable copyright infringement. No such case has yet been brought, and damages would be minimal in any event, the more so as copyright in the work is unlikely to have been registered either within three months of publication or prior to the infringement, as required by section 412 of the Copyright Act for the category into which most fanfics are likely to fall—works not commercially published and thus not pre-registered:

---

1 See 17 U.S.C. § 103(a).

2 See, for example, Casey Fiesler, *Everything I Need to Know I Learned from Fandom: How Existing Social Norms Can Help Shape the Next Generation of User-Generated Content*, 10 Vand. J. Ent. & Tech. L. 729, 748–50 (2008) (discussing several internal fandom disputes, including the Cassandra Claire/Clare controversy).

3 17 U.S.C. § 103(b).

> In any action under this title, other than an action brought for a violation of the rights of the author under section 106A(a), an action for infringement of the copyright of a work that has been preregistered under section 408(f) before the commencement of the infringement and that has an effective date of registration not later than the earlier of 3 months after the first publication of the work or 1 month after the copyright owner has learned of the infringement, or an action instituted under section 411(c), no award of statutory damages or of attorney's fees, as provided by sections 504 and 505, shall be made for —
> (1) any infringement of copyright in an unpublished work commenced before the effective date of its registration; or
> (2) any infringement of copyright commenced after first publication of the work and before the effective date of its registration, unless such registration is made within three months after the first publication of the work.[4]

Section 106A, the Visual Artists' Rights Act, is an oddity in U.S. copyright law: it protects the moral rights of authors of works of visual art. This might extend to the physical originals, if any, of works of fan art, or at least to those elements of a work of fan art that are original works of the fan artist, where the use of the elements of the underlying work is not unlawful. In other words, if one fan copies another fan artist's work (and the copied work is eligible for protection under section 106A) and presents it as his or her own in violation of Section 106A(a)(1)(a)'s protection of the artist's right of attribution, or violates any of the other protections in section 106A, the plaintiff may still be able to recover attorney's fees and statutory damages even though the copyright had not been registered before the infringement took place.[5]

---

4 17 U.S.C. § 412 (2008).

5 For other fanworks, including fanfic, infringement of most fan works would only entitle the copyright holder to attorney's fees and statutory damages if registered within three months of first publication or before the infringement, whichever is later. Section 408(f) allows preregistration of works to be commercially published; in the case of most fanfic, it is inapplicable, and the much smaller category of commercially published fanfic will be treated as any other commercially published work. Section 411(c) deals with "the case of a work consisting of sounds, images, or both, the first fixation of which is made simultaneously with its transmission"—that is, television or radio broadcasts, not a common venue for amateur fan works. Webcasts (but not, perhaps, podcasts) would be covered as well, but videos posted on YouTube or other websites would not. See *Live Nation Motor Sports, Inc.* v. *Davis*, No. 3:06-CV-276, 2007 WL 79311, at *3 (N.D.Tex. January 9, 2007) (defining "live broadcasts of the racing [event]" as those "via television, radio or internet websites"). Courts dealing with prerecorded segments in live television broadcasts have denied statutory damages and attorney's fees where the bulk of the work has been prerecorded, even with a live lead in (see *NBC Subsidiary (KCNC-TV), Inc.* v. *Broadcast Info. Servs., Inc.*, 717 F.Supp. 1449, 1452–53 (D.Colo. 1988); see also *Pac. & S. Co.* v. *Duncan*, 572 F.Supp. 1186, 1190, 1997–98 (N.D.Ga. 1983), *modified*, 744 F.2d 1490 (11th Cir. 1984)), but have carved out an apparent partial exception for news broadcasts: "Reports

With statutory damages and attorney's fees unavailable, and actual damages under 17 U.S.C. § 504(b) likely to be nil or negligible, fanfic-on-fanfic infringement is unlikely to become a significant source of litigation. Such disputes are more often about plagiarism than about actual copyright infringement, although the two are often confused and conflated by non-lawyers—perhaps further evidence of the distance between copyright law and those it attempts to regulate. Where no money is at stake, litigation is unlikely, even when there is a cognizable copyright claim; these disputes will continue to be resolved through the informal social structures of each fandom. Given the sometimes incandescent degree to which tempers can be heated in fan disputes, however, it is not impossible that some fans will ignore economic common sense and pursue litigation out of a need to be recognized as being in the right. In addition, as the outcome of fan disputes sometimes results in the ostracism of those determined by fan consensus to be in the wrong, secondary litigation—a defamation or intentional infliction of emotional distress action, for example—is possible as a result of a fanfic plagiarism/copyright dispute.

The three interests and their meaning for fanfic authors

As we have seen, three interests motivate attempts to suppress fanfic. The first, Niven's concern, is about misuse or misrepresentation of the story elements created by the author. Authors may feel quite strongly about this, but under U.S. copyright law, at least, it is a problem without a remedy. Niven has sought to address the problem while continuing to engage fandom by exerting some measure of control over fanfic through an approved, commercially published series, publishing stories about the kzinti by unknown as well as commercially established writers.[6]

The second, MZB's concern, is economic, but may also have no remedy. MZB issued a blanket prohibition on fanfic set in her Darkover universe because she was unable to publish a work that resembled a fan's story. This reaction seems excessive; many successful works of fiction become the subject of lawsuits claiming that some other author's idea was stolen, and the works on which these claims are based are rarely fanfic. J.K. Rowling herself was sued by an author named N.K. Stouffer, who claimed that the Harry Potter works copied important story elements, including the (non-copyrightable) word "Muggles," from her

---

of news stories, particularly stories breaking near broadcast time, cannot be registered in the copyright office prior to their transmission on a news program." *Georgia Television Co. v. TV News Clips of Atlanta, Inc.*, 718 F.Supp. 939, 952 (N.D.Ga. 1989), reconsideration denied 19 U.S.P.Q.2d 1372. Fan works, however, are unlikely to fall into this "breaking news" category.

6 Coincidentally, one of these authors is Jean Lamb, whose fanfic story "Masks" led to the Darkover fanfic ban. *See* Jean Lamb, *Galley Slave*, ANALOG, August 1996, reprinted in CHOOSING NAMES: MAN-KZIN WARS VIII 129 (Larry Niven, ed. 1998).

stories *The Legend of Rah and the Muggles*[7] and its sequels, including *Larry Potter and His Best Friend Lilly*.[8] Similar suits involving successful works are not uncommon, as we saw in Chapter 2 with the dispute between Georges Lewys and Eugene O'Neill. (It's not even the last such suit for Harry Potter; Rowling has since been sued by the estate of the late Adrian Jacobs, author of *The Adventures of Willy the Wizard: Livid Land*.[9]) The suit may involve a single story element, like the allegedly infringing Ewoks in *Preston* v. *20th Century Fox Canada*,[10] or multiple elements, as in *Rowling* v. *Stouffer* and in a claim that the baseball-themed fantasy novel *Summerland*,[11] published by Disney's subsidiary Miramax Books, infringed a similar story rejected by Disney.[12] While neither suit was successful, a distantly related suit was: author Art Buchwald, who had optioned a movie script, *King for a Day*, to Paramount, successfully claimed that Paramount had stolen the idea for the movie *Coming to America*.[13]

None of these claims were based on works of fanfic and banning fanfic did nothing to protect MZB against similar claims by authors who were not fanfic authors. The fourth prong, at least, of the section 107 test for fair use recognized MZB's right to control works that harm "the potential market for or value of" her work.[14] But most fanfic will not cause this particular type of market harm, which we can call story preemption, and most works that do cause such harm will not be fanfic. As ideas alone are not protected by copyright, damages, if any, would be minimal unless an author also copied a fan's expression. Ultimately the ban, and the subsequent decline of Darkover fandom, probably did more economic harm than the loss of *Contraband*—and had MZB sought to enforce the ban, many

---

7 Nancy K. Stouffer, The Legend of Rah and the Muggles (Thurman House, 2001) (1986). Thurman House was created by Ottenheimer Publishers "to republish the works of Nancy Stouffer." See Jim Milliott, *Ottenheimer Closing Down*, Publishers Weekly, June 17, 2002, available at www.publishersweekly.com/article/CA222465.html; see also *Scholastic, Inc.* v. *Stouffer*, 221 F. Supp.2d 425 (S.D.N.Y. 2002).

8 Nancy K. Stouffer, Larry Potter and His Best Friend Lilly (Thurman House, 2001) (original publication date disputed; the court found that Stouffer had submitted falsified evidence on this point); see *Stouffer*, 221 F. Supp. at 432–33.

9 Adrian Jacobs, The Adventures of Willy the Wizard: Livid Land (Bachman & Turner, 1987); Willy the Wizard home page, www.willythewizard.com; James Lumley, *'Willy the Wizard' Can Continue U.K. Court Duel Over 'Harry Potter' Novels*, Bloomberg, October 14, 2010, www.bloomberg.com/news/2010-10-14/-willy-the-wizard-can-continue-u-k-court-duel-over-harry-potter-novels.html.

10 *Preston* v. *20th Century Fox Canada, Ltd.*, 33 C.P.R. (3d) 242 (Fed. T.D. 1990), aff'd, 53 C.P.R. (3d) 407 (Fed. Ct. 1993).

11 Michael Chabon, Summerland (2002).

12 *Shanghold* v. *Walt Disney Co.*, No. 03 Civ. 9522 (WHP), 2006 WL 71672, at *5 (S.D.N.Y. January 12, 2006) (finding that the plaintiffs had fabricated evidence); see, for example, *Stouffer*, 246 F. Supp.2d 355.

13 *Buchwald* v. *Paramount Pictures Corp.*, 1990 WL 357611 (Cal. Super. Ct. 1990).

14 17 U.S.C. § 107(4) (2006).

or most fanfic authors would have been able to show that their works posed no economic harm. Had she not died prematurely at the age of 59 and instead lived to see the full flowering of online fandom, she might well have reversed her earlier decision.

The third, Rowling's concern, is related to but not identical to MZB's concern. As with MZB's, it may have been a mistake; Rowling owes her unprecedented commercial success to the global Harry Potter fandom phenomenon, which in turn owes its intensity to years of unpaid work by people like Vander Ark.[15] MZB would have had a more difficult time showing that *Masks* infringed any copyright interest of hers, because it copied no text from her works; she would have had to rely on a claim of copyright in the setting and characters. Rowling could show that large blocks of her text were copied verbatim; had this been done in a (non-parody) work of fiction, she would have had little trouble showing that the work was derivative and not fair use. Because the text was used in a reference work, however, the use was not derivative and was, for the most part, transformative.

Judge Patterson's decision seems to have been a relatively close call; he saw significant weaknesses in the plaintiffs' arguments, and indicated that a modified version of the Lexicon would not infringe. Although it was a setback for the Lexicon and left open the problem of fanfic using copyrighted characters, *Warner Brothers* v. *RDR Books* may yet point the way to a world in which most fan works, so long as it is not commercially published and does not simply copy stories or text, is fair use. In particular, the court's reinforcement of the idea that "based upon" does not equal derivative in a legal (as opposed to literary) sense should be welcomed by fans.

Whose fandom is it, anyway? Copyright law and the one-sided discourse

H.G. Wells' science fiction classic *The Time Machine*[16] has featured in countless latter-day works of fiction, commercially published or otherwise. Like Arthur Conan Doyle's Sherlock Holmes stories, it has become one of the taproot texts of the steampunk subgenre. *The Time Machine* was published in 1895; Wells died in 1946. *The Time Machine* is in the public domain in the United States and several other countries, but incredibly still in copyright in the United Kingdom and the other countries of the European Union, where the copyright will not expire until midnight on December 31, 2016—the end of the seventieth year after Wells' death.

Thus when the legendary Viennese actor, critic, and latter-day Renaissance man Egon Friedell wrote *Die Rückkehr der Zeitmaschine*, a sequel to *The Time Machine*, he was infringing Wells' copyright. At the time (the 1920s or 1930s) he seems not to have intended it to be published; it was, though the term did not

15 On the economics of a similar situation, see Derek E. Bambauer, *Faulty Math: The Economics of Legalizing the Grey Album*, 59 Ala. L. Rev. 345 (2008).

16 H.G. Wells, The Time Machine (London: Heinemann, 1895).

yet exist, fanfic. When it was finally published, in the year of Wells' death, it was no less (and no more) infringing than when he wrote it. (Friedell himself, sadly, was no longer alive to see the work published, having jumped to his death from his window to avoid arrest by the Nazis, his last words a warning to those on the sidewalk below.)

Friedell is known to modern readers not so much from his own work as from Peter Haage's Friedell-centered depiction of the literary and cultural scene in pre-war Vienna: *Der Partylöwe, der nur Bücher fraß: Egon Friedell und sein Kreis*.[17] Friedell, whose critical pen could strike fear into the authors of Vienna, was well aware of the incongruity in his writing fanfic based on the work of a foreign—British, no less!—author of socialist science fiction: though the central third of *Die Rückkehr der Zeitmaschine* is a straight-faced Wells pastiche, in its beginning and end sections the work takes the form of an epistolary novel in which a bumptious Friedell attempts to write to Wells, only to be intercepted by other members of Wells' circle who heap the most outrageous abuse upon him. This framework serves as a trellis on which Friedell's particular brand of snarky humor can blossom, as in this aside dismissing the German translation of *The Time Machine*: "Mr. Wells kann nämlich nicht Deutsch: dies dürfte die einzige Eigenschaft sein, die er mit seinem Übersetzer gemeinsam hat."[18] ["Mr. Wells does not know German: this may be the only property that he shares with his translator."][19]

Friedell's parody of a correspondence seeking permission to publish fanfic is a fairly accurate representation of what often happens between authors and fans in real life: to Friedell, Wells remains forever distant, unreachable. Many a popular author is similarly insulated from fandom by a coterie of hangers-on, employees, and others with a financial and/or emotional stake in the author's work; these secondary interest-holders are often far fiercer in their pursuit of perceived copyright infractions than the author himself or herself might have been. Even Tolkien, an author rather than a secondary interest-holder, was moved to protest when Ace Books reprinted all three volumes of the Lord of the Rings without seeking or obtaining permission, or paying royalties, and sold over a million

17 Peter Haage, Der Partylöwe, der nur Bücher frass: Egon Friedell und sein Kreis (Berlin: Claassen-Verlag, 1984).

18 Egon Freidell, Die Rückkehr der Zeitmaschine 6 (Berlin: Piper Verlag, 1946); the title is also sometimes given as Die Reise mit der Zeitmaschine, and should not be confused with the 1983 German TV film "Die Rückkehr der Zeitmaschine." An English translation, The Return of the Time Machine (Eddy C. Bertin, trans., New York: DAW Books, 1972; reprinted San Bernardino, CA: Borgo Press, 1987), exists but is hard to find. The German original is available at www.mobileread.com/forums/showthread.php?t=44938 (last visited October 19, 2010). (Note that the original is still in copyright in many countries, including the United Kingdom, Germany and Austria.)

19 Don't you hate it when authors throw passages in foreign languages into the middle of the text, and then make you look to the endnotes for a translation—or worse yet, don't provide one at all? I know I do.

copies.[20] (Ace's action seems astonishing today, and perhaps seemed astonishing when it happened in 1965, but was the norm in the days of Dickens and Trollope: before 1891 the U.S. provided no protection to foreign works.) But confronted with the noncommercial excesses and eccentricities of fandom, he only observed, perhaps a trifle condescendingly, that "Many young Americans are involved in the stories in a way that I'm not."[21]

The treatment of fanfic by content owners reflects a one-sided view of the conversation between authors and fans. This is not surprising, as that view has been embodied and embedded in Anglo-American copyright law since the Stationers' Company was first given a monopoly on printing books. Copyright law views the publication of works of fiction (or any works, for that matter, but fiction is our concern here) not as discourse but as monologue: the author delivers the content, and the audience passively receives it, with no part in shaping it. The world of commercially published works is akin to a classroom in which the teacher lectures without the inconvenience of interruption by questions or the effort of calling on students. This would be a terrible way to teach a class; at one time it might have been a valid way to publish fiction, but the communications and publication revolution brought about by the Internet has changed that.

Writers of fiction, or some of them, have always been in dialogue with fandom; as we have seen above, L. Frank Baum, Larry Niven, and Marion Zimmer Bradley all listened to and responded to their fandoms, at times incorporating fan ideas into their work, in the days before Netscape Navigator and Internet Explorer changed the world of words forever. Even Arthur Conan Doyle, whose Sherlock Holmes stories inspired the Baker Street Irregulars and the Sherlock Holmes Society, precursors to all modern fandoms, brought his fictional detective back from an apparently fatal fall over Switzerland's Reichenbach Falls in response to fan demand.[22]

But today the interaction between authors and fans is not limited to those fans who seek to impinge themselves on an author's attention. Fans post their creations online, accessible to all the world—and authors browse the Internet. While some may be able to resist the temptation to see what their own fandom has generated, others surely are not. Many, such as J.K. Rowling, speak approvingly of online fan content.

And fan content is reflected as an author's work progresses. J.K. Rowling's treatment of Harry's cousin Dudley Dursley provides an illustration. Dudley is Harry's chief tormentor for 10 of the first 11 years of his life. He is a bully who

---

20 Lev Grossman et al., *Feeding on Fantasy*, TIME, December 2, 2002, available at www.time.com/time/magazine/article/0,9171,1003803-2,00.html#ixzz0Zz5sPOj6 (last visited October 19, 2010).

21 Ibid.

22 Nor were they the first; the demand for more stories about a favorite character is probably as old as storytelling itself. See, for example, KENNETH MACLEISH, *Falstaff*, LONGMAN GUIDE TO SHAKESPEARE'S CHARACTERS 87–88 (Harlow: Longman, 1986).

beats up children younger and smaller than himself. And he is fat. When we first meet Dudley, his fatness is the first thing we learn about: "Ten years ago, there had been lots of pictures of what looked like a large pink beach ball wearing different-colored bonnets[.]"[23] The word "fat" is used repeatedly to describe him: "Dudley was very fat and hated exercise"; "He had a … thick, fat head"[24] and "fat legs"[25] on which he is seen not walking or running, but "waddling."[26] Dudley's greed for food, especially sweets, gets him in trouble, enabling Fred and George Weasley to play a rather dangerous prank on him by tricking him into eating Ton-Tongue Toffee.[27] Harry says Dudley looks "like a pig in a wig."[28] Hagrid agrees; after giving Dudley a pig's tail, he says "Meant ter turn him into a pig, but I suppose he was so much like a pig anyway there wasn't much left ter do."[29] Later we hear that Dudley is "roughly the size and weight of a young killer whale."[30] He has "piggy little eyes" and "five chins wobbling as he ate continually."[31]

All of this is part of the depiction of the Dursleys as a family of cartoon grotesques, but in the eyes of many fans it showed some serious fat acceptance and body image issues. When Rowling posted an opinion piece on her website attacking the media's obsession with thinness as an ideal, some fans responded with anger at the perceived hypocrisy. On her site, Rowling criticized language much like that she used to describe Dudley:

> "'Fat' is usually the first insult a girl throws at another girl when she wants to hurt her," I said; I could remember it happening when I was at school, and witnessing it among the teenagers I used to teach …
>
> [T]his everyday feature of female existence reminded me how strange and sick the "fat" insult is. I mean, is "fat" really the worst thing a human being can be? Is "fat" worse than "vindictive", "jealous", "shallow", "vain", "boring" or "cruel"?

Those words are also used as insults, of course; to be called "boring" is rarely considered a compliment, even if one might prefer, ever so slightly, to be among the Bores than among the Bored:

---

23 J.K. Rowling, Harry Potter and the Sorcerer's Stone 18 (New York: Scholastic, 1997).

24 Ibid., 20, 21.

25 J.K. Rowling, Harry Potter and the Chamber of Secrets 8 (New York: Scholastic, 1998).

26 Ibid., 8.

27 J.K. Rowling, Harry Potter and the Goblet of Fire 47–53 (New York: Scholastic, 2000).

28 J. K. Rowling (Sorcerer's Stone) 20.

29 Ibid., 59.

30 J.K. Rowling (Goblet of Fire) 27.

31 J.K. Rowling, Harry Potter and the Prisoner of Azkaban 16 (New York: Scholastic, 1999).

> Society is now one polish'd horde,
> Form'd of two mighty tribes, the Bores and Bored.[32]

She makes haste, though, to point out that while she is speaking in defense of the Fat, she is not of their number:

> I went to the British Book Awards that evening. After the award ceremony I bumped into a woman I hadn't seen for nearly three years. The first thing she said to me? "You've lost a lot of weight since the last time I saw you!"
>
> "Well," I said, slightly nonplussed, "the last time you saw me I'd just had a baby."
>
> What I felt like saying was, "I've produced my third child and my sixth novel since I last saw you. Aren't either of those things more important, more interesting, than my size?" But no—my waist looked smaller! Forget the kid and the book: finally, something to celebrate![33]

The point, though, is that:

> It's about what girls want to be, what they're told they should be, and how they feel about who they are. I've got two daughters who will have to make their way in this skinny-obsessed world, and it worries me, because I don't want them to be empty-headed, self-obsessed, emaciated clones; I'd rather they were independent, interesting, idealistic, kind, opinionated, original, funny—a thousand things, before "thin". And frankly, I'd rather they didn't give a gust of stinking chihuahua flatulence whether the woman standing next to them has fleshier knees than they do. Let my girls be Hermiones, rather than Pansy Parkinsons. Let them never be Stupid Girls. Rant over.[34]

This plea for fat acceptance has its limits: the "fleshier knees" she envisions belong not to her own daughters but to "the woman standing next to them," and Hermione

---

32 George Gordon, Lord Byron, Don Juan, Canto XIII, stanza 95 (Halifax: Milner & Sowerby, 1837), itself both fan fiction and parody.

33 J.K. Rowling, *For Girls Only, Probably* ..., available at www.jkrowling.com/textonly/en/extrastuff_view.cfm?id=22 (last visited October 19, 2010). In this, too, she echoes Byron:

> But from being farmers, we turn gleaners, gleaning
> The scanty but right-well thresh'd ears of truth ...
> Don Juan, Canto XIII, stanza 96.

34 J.K. Rowling, *For Girls Only, Probably* ..., available at www.jkrowling.com/textonly/en/extrastuff_view.cfm?id=22 (last visited October 19, 2010). Even the title of the post is odd, suggesting a lack of awareness that boys also have body image issues, let alone that Dudley might reinforce them.

Granger is not described as being even slightly overweight. And to some fans it seemed that previously Dudley's weight had been scapegoated:

> I am troubled by what I see as an inconsistency between her comments in the aforementioned post and her portrayal of fat characters, namely, Dudley.[35]

The problem the writer (a fan posting as idratherdream) perceives is J.K. Rowling's use of Dudley's fatness as a shorthand for his moral and intellectual failings:

> Except for Lord Voldemort himself (whose evil is much, much worse in kind and degree), Dudley (and a few other fat characters, such as Crabbe and Goyle) are the only characters whose moral failings (greediness, bullying, stupidity) are manifested in physical appearance. Of course, Rowling may not be doing this intentionally. She's simply making use of a sort of cultural shorthand: all she has to do is write "his bottom drooped over either side of the kitchen chair" and we read "greedy & stupid."[36]

The treatment of Dudley and his weight reaches its nadir when Dudley is in turned bullied by Fred & George Weasley,

> who find Dudley a perfect target for a little bullying of their own … [T]he image of Dudley snatching candy off the floor when the twins drop it and stuffing it in his mouth is one of the most stereotypical and offensive fictional descriptions of a fat person I have ever read. As a fat person, Dudley will transgress all social and moral codes (by crawling, eating off the floor, stealing, breaking his diet, being rude to guests) in order to get food, making him unfit for society[.][37]

Predictably, fans lined up on both sides of the controversy. But the anger expressed over the authorial treatment of Dudley and his physique was strong and real, and perhaps not coincidentally the presentation of Dudley soon changed. By 2007 he was described as "Harry's large, blond, muscular cousin[.]"[38] Some may think Rowling missed the point of the objections: this change from pig in a wig to muscularity coincided with Dudley's spiritual transformation, apparently in progress since his encounter with the Dementors at the beginning of the fifth volume. (At the time of that encounter Dudley's muscularity was already emerging, and rather than "fat" he was "as vast as ever, but a year's hard dieting and the

---

35 "Why is Dudley Fat?" post by idratherdream, April 12, 2006, 11:40 PM, available at www.leakylounge.com/Dudley-Fat-t26515.html&pid=782162&mode=threaded#entry782162 (last visited October 19 2010).

36 Ibid.

37 Ibid.

38 J.K. Rowling, Harry Potter and the Deathly Hallows 30 (New York: Scholastic, 2007).

discovery of a new talent had wrought a change in his physique ... Dudley had recently become the Junior Heavyweight Inter-School Boxing Champion."[39]) It is impossible to know to what extent the change was influenced by fan dissatisfaction with the descriptions of Dudley—it seems likely, though, that there was at least some influence, and that Rowling became aware of the dissatisfaction by surfing Harry Potter fan sites. Fanfic and fan nonfiction are not always easily separable; both are vehicles through which fans engage in dialogue with the works and the author. By critically engaging the work and the author, idratherdream is able to enjoy it more fully; the nonfiction criticism of Rowling's statements serves much the same equalizing purpose as the criticism in the fanfic "Five Years Even Later" described in Chapter 1.[40]

Fans in the author's seat

Through fanfic and other fan works, fandom is now in discourse with authors as never before. Fanfic gives fans a voice, yet copyright law ensures that the fans remain outsiders. Pervading the discourse is the belief, accurate or not, that the authors can shut down the fans at any time, if they are willing to face the economic consequences, or if, like Rowling with Vander Ark, their creation has become an industry in itself, an unstoppable economic juggernaut. As we have seen, most fan works are in fact fair use or otherwise permissible; the problem that remains is that few fans have the resources to defend their uses in court, and if threatened with a lawsuit are likely to surrender rather than fight. The fact that the fans often idolize the authors, while the authors are rarely even aware of individual fans, further aggravates the inequality.

As the disputes we have examined show, informal agreements between individual authors and their fans won't work, or at least won't work forever.[41]

---

39 J.K. Rowling, Harry Potter and the Order of the Phoenix 11 (New York: Scholastic, 2007).

40 Alaskaravenclaw, Epi-epilogue: 5 Years Even Later, July 27, 2007, available at http://alaskaravenclaw.livejournal.com/963.html (last visited October 19, 2010), discussed in text accompanying notes29–30 in Chapter 1, *supra*.

41 For a variety of views on the often-uneasy accommodation between fans and content owners, see, for example, Sean Kirkpatrick, *Like Holding a Bird: What the Prevalence of Fansubbing Can Teach Us About the Use of Strategic Selective Copyright Enforcement*, 21 Temp. Envtl. L. & Tech. J. 131 (2003); Erika S. Koster & Jim Shatz-Akin, *Set Phasers on Stun: Handling Internet Fan Sites*, 15 No. 1 Computer Law. 18 (1998); Cecilia Ogbu, *I Put Up a Website About My Favorite Show and All I Got Was This Lousy Cease-and-Desist Letter: The Intersection of Fan Sites, Internet Culture, and Copyright Owners*, 12 S. Cal. Interdisc. L.J. 279 (2003); Edward Lee, *Warming Up to User-Generated Content*, 2008 U. Ill. L. Rev. 1459 (2008); Megan Richardson & David Tan, *The Art of Retelling: Harry Potter and Copyright in a Fan-Literature Era*, 14 Media & Arts L. Rev. 31 (2009); Steven A. Hetcher, *Using Social Norms to Regulate Fan Fiction and Remix Culture*, 157 U. Pa. L. Rev. 1869 (2009); Jordan Hatcher, *Of Otakus and Fansubs: A Critical Look at*

They fail in one of two ways. Either some fan goes too far for the author to tolerate, resulting in an attempt to crack down on fanfic in general (usually in the form of the announcement of a "no fanfic" policy by the author, but sometimes in the form of legal action, as in the case of Warner Brother's actions against some unauthorized Harry Potter novels and fan sites), or the copyright interests are passed on to the author's heirs or transferred to some corporate entity lacking the author's individual rapport with fandom. Ultimately a lasting accommodation will have to be reached, under which the economic rights of authors remain protected while fans, in turn, are protected from chilling-effect harassment or persecution over the production of fan works that, for any or all of the reasons we've explored, do not violate copyright.

The line between fan and author is already beginning to blur, as commercially published authors write fanblogs and fans become published authors. Some works, like Alexandre Philippe's documentary on Klingon speakers, *Earthlings: Ugly Bags of Mostly Water*, are hard to classify as fan works or works on fandom. More recently, with *The People vs. George Lucas*, Philippe has provided a voice for fans to express their frustrations with the later work of Star Wars creator George Lucas. Philippe is not simply a fan voicing his frustrations; the movie is composed partly of footage submitted by fans, as well as interviews with people on both the "fan" and "author" side of the equation.[42] Philippe watched over 600 hours of fan-submitted video, "every minute of it, several times," and says "the fan submissions gave the film a truly unique voice and personality. This film is just as much about the fans as it's about George; and it's dedicated to them, because they played a big part in it. They contributed their footage, ideas, information, and a great deal of passion; so it's a participatory doc in the truest sense."[43]

The People vs. George Lucas is an act of empowerment, but fandom is already powerful, and is just beginning to realize the fact. Fandom is big business. In San Diego Comic-Con is the city's largest annual convention, selling out its full

Anime Online in Light of Current Issues in Copyright Law, 2 SCRIPT-ED 551 (2005); Sean Leonard, *Celebrating Two Decades of Unlawful Progress: Fan Distribution, Proselytization Commons, and the Explosive Growth of Japanese Animation*, 12 UCLA ENT. L. REV. 189 (2005); Leanne Stendell, Comment, *Fanfic and Fan Fact: How Current Copyright Law Ignores the Reality of Copyright Owner and Consumer Interests in Fan Fiction*, 58 SMU L. REV. 1551 (2005); Justin Hughes, *Recoding Intellectual Property and Overlooked Audience Interest*, 77 TEX. L. REV. 923 (1999).

42 Philippe's interviewees include fan/author Neil Gaiman, who seems to have put in quite a few appearances in this book.

43 *Wendy Mitchell, Documentary Reveals the Love-Hate Relationship of George Lucas Fans*, ENTERTAINMENT WEEKLY, March 11, 2010, available at http://popwatch.ew.com/2010/03/11/george-lucas-documentary (last visited October 19, 2010); see also Alexandre O. Philippe, *The People vs. George Lucas* (2010); Erik Childress, *SXSW Interview: 'The People vs. George Lucas' Director Alexandre O. Philippe*, CINEMATICAL, March 11, 2010, available at www.cinematical.com/2010/03/11/sxsw-interview-the-people-vs-george-lucas-director-alexandre (last visited October 19, 2010).

2009 allotment of 126,000 tickets two months before opening day; the four days of the convention are the highest hotel-occupancy days of the year, during which visitors add over $16 million to the city's economy. San Diego now worries about losing Comic-Con as it once worried about losing its professional sports teams or military bases: Comic-Con's contract with the San Diego Convention Center runs out in 2012, and the city is considering expanding the Convention Center to entice Comic-Con to stay beyond that date.[44]

To infinity and beyond: we are all the author now

A personal anecdote may illustrate the interactive nature of published works in the Internet age: in the course of researching this book, I looked at the Wikipedia entry "Legal Issues with Fan Fiction." The last time I had seen this, it had not been a separate entry, but a brief paragraph or two within the "Fan fiction" entry. To my surprise, the entry now included a substantial amount of information that, to the best of my knowledge, had not been assembled into one place before an earlier article of mine,[45] including the information about the MZB and Larry Niven/Elf Sternberg controversies discussed in this book. While it's possible some other researcher had followed the same line of reasoning and research at the same time, a more likely explanation was that someone had read a draft of my article posted on the Social Science Research Network (SSRN) or the Berkeley Electronic Press, and adapted the ideas for Wikipedia.

There was no question of copyright infringement, of course. I could claim no copyright in facts or ideas, only in their expression—and it was not my particular expression of those facts and ideas that had been copied, but the underlying facts and ideas themselves. I might (or might not) have been the first to assemble them in one place, but as the Supreme Court made clear in *Feist Publications, Inc.* v. *Rural Telephone Service Co.*, copyright law provides no protection for the sweat of my brow.[46] And as someone who's always been unreceptive, to put it mildly, to the idea that U.S. copyright law should incorporate non-economic rights—that is, the "moral rights" described in Article 6*bis* of the Berne Convention,[47] particularly the right of attribution (or, if you must, the "right of paternity"), it would be hypocritical (not to mention pointless, under U.S. law) to argue that I should be acknowledged as the author of the work.

---

44 Conversation with San Diego City Council member Kevin Faulconer, February 19, 2010; Maria Connor, *Comic-Con Nudges Dollars North*, Del Mar Times, July 24, 2009, at 1.

45 Aaron Schwabach, *The Harry Potter Lexicon and the World of Fandom: Fan Fiction, Outsider Works, and Copyright*, 70 U. Pitt. L. Rev. (2009).

46 *Feist Publications, Inc.* v. *Rural Telephone Service Co.*, 499 U.S. 340 (1991).

47 Berne Convention for the Protection of Literary and Artistic Works, art. 6*bis*, September 9, 1886, as revised at Paris, July 24, 1971, and amended on September 29, 1979, 25 U.S.T. 1341, 828 U.N.T.S. 221.

Any griping against Wikipedia would have defeated the point of my own work in any case. The reason I had written the article was to get the knowledge out there, and having the information picked up by Wikipedia was a sign that I had succeeded. But a desire to stay involved in the discourse, or perhaps merely ego, left a persistent feeling of dissatisfaction. Then I remembered: Wikipedia is not a unidirectional communication; it is a pool for the knowledge of the entire human race. It is an interactive conversation, not a lecture; I can contribute too. So I took a step I'd never taken before: I edited the "External Links" section to include a link to my article on SSRN, and was content.

Wikipedia, of course, is designed and built as an open-source publication; it has no "author," or rather, all of us are the author. Surely it is different from, say, Harry Potter? Yet humanities scholars have known for ages that reading is an interactive process, with the result created in the mind of the reader as well as the mind of the author. As we saw, Judge Posner of the Seventh Circuit recognized this in *Gaiman* v. *McFarlane*: "A reader of unillustrated fiction completes the work in his mind."[48] To a lesser extent, the same may be true of works in other media, and works of nonfiction, as well. The communications revolution of the past two decades has made it possible for this conversation between author and reader to become not unilateral or even bilateral, but multilateral. (With that in mind, anyone wishing to contact me to discuss this work may do so by e-mail at aarons@tjsl.edu.) The nature of conversation has changed; far more of it now takes place online and in text. Readers want to talk about what they read, and audiences want to talk about what they've seen; any work of fiction is the starting point for multiple conversations. The fact that some participants in the conversation are getting paid (albeit not very much, in most cases) to take part while others are paying to take part should not allow the former to dictate the terms of the conversation to the latter.

I will not end with some naïve plea that copyright law should be revised to protect fanfic; indeed, as we have seen, in some cases—notably parody—it already does. In others, such as vidding, it probably does not; the best way to deal with the problem may be, as YouTube has already done, to license songs for vidding. So far fans have found YouTube's AudioSwap somewhat underwhelming due to technical issues and a poor selection of songs, but the proper remedy for that problem would seem to be the marketplace rather than legislation. Fanfic licenses might be included with other works as well, or offered at an additional cost.

However, intellectual property law in general, and copyright in particular, are in a greater state of upheaval and uncertainty than they have been in centuries. The future of content is likely to see some major changes. Textbooks, for example, can already be tailored to a particular class, adding, subtracting and modifying content without consulting the author.[49] Perhaps in the future authors will issue

48 *Gaiman* v. *McFarlane*, 360 F.3d 644, 661 (7th Cir. 2004).

49 See, for example, Motoko Rich, *Textbooks that Professors Can Rewrite Digitally*, N.Y. Times, February 22, 2010. On possible new directions in the fan/content owner

novels, and, when technology permits, even video entertainment, in this form as well, further erasing the line between author and audience. It is to be hoped that whatever new regime ultimately emerges will have a place in it for fan works and fandom.

relationship in copyright law, see, for example, Deborah Tussey, *From Fan Sites to File Sharing: Personal Use in Cyberspace*, 35 GA. L. REV. 1129 (2001); Jessica Litman, *Creative Reading*, 70 LAW & CONTEMP. PROBS. 175 (2007) ("by ignoring the central importance of readers, listeners, viewers, and players in the copyright scheme, we have all but conceded that the essential policy question in determining whether a use of copyrighted material should be lawful is the way the use looks from the viewpoint of the copyright owner"); Rebecca Tushnet, *User-Generated Discontent: Transformation in Practice*, 31 COLUM. J.L. & ARTS 497 (2008) ("User-generated fair use principles offer their own definitions of transformation, both implicit and explicit, that draw not only on formal copyright law but also on the practices of specific creative communities" and "Groups acting together can define and defend fair use from the perspective of individual creators.")

Appendices

I. G.K. Chesterton on parody

Parody is accorded a special status in U.S. copyright law, but as so often happens when words are defined by courts or legislatures for legal purposes, the definition differs somewhat from that used in the wider world. In this essay on Bret Harte, Gilbert Keith Chesterton provides a thoughtful analysis of the essence of parody.

Gilbert Keith Chesterton, Bret Harte, in Varied Types 179 (Project Gutenberg, ed., 2004) (1908), available at http://infomotions.com/etexts/gutenberg/dirs/1/4/2/0/14203/14203.htm (last visited March 2, 2010).

> America is under a kind of despotism of humour. Everyone is afraid of humour: the meanest of human nightmares … America has laughed at things magnificently, with Gargantuan reverberations of laughter. But she has not even begun to learn the richer lesson of laughing with them.

* * *

> Mere derision, mere contempt, never produced or could produce parody. A man who simply despises Paderewski for having long hair is not necessarily fitted to give an admirable imitation of his particular touch on the piano. If a man wishes to parody Paderewski's style of execution, he must emphatically go through one process first: he must admire it, and even reverence it. Bret Harte had a real power of imitating great authors, as in his parodies on Dumas, on Victor Hugo, on Charlotte Bronte. This means, and can only mean, that he had perceived the real beauty, the real ambition of Dumas and Victor Hugo and Charlotte Bronte. To take an example, Bret Harte has in his imitation of Hugo a passage like this: "M. Madeline was, if possible, better than M. Myriel. M. Myriel was an angel. M. Madeline was a good man." I do not know whether Victor Hugo ever used this antithesis; but I am certain that he would have used it and thanked his stars if he had thought of it. This is real parody, inseparable from admiration. It is the same in the parody of Dumas, which is arranged on the system of "Aramis killed three of them. Porthos three. Athos three." You cannot write that kind of thing unless you have first exulted in the arithmetical ingenuity of the plots of Dumas. It is the same in the parody of Charlotte Bronte, which opens with a dream of a storm-beaten cliff, containing jewels and pelicans. Bret Harte could not have written it unless he had really understood the triumph of the Brontes, the triumph

of asserting that great mysteries lie under the surface of the most sullen life, and that the most real part of a man is in his dreams.

This kind of parody is for ever removed from the purview of ordinary American humour. Can anyone imagine Mark Twain, that admirable author, writing even a tolerable imitation of authors so intellectually individual as Hugo or Charlotte Bronte? Mark Twain would yield to the spirit of contempt which destroys parody. All those who hate authors fail to satirise them, for they always accuse them of the wrong faults. The enemies of Thackeray call him a worldling, instead of what he was, a man too ready to believe in the goodness of the unworldly. The enemies of Meredith call his gospel too subtle, instead of what it is, a gospel, if anything, too robust. And it is this vulgar misunderstanding which we find in most parody—which we find in all American parody—but which we never find in the parodies of Bret Harte.

"The skies they were ashen and sober,
The streets they were dirty and drear,
It was the dark month of October,
In that most immemorial year.
Like the skies, I was perfectly sober,
But my thoughts they were palsied and sear,
Yes, my thoughts were decidedly queer."

This could only be written by a genuine admirer of Edgar Allan Poe, who permitted himself for a moment to see the fun of the thing. Parody might indeed be defined as the worshipper's half-holiday.

II. Selected excerpts from U.S. copyright statutes

U.S. copyright law is in flux; Congress and the courts are constantly called upon to tinker with it. Up-to-date versions of Title 17 of the United States Code—the Copyright Code—are available at many places online. Two reliable sources are the United States Copyright Office website at www.copyright.gov/title17/ and Cornell University's Legal Information Institute at www.law.cornell.edu/uscode/html/uscode17/usc_sup_01_17.html. The sections reproduced below may well be out of date by the time you read them; they are included here as a quick reference while reading the text.

17 U.S.C. § 101. Definitions

Except as otherwise provided in this title, as used in this title, the following terms and their variant forms mean the following:

An "anonymous work" is a work on the copies or phonorecords of which no natural person is identified as author.

* * *

"Audiovisual works" are works that consist of a series of related images which are intrinsically intended to be shown by the use of machines, or devices such as projectors, viewers, or electronic equipment, together with accompanying sounds, if any, regardless of the nature of the material objects, such as films or tapes, in which the works are embodied.

* * *

"Copies" are material objects, other than phonorecords, in which a work is fixed by any method now known or later developed, and from which the work can be perceived, reproduced, or otherwise communicated, either directly or with the aid of a machine or device. The term "copies" includes the material object, other than a phonorecord, in which the work is first fixed.

* * *

"Copyright owner", with respect to any one of the exclusive rights comprised in a copyright, refers to the owner of that particular right.

A work is "created" when it is fixed in a copy or phonorecord for the first time; where a work is prepared over a period of time, the portion of it that has been fixed at any particular time constitutes the work as of that time, and where the work has been prepared in different versions, each version constitutes a separate work.

A "derivative work" is a work based upon one or more preexisting works, such as a translation, musical arrangement, dramatization, fictionalization, motion picture version, sound recording, art reproduction, abridgment, condensation, or any other form in which a work may be recast, transformed, or adapted. A work consisting of editorial revisions, annotations, elaborations, or other modifications which, as a whole, represent an original work of authorship, is a "derivative work".

* * *

The term "financial gain" includes receipt, or expectation of receipt, of anything of value, including the receipt of other copyrighted works.

A work is "fixed" in a tangible medium of expression when its embodiment in a copy or phonorecord, by or under the authority of the author, is sufficiently permanent or stable to permit it to be perceived, reproduced, or otherwise communicated for a period of more than transitory duration. A work consisting of sounds, images, or both, that are being transmitted, is "fixed" for purposes of this title if a fixation of the work is being made simultaneously with its transmission.

* * *

A "joint work" is a work prepared by two or more authors with the intention that their contributions be merged into inseparable or interdependent parts of a unitary whole.

"Literary works" are works, other than audiovisual works, expressed in words, numbers, or other verbal or numerical symbols or indicia, regardless of the nature of the material objects, such as books, periodicals, manuscripts, phonorecords, film, tapes, disks, or cards, in which they are embodied.

"Motion pictures" are audiovisual works consisting of a series of related images which, when shown in succession, impart an impression of motion, together with accompanying sounds, if any.

* * *

To "perform" a work means to recite, render, play, dance, or act it, either directly or by means of any device or process or, in the case of a motion picture or other audiovisual work, to show its images in any sequence or to make the sounds accompanying it audible.

* * *

A "pseudonymous work" is a work on the copies or phonorecords of which the author is identified under a fictitious name.

"Publication" is the distribution of copies or phonorecords of a work to the public by sale or other transfer of ownership, or by rental, lease, or lending. The offering to distribute copies or phonorecords to a group of persons for purposes of further distribution, public performance, or public display, constitutes publication. A public performance or display of a work does not of itself constitute publication.

To perform or display a work "publicly" means—

(1) to perform or display it at a place open to the public or at any place where a substantial number of persons outside of a normal circle of a family and its social acquaintances is gathered; or
(2) to transmit or otherwise communicate a performance or display of the work to a place specified by clause (1) or to the public, by means of any device or process, whether the members of the public capable of receiving the performance or display receive it in the same place or in separate places and at the same time or at different times.

"Registration", for purposes of sections 205(c)(2), 405, 406, 410(d), 411, 412, and 506(e), means a registration of a claim in the original or the renewed and extended term of copyright.

"Sound recordings" are works that result from the fixation of a series of musical, spoken, or other sounds, but not including the sounds accompanying a motion picture or other audiovisual work, regardless of the nature of the material objects, such as disks, tapes, or other phonorecords, in which they are embodied.

* * *

For purposes of section 411, a work is a "United States work" only if—

(1) in the case of a published work, the work is first published—
  (A) in the United States;
  (B) simultaneously in the United States and another treaty party or parties, whose law grants a term of copyright protection that is the same as or longer than the term provided in the United States;
  (C) simultaneously in the United States and a foreign nation that is not a treaty party; or
  (D) in a foreign nation that is not a treaty party, and all of the authors of the work are nationals, domiciliaries, or habitual residents of, or in the case of an audiovisual work legal entities with headquarters in, the United States;
(2) in the case of an unpublished work, all the authors of the work are nationals, domiciliaries, or habitual residents of the United States, or, in the case of an unpublished audiovisual work, all the authors are legal entities with headquarters in the United States; or
(3) in the case of a pictorial, graphic, or sculptural work incorporated in a building or structure, the building or structure is located in the United States.

* * *

17 U.S.C. § 102. Subject matter of copyright: in general

(a) Copyright protection subsists, in accordance with this title, in original works of authorship fixed in any tangible medium of expression, now known or later developed, from which they can be perceived, reproduced, or otherwise communicated, either directly or with the aid of a machine or device. Works of authorship include the following categories:

(1) literary works;
(2) musical works, including any accompanying words;
(3) dramatic works, including any accompanying music;
(4) pantomimes and choreographic works;
(5) pictorial, graphic, and sculptural works;
(6) motion pictures and other audiovisual works;
(7) sound recordings; and
(8) architectural works.

(b) In no case does copyright protection for an original work of authorship extend to any idea, procedure, process, system, method of operation, concept, principle, or discovery, regardless of the form in which it is described, explained, illustrated, or embodied in such work.

17 U.S.C. § 106. Exclusive rights in copyrighted works

Subject to sections 107 through 122, the owner of copyright under this title has the exclusive rights to do and to authorize any of the following:

(1) to reproduce the copyrighted work in copies or phonorecords;
(2) to prepare derivative works based upon the copyrighted work;
(3) to distribute copies or phonorecords of the copyrighted work to the public by sale or other transfer of ownership, or by rental, lease, or lending;
(4) in the case of literary, musical, dramatic, and choreographic works, pantomimes, and motion pictures and other audiovisual works, to perform the copyrighted work publicly;
(5) in the case of literary, musical, dramatic, and choreographic works, pantomimes, and pictorial, graphic, or sculptural works, including the individual images of a motion picture or other audiovisual work, to display the copyrighted work publicly; and
(6) in the case of sound recordings, to perform the copyrighted work publicly by means of a digital audio transmission.

17 U.S.C. § 106A. Rights of certain authors to attribution and integrity

(a) Rights of attribution and integrity.--Subject to section 107 and independent of the exclusive rights provided in section 106, the author of a work of visual art—

(1) shall have the right—

(A) to claim authorship of that work, and

(B) to prevent the use of his or her name as the author of any work of visual art which he or she did not create;

(2) shall have the right to prevent the use of his or her name as the author of the work of visual art in the event of a distortion, mutilation, or other modification of the work which would be prejudicial to his or her honor or reputation; and

(3) subject to the limitations set forth in section 113(d), shall have the right—

(A) to prevent any intentional distortion, mutilation, or other modification of that work which would be prejudicial to his or her honor or reputation, and any intentional distortion, mutilation, or modification of that work is a violation of that right, and

(B) to prevent any destruction of a work of recognized stature, and any intentional or grossly negligent destruction of that work is a violation of that right.

* * *

17 U.S.C. § 107. Limitations on exclusive rights: fair use

Notwithstanding the provisions of sections 106 and 106A, the fair use of a copyrighted work, including such use by reproduction in copies or phonorecords or by any other means specified by that section, for purposes such as criticism, comment, news reporting, teaching (including multiple copies for classroom use), scholarship, or research, is not an infringement of copyright. In determining whether the use made of a work in any particular case is a fair use the factors to be considered shall include—

(1) the purpose and character of the use, including whether such use is of a commercial nature or is for nonprofit educational purposes;

(2) the nature of the copyrighted work;

(3) the amount and substantiality of the portion used in relation to the copyrighted work as a whole; and

(4) the effect of the use upon the potential market for or value of the copyrighted work.

The fact that a work is unpublished shall not itself bar a finding of fair use if such finding is made upon consideration of all the above factors.

17 U.S.C. § 408. Copyright registration in general

(a) Registration Permissive.—At any time during the subsistence of the first term of copyright in any published or unpublished work in which the copyright was secured before January 1, 1978, and during the subsistence of any copyright secured on or after that date, the owner of copyright or of any exclusive right in the work may obtain registration of the copyright claim by delivering to the Copyright Office the deposit specified by this section, together with the application and fee specified by sections 409 and 708. Such registration is not a condition of copyright protection.

(b) Deposit for Copyright Registration.—Except as provided by subsection (c), the material deposited for registration shall include—

(1) in the case of an unpublished work, one complete copy or phonorecord;

(2) in the case of the published work, two complete copies or phonorecords of the best edition;

(3) in the case of a work first published outside the United States, one complete copy or phonorecord as so published;

(4) in the case of a contribution to a collective work, one complete copy or phonorecord of the best edition of the collective work.

Copies or phonorecords deposited for the Library of Congress under section 407 may be used to satisfy the deposit provisions of this section, if they are accompanied by the prescribed application and fee, and by any additional identifying material that the Register may, by regulation, require. The Register shall also prescribe regulations establishing requirements under which copies or phonorecords acquired for the Library of Congress under subsection (e) of section 407, otherwise than by deposit, may be used to satisfy the deposit provisions of this section.

* * *

(f) Preregistration of works being prepared for commercial distribution.—

(1) Rulemaking.—Not later than 180 days after the date of enactment of this subsection, the Register of Copyrights shall issue regulations to establish procedures for preregistration of a work that is being prepared for commercial distribution and has not been published.

(2) Class of works.—The regulations established under paragraph (1) shall permit preregistration for any work that is in a class of works that the Register determines has had a history of infringement prior to authorized commercial distribution.

(3) Application for registration.—Not later than 3 months after the first publication of a work preregistered under this subsection, the applicant shall submit to the Copyright Office—

(A) an application for registration of the work;

(B) a deposit; and

(C) the applicable fee.

(4) Effect of untimely application.—An action under this chapter for infringement of a work preregistered under this subsection, in a case in which the infringement commenced no later than 2 months after the first publication of the work, shall be dismissed if the items described in paragraph (3) are not submitted to the Copyright Office in proper form within the earlier of—

(A) 3 months after the first publication of the work; or
(B) 1 month after the copyright owner has learned of the infringement.

17 U.S.C. § 409. Application for copyright registration

The application for copyright registration shall be made on a form prescribed by the Register of Copyrights and shall include--

(1) the name and address of the copyright claimant;
(2) in the case of a work other than an anonymous or pseudonymous work, the name and nationality or domicile of the author or authors, and, if one or more of the authors is dead, the dates of their deaths;
(3) if the work is anonymous or pseudonymous, the nationality or domicile of the author or authors;
(4) in the case of a work made for hire, a statement to this effect;
(5) if the copyright claimant is not the author, a brief statement of how the claimant obtained ownership of the copyright;
(6) the title of the work, together with any previous or alternative titles under which the work can be identified;
(7) the year in which creation of the work was completed;
(8) if the work has been published, the date and nation of its first publication;
(9) in the case of a compilation or derivative work, an identification of any preexisting work or works that it is based on or incorporates, and a brief, general statement of the additional material covered by the copyright claim being registered;
(10) in the case of a published work containing material of which copies are required by section 601 to be manufactured in the United States, the names of the persons or organizations who performed the processes specified by subsection (c) of section 601 with respect to that material, and the places where those processes were performed; and
(11) any other information regarded by the Register of Copyrights as bearing upon the preparation or identification of the work or the existence, ownership, or duration of the copyright.

If an application is submitted for the renewed and extended term provided for in section 304(a)(3)(A) and an original term registration has not been made, the Register may request information with respect to the existence, ownership, or duration of the copyright for the original term.

17 U.S.C. § 411. Registration and civil infringement actions

(a) Except for an action brought for a violation of the rights of the author under section 106A(a), and subject to the provisions of subsection (b), no civil action for infringement of the copyright in any United States work shall be instituted until preregistration or registration of the copyright claim has been made in accordance with this title. In any case, however, where the deposit, application, and fee required for registration have been delivered to the Copyright Office in proper form and registration has been refused, the applicant is entitled to institute a civil action for infringement if notice thereof, with a copy of the complaint, is served on the Register of Copyrights. The Register may, at his or her option, become a party to the action with respect to the issue of registrability of the copyright claim by entering an appearance within sixty days after such service, but the Register's failure to become a party shall not deprive the court of jurisdiction to determine that issue.

*   *   *

17 U.S.C. § 412. Registration as prerequisite to certain remedies for infringement

In any action under this title, other than an action brought for a violation of the rights of the author under section 106A(a), an action for infringement of the copyright of a work that has been preregistered under section 408(f) before the commencement of the infringement and that has an effective date of registration not later than the earlier of 3 months after the first publication of the work or 1 month after the copyright owner has learned of the infringement, or an action instituted under section 411(c), no award of statutory damages or of attorney's fees, as provided by sections 504 and 505, shall be made for—

(1) any infringement of copyright in an unpublished work commenced before the effective date of its registration; or

(2) any infringement of copyright commenced after first publication of the work and before the effective date of its registration, unless such registration is made within three months after the first publication of the work.

17 U.S.C. § 504. Remedies for infringement: damages and profits

(a) In General.—Except as otherwise provided by this title, an infringer of copyright is liable for either—

(1) the copyright owner's actual damages and any additional profits of the infringer, as provided by subsection (b); or

(2) statutory damages, as provided by subsection (c).

(b) Actual Damages and Profits.—The copyright owner is entitled to recover the actual damages suffered by him or her as a result of the infringement, and any profits of the infringer that are attributable to the infringement and are not taken into account in computing the actual damages. In establishing the infringer's profits, the copyright owner is required to present proof only of the infringer's gross revenue, and the infringer is required to prove his or her deductible expenses and the elements of profit attributable to factors other than the copyrighted work.

(c) Statutory Damages.—

(1) Except as provided by clause (2) of this subsection, the copyright owner may elect, at any time before final judgment is rendered, to recover, instead of actual damages and profits, an award of statutory damages for all infringements involved in the action, with respect to any one work, for which any one infringer is liable individually, or for which any two or more infringers are liable jointly and severally, in a sum of not less than $750 or more than $30,000 as the court considers just. For the purposes of this subsection, all the parts of a compilation or derivative work constitute one work.

(2) In a case where the copyright owner sustains the burden of proving, and the court finds, that infringement was committed willfully, the court in its discretion may increase the award of statutory damages to a sum of not more than $150,000. In a case where the infringer sustains the burden of proving, and the court finds, that such infringer was not aware and had no reason to believe that his or her acts constituted an infringement of copyright, the court in its discretion may reduce the award of statutory damages to a sum of not less than $200. The court shall remit statutory damages in any case where an infringer believed and had reasonable grounds for believing that his or her use of the copyrighted work was a fair use under section 107, if the infringer was: (i) an employee or agent of a nonprofit educational institution, library, or archives acting within the scope of his or her employment who, or such institution, library, or archives itself, which infringed by reproducing the work in copies or phonorecords; or (ii) a public broadcasting entity which or a person who, as a regular part of the nonprofit activities of a public broadcasting entity (as defined in subsection (g) of section 118) infringed by performing a published nondramatic literary work or by reproducing a transmission program embodying a performance of such a work.

(3) (A) In a case of infringement, it shall be a rebuttable presumption that the infringement was committed willfully for purposes of determining relief if the violator, or a person acting in concert with the violator, knowingly provided or knowingly caused to be provided materially false contact information to a domain name registrar, domain name registry, or other domain name registration authority in registering, maintaining, or renewing a domain name used in connection with the infringement.

(B) Nothing in this paragraph limits what may be considered willful infringement under this subsection.

* * *

17 U.S.C. § 506. Criminal offenses

(a) Criminal infringement.—

(1) In general.—Any person who willfully infringes a copyright shall be punished as provided under section 2319 of title 18, if the infringement was committed—

(A) for purposes of commercial advantage or private financial gain;

(B) by the reproduction or distribution, including by electronic means, during any 180-day period, of 1 or more copies or phonorecords of 1 or more copyrighted works, which have a total retail value of more than $1,000; or

(C) by the distribution of a work being prepared for commercial distribution, by making it available on a computer network accessible to members of the public, if such person knew or should have known that the work was intended for commercial distribution.

* * *

(c) Fraudulent Copyright Notice.—Any person who, with fraudulent intent, places on any article a notice of copyright or words of the same purport that such person knows to be false, or who, with fraudulent intent, publicly distributes or imports for public distribution any article bearing such notice or words that such person knows to be false, shall be fined not more than $2,500.

(d) Fraudulent Removal of Copyright Notice.—Any person who, with fraudulent intent, removes or alters any notice of copyright appearing on a copy of a copyrighted work shall be fined not more than $2,500.

(e) False Representation.—Any person who knowingly makes a false representation of a material fact in the application for copyright registration provided for by section 409, or in any written statement filed in connection with the application, shall be fined not more than $2,500.

(f) Rights of Attribution and Integrity.—Nothing in this section applies to infringement of the rights conferred by section 106A(a).

III. Websites discussing the rights and responsibilities of fanfic authors

Several organizations have taken on the cause of fanfic. Many of these organizations, and many individuals, offer information about specific content owners' attitudes toward fanfic, opinions about copyright law, more general advice, and advocacy. Much of this information, especially about copyright law, is incorrect; there is probably more misinformation than correct information on this topic floating around the web. The sites below, at last inspection, offered responsible advice. Keep in mind, though, that very little is definite in this area.

The Electronic Frontier Foundation, www.eff.org

The most widely-recognized advocacy group for online information rights, the Electronic Frontier Foundation, provides advice on fair use at www.eff.org/issues/intellectual-property.

Chilling Effects Clearinghouse, www.chillingeffects.org

The Chilling Effects Clearinghouse is a project of the Electronic Frontier Foundation in conjunction with legal clinics at several law schools; it aims to help web users stay out of trouble while at the same time monitoring overzealous copyright enforcement. It provides answers to a number of common fan author questions at www.chillingeffects.org/fanfic.

Fan Works Inc., www.fanworks.org

This site, sadly not frequently updated, provides an extensive and detailed list of individual authors and their approaches to fanfic at www.fanworks.org/writersresource/?tool=fanpolicy.

The Organization for Transformative Works, http://transformativeworks.org

The Organization for Transformative Works takes an unambiguously pro-fanfic stance on questions of copyright law. It addresses legal questions arising from fanfic at http://transformativeworks.org/faq-277.

Selected Bibliography

Law review articles

Chander, Anupam & Sunder, Madhavi, *Everyone's a Superhero: A Cultural Theory of "Mary Sue" Fan Fiction as Fair Use*, 95 CAL. L. REV. 597 (2007).

Chua, Ernest, *Fan Fiction and Copyright: Mutually Exclusive, Able to Coexist or Something Else?*, 14 ELAW JOURNAL 215 (2007).

Chung, Jacqueline Lai, *Drawing Idea from Expression: Creating a Legal Space for Culturally Appropriated Literary Characters*, 49 WM. & MARY L. REV. 903 (2007).

Coombe, Rosemary, *Authorizing the Celebrity: Publicity Rights, Postmodern Politics, and Unauthorized Genders*, 10 CARDOZO ARTS & ENT. L.J. 365 (1992).

Daniels, Joshua M., *"Lost in Translation": Anime, Moral Rights, and Market Failure*, 88 B.U. L. REV. 709 (2008).

D'Agostino, Giuseppina, *Comparative Copyright Analysis of Canada's Fair Dealing to U.K. Fair Dealing and U.S. Fair Use*, 53 MCGILL L.J. 309 (2008).

Elliott, Jessica, *Copyright Fair Use and Private Ordering: Are Copyright Holders and the Copyright Law Fanatical for Fansites?*, 11 DEPAUL-LCA J. ART & ENT. L. & POL'Y 329 (2001).

Fiesler, Casey, *Everything I Need to Know I Learned from Fandom: How Existing Social Norms Can Help Shape the Next Generation of User-Generated Content*, 10 VAND. J. ENT. & TECH. L. 729 (2008).

Foley, Kathryn M., *Protecting Fictional Characters: Defining the Elusive Trademark-Copyright Divide*, 41 CONN. L. REV. 921 (2009).

Freedman, Matthew Brett, *Machinima and Copyright Law*, 13 J. INTELL. PROP. L. 235 (2005).

Geary-Boehm, Krissi J., *Cyber Chaos: The Clash Between Band Fansites and Intellectual Property Holders*, 30 S. ILL. U. L.J. 87 (2005).

Gerber, Robert S., *Mixing It Up on The Web: Legal Issues Arising from Internet "Mashups,"* 18 INTELL. PROP. & TECH. L.J. 11 (2006).

Goldman, Eric, *A Road to No Warez: The No Electronic Theft Act and Criminal Copyright Infringement*, 82 OREGON L. REV. 369 (2003).

Hatcher, Jordan, *Of Otakus and Fansubs: A Critical Look at Anime Online in Light of Current Issues in Copyright Law*, 2 SCRIPT-ED 551 (2005).

Hayes, Christina J., *Note, Changing the Rules of the Game: How Video Game Publishers Are Embracing User-Generated Derivative Works*, 21 HARV. J.L. & TECH. 567 (2008).

Helfand, Michael Todd, *When Mickey Mouse Is As Strong As Superman: The Convergence of Intellectual Property Laws to Protect Fictional Literary and Pictorial Characters*, 44 Stan. L. Rev. 623 (1992).

Hetcher, Steven A., *Using Social Norms to Regulate Fan Fiction and Remix Culture*, 157 U. Pa. L. Rev. 1869 (2009).

Hughes, Justin, *Recoding Intellectual Property and Overlooked Audience Interest*, 77 Tex. L. Rev. 923 (1999).

Katyal, Sonia, *Performance, Property, and the Slashing of Gender in Fan Fiction*, 14 Am. U. J. Gender Soc. Pol'y & Law 463 (2006).

Katz, Jonathan S., *Expanded Notions of Copyright Protection: Idea Protection Within the Copyright Act*, 77 B.U. L. Rev. 873 (1997).

Kirkpatrick, Sean, *Like Holding a Bird: What the Prevalence of Fansubbing Can Teach Us About the Use of Strategic Selective Copyright Enforcement*, 21 Temp. Envtl. L. & Tech. J. 131 (2003).

Koster, Erika S. & Shatz-Akin, Jim, *Set Phasers on Stun: Handling Internet Fan Sites*, 15 No. 1 Computer Law. 18 (1998).

Kurtz, Leslie A., *The Independent Legal Lives of Fictional Characters*, 1986 Wis. L. Rev. 429 (1986).

Lee, Edward, *Warming Up to User-Generated Content*, 2008 U. Ill. L. Rev. 1459 (2008).

Lemley, Mark, *Should a Licensing Market Require Licensing?*, 70 Law & Contemp. Probs. 185 (2007).

Leonard, Sean, *Celebrating Two Decades of Unlawful Progress: Fan Distribution, Proselytization Commons, and the Explosive Growth of Japanese Animation*, 12 UCLA Ent. L. Rev. 189 (2005).

Litman, Jessica, *Creative Reading*, 70 Law & Contemp. Probs. 175 (2007).

Long, Andrew S., *Mashed Up Videos and Broken Down Copyright: Changing Copyright to Promote the First Amendment Values of Transformative Video*, 60 Okla. L. Rev. 317 (2007).

McCardle, Meredith, *Fandom, Fan Fiction and Fanfare: What's All the Fuss?*, 9 B.U. J. Sci. & Tech. L. 443 (2003).

Murray, Simone, *"Celebrating the Story the Way It Is": Cultural Studies, Corporate Media, and the Contested Utility of Fandom*, 18 Continuum: J. Media & Cult. Studies 7 (2004).

Muscar, Jaime E., *A Winner is Who? Fair Use and the Online Distribution of Manga and Video Game Fan Translations*, 9 Vand. J. Ent. & Tech. L. 223 (2006).

Nemetz, Steven L., *Copyright Protection of Fictional Characters*, 14 Intell. Prop. J. 59 (2000).

Nevins, Jr., Francis M., *Copyright + Character = Catastrophe*, 39 J. Copyright Soc'y U.S.A. 303 (1992).

Niro, Dean D., *Protecting Characters Through Copyright Law: Paving a New Road Upon Which Literary, Graphic, and Motion Picture Characters Can All Travel*, 41 DePaul L. Rev. 359 (1992).

Noda, Nathaniel T., *When Holding On Means Letting Go: Why Fair Use Should Extend to Fan-Based Activities*, 5 U. DENVER SPORTS & ENT. L.J. (2008).

Nolan, Mollie E., *Search for Original Expression: Fan Fiction and the Fair Use Defense*, 30 S. ILL. L.J. 533 (2006).

Note, *"Recoding" and the Derivative Works Entitlement: Addressing the First Amendment Challenge*, 119 HARV. L. REV. 1488 (2006).

Ogbu, Cecilia, *I Put Up a Website About My Favorite Show and All I Got Was This Lousy Cease-and-Desist Letter: The Intersection of Fan Sites, Internet Culture, and Copyright Owners*, 12 S. CAL. INTERDISC. L.J. 279 (2003).

Peltz, Richard, *Global Warming Trend? The Creeping Indulgence of Fair Use in the International Copyright Law*, 17 TEX. INTELL. PROP. L.J. 267 (2009).

Phillips, Anna, *Copyright or Trademark? Can One Boy Wizard Prevent Film Title Duplication?*, 11 SAN DIEGO INT'L L.J. 319 (2009).

Ranon, Christina Z., *Honor Among Thieves: Copyright Infringement in Internet Fandom*, 8 VAND. J. ENT. & TECH. L. 421 (2006).

Reid, Christopher, *Fair Game: The Application of Fair Use Doctrine to Machinima*, 19 FORDHAM INTELL. PROP. MEDIA & ENT. L.J. 831 (2009).

Richardson, Megan & Tan, David, *The Art of Retelling: Harry Potter and Copyright in a Fan-Literature Era*, 14 MEDIA & ARTS L. REV. 31 (2009).

Schwabach, Aaron, *The Harry Potter Lexicon and the World of Fandom: Fan Fiction, Outsider Works, and Copyright*, 70 U. PITT. L. REV. 387 (2009).

Seville, Catherine, *Peter Pan's Rights: "To Die Will Be an Awfully Big Adventure"*, 51 J. COPYRIGHT SOC'Y U.S.A. 1 (2003).

Siskind, Shira, *Crossing the Fair Use Line: The Demise and Revival of the Harry Potter Lexicon and Its Implications for the Fair Use Doctrine in the Real World and on the Internet*, 27 CARDOZO ARTS & ENT. L.J. 291 (2009).

Stendell, Leanne, *Comment, Fanfic and Fan Fact: How Current Copyright Law Ignores the Reality of Copyright Owner and Consumer Interests in Fan Fiction*, 58 SMU L. REV. 1551 (2005).

Trombley, Sarah, *Visions and Revisions: Fanvids and Fair Use*, 25 CARDOZO ARTS & ENT. J. 647 (2008).

Tushnet, Rebecca, *Legal Fictions: Copyright, Fan Fiction and a New Common Law*, 17 LOY. L.A. ENT. L. REV. 651 (1997).

Tushnet, Rebecca, *My Fair Ladies: Sex, Gender, and Fair Use in Copyright*, 15 AM. U.J. GENDER SOC. POL'Y & L. 273 (2007).

Tushnet, Rebecca, *Payment in Credit: Copyright Law and Subcultural Creativity*, 70 LAW & CONTEMP. PROBS. 135 (2007).

Tushnet, Rebecca, *User-Generated Discontent: Transformation in Practice*, 31 COLUM. J.L. & ARTS 497 (2008).

Tushnet, Rebecca, *I Put You There: User-Generated Content and Anticircumvention*, 12 VANDERBILT J. ENT. & TECH. L. 889 (2010).

Tussey, Deborah, *From Fan Sites to File Sharing: Personal Use in Cyberspace*, 35 GA. L. REV. 1129 (2001).

Williams, Jo-Na, *The New Symbol of "Hope" for Fair Use: Shepard Fairey v. The Associated Press*, LANDSLIDE, Sept./Oct. 2009, at 55.

Books

ADITYO, YOKIE, HAPPY PORTER: PENYUSUP DI SEKOLAH SIHIR HOMEWORK (2007).

AUSTEN, JANE & GRAHAME-SMITH, SETH, PRIDE AND PREJUDICE AND ZOMBIES (Philadelphia: Quirk Books, 2009).

AUSTEN, JANE & WINTERS, BEN H., SENSE & SENSIBILITY & SEA MONSTERS (Philadelphia: Quirk Books, 2009).

BAUM, L. FRANK, THE WONDERFUL WIZARD OF OZ (1900).

BAUM, L. FRANK, *Prologue* to THE PATCHWORK GIRL OF OZ (1913).

BARTHELME, DONALD, SNOW WHITE (1967).

BRADLEY, MARION ZIMMER, *Introduction* to THE KEEPER'S PRICE (Marion Zimmer Bradley, ed., 1980).

BRADLEY, MARION ZIMMER, THE MISTS OF AVALON (1982).

BREWER, DAVID A., THE AFTERLIFE OF CHARACTER, 1726–1825 (Philadelphia: University of Pennsylvania Press, 2005).

BRODIE, FAWN M., THOMAS JEFFERSON: AN INTIMATE HISTORY (New York: Bantam, 1974).

BROWN, WILLIAM WELLS, CLOTEL; OR, THE PRESIDENT'S DAUGHTER: A NARRATIVE OF SLAVE LIFE IN THE UNITED STATES (London: Partridge & Oakey, 1853).

BURGESS, GRANVILLE , DUSKY SALLY (New York: Broadway Play Publishing, 1987).

BYRD, MAX, JEFFERSON: A NOVEL (1993).

CHABON, MICHAEL, SUMMERLAND (2002).

CHASE-RIBOUD, BARBARA, SALLY HEMINGS: A NOVEL (New York: Viking Press, 1979).

CHESTERTON, GILBERT KEITH, THE MAN WHO WAS SUNDAY: A NIGHTMARE (1908).

CHESTERTON, GILBERT KEITH, VARIED TYPES (Project Gutenberg, ed., 2004) (1908).

CHESTERTON, GILBERT KEITH, THE COMPLETE FATHER BROWN STORIES (1998).

CRICHTON, MICHAEL, JURASSIC PARK (1990).

CRICHTON, MICHAEL, THE LOST WORLD (1995).

CONAN DOYLE, ARTHUR, THE LOST WORLD (1912).

ERICKSON, STEVE, ARC D'X (1993).

FAN FICTION AND FAN COMMUNITIES IN THE AGE OF THE INTERNET (Kristina Busse and Karen Hellekson, eds., Jefferson, NC: McFarland, 2006).

FRIEDELL, EGON, DIE RÜCKKEHR DER ZEITMASCHINE (Berlin: Piper Verlag, 1946); in English as THE RETURN OF THE TIME MACHINE (Eddy C. Bertin, trans., New York: DAW Books, 1972; reprinted in San Bernardino, CA: Borgo Press, 1987).

GERBER, MICHAEL, BARRY TROTTER AND THE UNAUTHORIZED PARODY (2001).

GORDON, GEORGE, LORD BYRON, DON JUAN, Canto XIII, stanza 95 (Halifax: Milner & Sowerby, 1837).

HAAGE, PETER, DER PARTYLÖWE, DER NUR BÜCHER FRASS: EGON FRIEDELL UND SEIN KREIS (Berlin: Claassen-Verlag, 1984).

HAGGARD, H. RIDER, SHE (1887).

HUDSON, WILLIAM HENRY, GREEN MANSIONS: A ROMANCE OF THE TROPICAL FOREST (1904).

HUELLE, PAWEŁ, CASTORP (Antonia Lloyd-Junes, trans., London: Serpent's Tail, 2007).

JOLIN, PETER, HARRY POUTER AND PHIL O'DENDRON'S STONE: PARODY OF HARRY POTTER AND THE PHILOSOPHER'S STONE, SOMEWHERE ON THE EDGE OF GOOD TASTE (2005).

Lamb, Jean, *Galley Slave*, ANALOG, Aug. 1996, reprinted in CHOOSING NAMES: MAN-KZIN WARS VIII 129 (Larry Niven, ed., 1998).

Lamb, Jean, *Shut-In*, in RENUNCIATES OF DARKOVER (Marion Zimmer Bradley, ed., 1991).

LANDES, WILLIAM M. & POSNER, RICHARD A., THE ECONOMIC STRUCTURE OF INTELLECTUAL PROPERTY LAW (2003).

THE LAW & HARRY POTTER (Jeffrey Thomas and Franklin Snyder, eds., Durham: Carolina Academic Press, 2010).

MCHALE, BRIAN, POSTMODERNIST FICTION (1987).

MCLEOD, KEMBREW, FREEDOM OF EXPRESSION®: OVERZEALOUS COPYRIGHT BOZOS AND OTHER ENEMIES OF CREATIVITY (New York: Doubleday, 2005).

NIVEN, LARRY, RINGWORLD (1970).

NIVEN, LARRY, THE RINGWORLD ENGINEERS vii–viii (1980).

NIVEN, LARRY, THE PATCHWORK GIRL (1984).

NIVEN, LARRY, *Introduction* to MAN-KZIN WARS IV (Larry Niven, ed., 1991).

NIVEN, LARRY, RAINBOW MARS (New York: Tor Books, 1999).

NIVEN, LARRY, L'ANNEAU-MONDE (Fabrice Lamidey, trans., 2005).

NIVEN, LARRY & POURNELLE, JERRY, INFERNO (New York: Pocket Books, 1976).

O'DONOHOE, NICK, TOO, TOO SOLID FLESH (Wizards of the Coast, 1989).

ORY, PASCAL, LA CULTURE COMME AVENTURE : TREIZE EXERCICES D'HISTOIRE CULTURELLE 227 (Paris: Editions Complexe, 2008).

PAUL, GREGORY S., PREDATORY DINOSAURS OF THE WORLD: A COMPLETE ILLUSTRATED GUIDE (New York: Simon & Schuster, 1988).

PENLEY, CONSTANCE, NASA/TREK: POPULAR SCIENCE AND SEX IN AMERICA (1997).

PIPER, H. BEAM, LITTLE FUZZY (New York: Avon, 1962); THE OTHER HUMAN RACE (1964), republished as FUZZY SAPIENS; FUZZIES AND OTHER PEOPLE (1984).

PUSHKIN, ALEXANDER, СКАЗКА О ЦАРЕ САЛТАНЕ (1831).

PUSHKIN, ALEXANDER, THE TALE OF TSAR SALTAN (Louis Zellikoff, trans., Moscow: Progress Publishers, 1970).

PYNCHON, THOMAS, MASON & DIXON (New York: Henry Holt & Co. Publishers, 1997).

RINALDI, ANN, WOLF BY THE EARS (New York: Scholastic, 1993).

ROTTRING, K.B., HERI KÓKLER ÉS AZ EPEKÖVE (2005).

ROWLING, J.K., HARRY POTTER AND THE SORCERER'S STONE (New York: Scholastic, 1997).

Rowling, J.K., Harry Potter and the Chamber of Secrets (New York: Scholastic, 1998).

Rowling, J.K., Harry Potter and the Prisoner of Azkaban (New York: Scholastic, 1999).

Rowling, J.K., Harry Potter and the Goblet of Fire (New York: Scholastic, 2000).

Rowling, J.K., Harry Potter and the Half-Blood Prince (2005).

Rowling, J.K., Harry Potter and the Deathly Hallows (New York: Scholastic, 2007).

Rowling, J.K., Harry Potter and the Order of the Phoenix (New York: Scholastic, 2007).

Sheppard, Franklin L., Alleluia (Baltimore: Presbyterian Board of Publications and Sabbath School Work, 1915).

Souza, Marcio, Lost World II: The End of the Third World (Lana Santamaria, trans., 1993), originally published as O Fim Do Terceiro Mundo (Marco Zero, ed., 1989).

Snows of Darkover (Marion Zimmer Bradley, ed., 1980).

Star Trek: The New Voyages (Sondra Marshak & Myrna Culbreath, eds., 1976).

Sterling, Bruce, We See Things Differently, reprinted in Globalhead (1992).

Stouffer, Nancy K., Larry Potter and His Best Friend Lilly (Thurman House, 2001).

Stouffer, Nancy K., The Legend of Rah and the Muggles (Thurman House, 2001) (1986).

Theorizing Fandom: Fans, Subculture and Identity (Cheryl Harris & Alison Alexander, eds., 1998).

Tolkien, J.R.R., The Two Towers (New York: Ballantine Books, 1965).

Tolkien, J.R.R., *Tree and Leaf*, in The Tolkien Reader (1966).

Tuten, Frederic, Tintin in the New World (Baltimore: Black Classic Press, 1993).

Vander Ark, Steve, The Lexicon: An Unauthorized Guide to Harry Potter Fiction and Related Materials (Muskegon: RDR Books, 2009).

Veys, Pierre, Harry Cover: L'ensorcelante parodie (2005).

Veys, Pierre, Harry Cover: Les mangeurs d'anglais (2007).

Во́лков, Алекса́ндр Меле́нтьевич [Volkov, Alexander Melentyevich], Волшебник Изумрудного Города [The Wizard of the Emerald City] et seq. (1939), available in English translation as Tales of Magic Land (Peter L. Blystone, trans, 2nd revised edition, Red Branch Press, 2010).

Want, Robert S., Harry Potter and the Order of the Court: The J.K. Rowling Copyright Case and the Question of Fair Use (2008).

Wells, H.G., The Time Machine (London: Heinemann, 1895).

Емец, Дмитрий [Yemets, Dmitri], Таня Гроттер и магический контрабас [Tanya Grotter and the Magical Double Bass] et seq. (Moscow: Eksmo, 2002).

Жвалевский, Андрей [Zhvalevskiyi, Andreyi], Порри Гаттер и Каменный Философ [Porri Gatter and the Stone Philosopher] (Vremnya, 2002).

Жвалевский, Андрей [Zhvalevskiyi, Andreyi], Порри Гаттер : Личное дело Мергионы [Porri Gatter: Merlioniy's Personal File] (Vremnya, 2003).
Жвалевский, Андрей [Zhvalevskiyi, Andreyi], Порри Гаттер : 9 подвигов Сена Аесли [Porri Gatter: 9 Feats of Hay Aesli] (Vremnya, 2004).

Index